# THE GARDEN IN THE MACHINE

Midcentury: Architecture, Landscape, Urbanism, and Design

Richard Longstreth, Editor

# THE GARDEN IN THE MACHINE

## Planning and Democracy in the Tennessee Valley Authority

Avigail Sachs

University of Virginia Press
CHARLOTTESVILLE AND LONDON

University of Virginia Press

Printed in the United States of America on acid-free paper

*First published 2023*

9 8 7 6 5 4 3 2 1

Library of Congress Cataloging-in-Publication Data

Names: Sachs, Avigail, author.
Title: The garden in the machine : planning and democracy in the Tennessee Valley Authority / Avigail Sachs.
Description: Charlottesville : University of Virginia Press, 2023. | Series: Midcentury: architecture, landscape, urbanism, and design | Includes bibliographical references and index.
Identifiers: LCCN 2022026295 (print) | LCCN 2022026296 (ebook) | ISBN 9780813948911 (hardcover) | ISBN 9780813948959 (paperback) | ISBN 9780813948966 (ebook)
Subjects: LCSH: Regional planning—Social aspects—Tennessee River Valley. | Landscape design—Social aspects—Tennessee River Valley. | Architecture—Human factors—Tennessee River Valley. | Tennessee Valley Authority.
Classification: LCC NA9053.H76 S23 2023 (print) | LCC NA9053.H76 (ebook) | DDC 711/.309768—dc23/eng/20220719
LC record available at https://lccn.loc.gov/2022026295
LC ebook record available at https://lccn.loc.gov/2022026296

*Cover photo:* Norris Dam, Clinch River, Tennessee. (Photo by Avigail Sachs)

*For Shai, Itamar, Uri and their parents, with all my love*

# CONTENTS

# ACRONYMS AND ABBREVIATIONS

| | |
|---|---|
| AIA | American Institute of Architects |
| AIP | American Institute of Planners |
| ALCOA | Aluminum Company of America |
| APHA | American Public Health Association |
| ARD | Architecture Research Division (TVA) |
| ASLA | American Society of Landscape Architects |
| ASME | American Society of Mechanical Engineers |
| CCC | Civilian Conservation Corps |
| DRPM | Department of Reservoir Property Management (TVA) |
| DRPS | Department of Regional Planning Studies (TVA) |
| DRPG | Division of Recreation and Public Grounds (TVA) |
| DRS | Department of Regional Studies (TVA) |
| FHA | Federal Housing Administration |
| FWA | Federal Works Administration |
| LP&H | Land Planning and Housing Division (TVA) |
| MVA | Mississippi Valley Archives, Brister Library, Memphis State |
| NAA | The National Archives at Atlanta |
| NAACP | National Association for the Advancement of Colored People |

| | |
|---|---|
| NAHB | National Association of Home Builders |
| NHA | National Housing Agency |
| NPS | National Park Service |
| NRC | National Resource Committee |
| NRPB | National Resources Planning Board |
| REA | Rural Electrification Administration |
| RPAA | Regional Planning Association of America |
| TVA | Tennessee Valley Authority |
| USHA | United States Housing Authority |

# ACKNOWLEDGMENTS

Micah Rutenberg's name is not on the cover of this book, but it would be a very different project without his willingness to discuss anything and everything TVA. We have been collaborating on a visual representation—maps and photographs—of the *machines* described here and hope to be able to share it soon. Many colleagues at the College of Architecture and Design at the University of Tennessee, Knoxville, have also supported this project, especially by allowing me to bombard them with TVA musings for several years. Dean Jason Young's contribution, as Director of the School of Architecture, was invaluable, not least in asking me to guide the school's guests on the "dam tour" again and again. Both Jason and Gale Fulton, Director of the School of Landscape Architecture, used their managerial acumen to promote this project with much-needed intellectual and financial resources. Tracy Moir-McClean shared her TVA insights with me, Robert French urged me on, and Brad Collett helped arrange visits to the visitors' centers that have been closed since the 1990s; thank you to all the TVA'ers who proudly showed me the environments they preside over. This project would have been impossible without support from Maureen Hill and the staff at the National Archives at Atlanta. Their collection is enormous, but so is their patience. I am also indebted to Clare Wolfowitz, Mark Mones, Ellen Satrom, and Leslie Tingle for their support, and to Richard

Longstreth and two anonymous readers for thoughtful comments. The late Boyd Zenner was essential in making this project into a book; she is truly missed.

This book was written with my students in mind. In the past decade it has been my privilege to accompany them as they navigate the diverse career paths open to architects and landscape architects. My efforts to show them that there are creativity and imagination in every stage of the design and construction process form the bedrock of this study. There is no reason for them to repeat the TVA's specific projects, and I sincerely hope we will be able to overcome the gender, race, and class biases that shaped its program. The TVA architects and planners' commitment to both theory and practice, however, should continue to inspire us. It is easy to get lost in the humdrum, but the utopian is always there if you look for it. Marianela D'Aprile, Dillon Dunn, Mike Lidwin, and DeMauri Mumphrey have been wonderful partners in this process.

I wrote the first draft of this study in Jerusalem as a fellow at the Israel Institute for Advanced Studies. Thank you to Yael Alweil for inviting me to join the research group "Re-theorizing the Architecture of Housing as Grounds for Research and Practice" and to Gaia Caramellino and Susanne Schindler for organizing it with her. Our group work was marred by a global pandemic, but Yael, Tzafrir Fainholtz, Mariana Fix, Dana Vais, Jesse Lockard, and I managed to eke out a short but wonderful collegial experience. Elisheva Baumgarten, a dear friend, gave me an intellectual sanctuary when our group was disbanded. Being in Israel allowed me to reconnect with many friends I met through the Israeli Nature Society. Hiking again with Ami, Shmulik, Yaron, Ofra, Amnon, Boaz, Dvir, Elisheva, Guy, Tidhar and Shachar, as well as Ariel Libman and Ariel and Nurit Novoplansky, was fulfilling and inspiring. More sedentary, but no less important, was time spent with Tabi Shapira, Ayelet Landau, Amir Engel, Hadas Ragolsky, Hadas Shasha-Lavski, Adi Sela-Wiener, Osnat Dinur, Noam Austerlitz, Tal Einhorn, Miri Lavi, and Noam Shoked.

Andrew Shanken first discussed architects in World War II, and I continue to benefit from his intellectual and emotional support. Thaïsa Way, Zeynep Kezer, and Liz Wardinski weighed in on *gardens, machines* and other matters. They continue to inspire me, as do Kathy Wheeler, Scott Wall, Marcia Goldstein, Tom Riesing, Liz Teston, Rana Abudayyeh, Lyn Hartman, Tina Shepardson, Piper Mullins, Yael Perez, Sharone Tomer, Erica Leak, Maria Moreno, Lavina Liburd, Aparna Datey, Valerie Friedman, Tim Sundell, Cheri Elliot Torano, Einat Lev, Jane Crudden

Carson, Jason Shoemaker, and Jacob Stanley. My family has expanded as this book matured, and it has been wonderful to welcome Ava, Alden, Yael, Tal, Aryeh, and Eitan. My love also to the adults: Rahel, Hanan, Tanya, Tamar, Peter, Clare, Paul, Shaha, Sara, Francisco, David, Rachel, Mark, Louis, Leslie, Lee, and Fanny.

My mother, Laura Sachs, has seen more TVA dams than most Tennessee Valley residents and never lost her enthusiasm for the project. As an unofficial research assistant, she has contributed to this book more than she knows. Visiting Norris Dam with my niece Shai and nephew Itamar was eye-opening—not least because we saw it from the reservoir. My nephew Uri is already interested in engineering and architectural projects, and I hope to share these with him soon. Shai, Itamar, Uri, and their parents, Rachel and Nir, Natan and Avril, have grounded me as I wrote this book. It is dedicated to them with all my love.

# INTRODUCTION

Architects and landscape architects do pursue utopian ideals, but they do so through the institutions in which they work; the ideological and social contexts of these environments shape the scope and method of their practice. This process is particularly evident in new and radical institutions, such as the audacious agencies created by President Franklin D. Roosevelt as part of the New Deal. Within these complex organizations progressive ideas, previously theoretical, were given legal and physical form. This study explores this dramatic undertaking by following the architects and landscape architects who worked on the staff of the Tennessee Valley Authority (TVA), established in 1933. The TVA, unique among these new federal entities, was given responsibility for a region rather than for a single project—even exercising full authority to buy land and implement its own proposals. As an environmental project, the TVA offered architects and landscape architects an exceptionally wide sphere to exercise their professional creativity. Keenly aware of the unprecedented opportunity, they took on new challenges and gladly expanded their professional practice. This was especially true in the first two decades of the TVA's operation, discussed here. The range of projects in which the TVA staff engaged is thus a microcosm of how American architecture and landscape were transformed in the context of the Great Depression and World War II.

The TVA united several threads of resource conservation ideologies and was responsible, simultaneously, for flood prevention, soil conservation, reforestation, power production, and rural electrification. As Samuel P. Hays shows, the key to resource conservation was maximum efficiency based in scientific and technological knowledge.[1] Underlying this emphasis was the belief that America's history was one of progress in which the "continuous expansion of knowledge of—and power over—nature" provided individuals with opportunities to sustain their bodies and minds through their labor.[2] In the nineteenth century this progress was predicated on the westward-moving frontier and its abundant resources and opportunities. The closing of the frontier, as Frederick Jackson Turner argued, diminished this unique condition, which had allowed American democracy to flourish.[3] Resource conservation was thus not only about managing public resources but also about extending individual opportunities and safe-guarding the American way of life.[4] Such management, however, entailed moving away from the individual pioneer and entrepreneur—the heroes of capitalist expansion—and placing the responsibility of supporting human labor in the hands of scientists and engineers.[5] These professionals were expected to form an elite corps within government; the TVA was an exemplar of this worldview.[6] As an institution it was characterized by scientific and technical knowledge, hierarchical organization, and interdisciplinary collaboration, which became the hallmarks of its regional development.

The Tennessee Valley was a prime candidate for federal efforts at resource conservation. Valley residents had long been subject to severe flooding by the wild Tennessee River, regularly suffering damage and loss of life.[7] At the same time, natural rain patterns supported, rather than undermined, the human effort to maximize flood control, navigation, and power production simultaneously.[8] The region was also plagued by severe soil erosion, the outcome of outdated farming practices and the cultivation of steep hillside farms, but the majority of local farmers could not afford to buy the fertilizer or make the adjustments needed to counteract this trend.[9] A government role also suited the anticorporate theme of progressive discourse: the logging industry had long recognized the value of the old-growth forests in the region, and its operations had left behind bare mountains and widespread erosion. In addition, the federal government already owned industrial land in the region, an anomaly in American politics. During World War I, Washington had constructed a large electricity-producing dam and two nitrate plants in Muscle Shoals, Alabama, a dominant landmark on the Tennessee River. In the 1920s, building on regional and federal legislative attempts of the previous decades, progressive senator George Norris of Nebraska lobbied tirelessly to convince Congress to retain control of this land and the dam and to make them the kernel of a public project. The establishment of the TVA signaled ultimate success following his "years of agitation."[10]

The TVA Act of May 1933 clearly outlined the three core responsibilities of the new agency. First, the Authority was legally required to transform the erratic Tennessee River into a navigable waterway and to protect communities and farmers from floods. The TVA proposed, accordingly, a series of nine river dams as well as storage dams on the tributaries, and this "unified system" became the core of its work in its first two decades (fig. 1). I refer to this core project as the *river machine:* "No other major stream was so completely controlled for the protection and benefit of man."[11] Second, the Authority was given responsibility for the nitrate factories and directed to prepare them for future conflict. In the interim they would be used to produce fertilizers to be distributed to farmers across the Tennessee Valley at cost. These fertilizers supported a modernization of farming and forestry practices—and through them, erosion control and reforestation—powering what I call the *land machine.* Third, the act allowed the TVA to generate and sell electricity, a controversial authorization that was upheld by the Supreme Court in the late 1930s.[12] The infusion of electric power, together with enhanced river navigation, was expected to support the rural electrification of the region and the growth of industry and commerce along the Tennessee River. I call this third component the *power machine.* This machine took the energy embodied in the wild river and transformed it into human commodities, as regional planner Benton MacKaye commented: the "*power lines* are in effect extensions of the river wherein the flow, converted into electric juice, moved on through copper wires from power-plant to smokeless factory and home."[13]

The TVA was also imbued with social and symbolic roles; historian Walter Creese refers to them as the allegorical enterprise of the TVA.[14] President Roosevelt, in a message to Congress supporting the TVA Act, hailed it as a model for the regeneration of the entire United States and referred to it as a new form of pioneering.[15] In this utopian vision the resources developed through conservation efforts would be distributed fairly, engendering widespread prosperity. The assumption was that the technical and scientific approach to management would create a new political

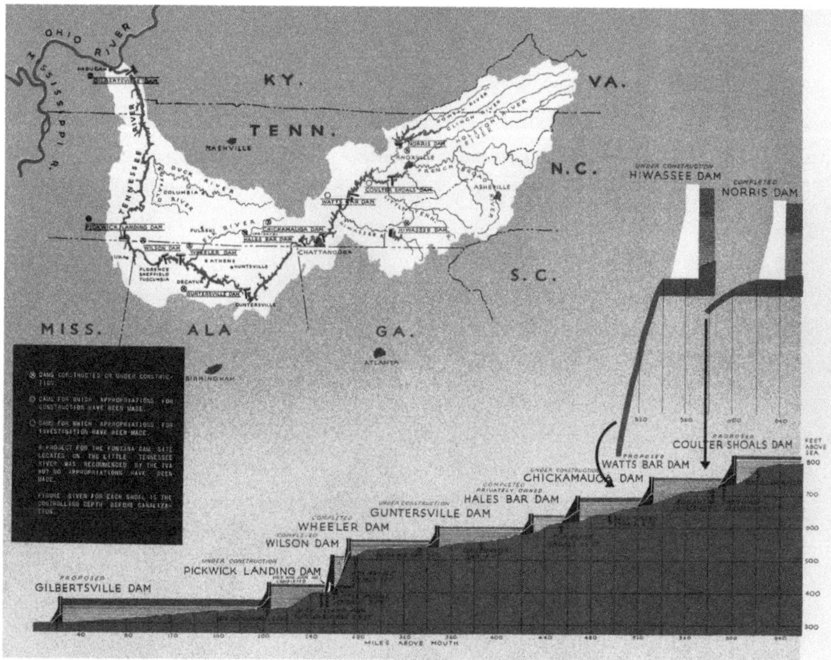


**Figure 1.** Map of the Tennessee Valley and the TVA river machine prepared by the Office of Information, from *The Development of the Tennessee Valley* (Washington, DC: Government Printing Office, 1936). The map illustrates how the river gathers tributaries in the eastern, mountainous portion of the Valley before flowing past Chattanooga, Tennessee, into northern Alabama and then northward toward its confluence with the Ohio River at Paducah, Kentucky.

order based on universal fairness rather than narrow, "pork-barrel" interests. Resource conservation was thus conceived as the basis for repairing nothing less than American democracy and the Western world order.[16] The TVA Act itself, however, was vague about these social aspirations, focusing on method rather than goals. Only two sections, briefly and rather cryptically, allowed the president to direct the new agency to conduct "surveys of and general plans for said Tennessee Basin and adjoining territory as may be useful to the Congress and to the several States in guiding and controlling the extent, sequence, and nature of development that may be equitably and economically advanced through the expenditure of public funds, or through the guidance or control of public authority, all for the general purpose of fostering an orderly and proper physical, economic, and social development of said areas."[17]

For most TVA staff the act was sufficient—they focused on building the machines, confident that resource conservation and good management would, in and of themselves, yield "orderly and proper" results. For a small but important group, however, the social aspiration represented the very core of the TVA project. These reformers, the architects and landscape architects among them, subscribed to another strand of progressive thought—regional planning. In this view, intelligent action—that is, planning—was to be used to create spiritual harmony, not merely material prosperity and efficient political order.[18] They also believed, with John Dewey and other pragmatist philosophers, that democracy did not emerge naturally from material conditions but needed to be taught and practiced so as to endure. In their quest for this utopian vision, these TVA reformers emphasized two mechanisms. First was a specific environment, what Leo Marx describes in his seminal book *The Machine in the Garden* as the "pastoral ideal."[19] Second was an insistence on life in small communities, which would foster "cooperation and mutual helpfulness."[20] These intertwined goals—a harmonious balance between individuals, nature, and society—are here referred to as the utopian goal of the *garden*.

The "pastoral ideal," like resource conservation, was rooted in a conception of the American frontier and its role in American society, but here the westward expansion was as destructive as it was beneficial. In this view, human life and society thrive best in the "middle landscape," an idealized place that provides both the advances of civilization and a continual access to the healing properties of nature. The middle landscape is a modified landscape, the result of thoughtful, rather than exploitative, human action. It is also inherently contradictory: it is "a dynamic and changing landscape that draws on both ideas of an Edenic, pastoral garden and the power of the 'technological sublime.'"[21] In other words, even as what Marx calls the "machine in the garden"—the inexorable move of technology into new landscapes—destroys nature, it is also expected to create a new, utopian, garden—the middle landscape. Marx traces the roots of the pastoral ideal to Greek and Roman philosophy and poetry, but he recognizes that it had particular impact in North America, where the westward-moving frontier seemed to offer an opportunity to realize it in truth. This impact was strengthened by the Jeffersonian idealization of the yeoman farmer "as an incorruptible and independent citizen," who also was seen to live in the middle landscape.[22]

The ideology of regional planning was also rooted in the work of Scottish biologist Patrick Geddes. For Geddes, the central threat to human spiritual fulfillment were the conditions in industrial cities. He describes these cities—with their collieries, steam engines, railways, markets, and, above all, monotony—as a progression of "Slum, Semi-slum, Superslum."[23] The antidote to this situation was to be found in the discipline of town planning, which Geddes describes as a "master-art; vaster than that of street planning, it is *landscape making*."[24] Geddes's ideas were reframed for an American audience by the Regional Planning Association of America (RPAA). It called for a dispersal of populations across regions in small, self-sufficient but well-connected settlements, in which inhabitants could engage with other members of their community and balance their lives between agricultural and industrial pursuits, cooperating rather than competing. Proponents referred to these settlements as the "democratic community."[25] The RPAA and other regional planners found a blueprint for this idea in the work of Ebenezer Howard, who in 1902 published *Garden Cities of To-morrow*.[26] Howard described a region of contained towns protected by "greenbelts," which he referred to as "garden cities."[27] Regional planners argued that the development of technological infrastructure, particularly roads and electricity, would allow the proper dispersal of these garden cities.[28] The American frontier had been set in a primeval garden; in the new pioneering the garden would have to be set within a machine.

The progressive ideas of community were limited; they were shaped by yet another aspect of American history—the deep racism and discrimination practiced against African Americans after the Civil War. As Derek H. Alderman and Robert N. Brown explain: "Jim Crow ideology . . . saw social reform (for whites) and social control (of blacks) as one and the same."[29] The TVA was a federal project, but its directors and professionals did not counteract southern segregation, instead developing a metric for hiring African Americans in TVA projects based on local population. They thus took advantage of the region's demographics: most of the Black citizens lived in the cities or in northern Alabama.[30] In many of the Appalachian counties—the eastern, rural, and mountainous parts of the Tennessee Valley—there were few if any Black residents at all. This condition allowed the promoters of the TVA's efforts to cast their work as a laboratory for the entire nation, despite actual conditions. The white "folk" in the mountainous areas, moreover, were eking out a subsistence living, if that. Descriptions of their lives emphasized widespread poverty, disease, and deprivation. As Henry D. Shapiro shows, by the 1930s American public consciousness had come to see the residents of Appalachia as frozen in the first stages of conquering the wilderness and in dire need of the boost of reform, scientifically improved farming practices, and electrification.[31]

The tensions both within and between resource conservation and regional planning shaped TVA policy. Democracy, especially as imagined by the resource conservationists, was dependent on the actions of individuals; planning by its very nature is collective and public. Philip Selznick and Erwin C. Hargrove speak of two "organizational myths" and examine their impact.[32] The differences of opinion were evident at the top: the three-person board of directors appointed by Roosevelt held sharply competing views. Arthur E. Morgan believed that planning must supersede the politics of the democratic system and was best achieved through demonstration and centralized action. In his view, the enlightened elite—composed of professionals and visionaries such as himself—had a responsibility to lead through example. His goal was to produce a model that could emulated across the nation.[33] Included in this vision were buildings and landscapes designed by trained and dedicated professionals. Morgan was the first director appointed by the president, and he strode ahead and appointed a talented group of regional planners, architects, and landscape architects to the TVA, charging them with bringing his vision to reality. The TVA thus included, from its inception, a core group of professionals committed to the outright manifestation of its garden goals.

Arthur Morgan's fellow board members, Harcourt A. Morgan and David E. Lilienthal, objected to his approach: planning, they argued, ought rather to be undertaken by "the people" of the Valley, using knowledge provided by professionals. Lilienthal, the more articulate of the two, coined the term "grass roots democracy" to describe this approach, and spoke of a *planning* region instead of a *planned* one. Here was the idea of a modified capitalist society translated in an actionable plan: scientists and professionals would conserve and create resources, and citizens—particularly white citizens—would use them to build independent and fulfilling lives. In this approach the "proper" environment for a democratic society was open to interpretation. This was a powerful rhetoric, especially compared to Arthur Morgan's top-down approach, but it was often indistinguishable from economic development that did not aspire to the more utopian goal of "democracy."

In the TVA's first years these arguments (aligning with personal differences) erupted into a strong disagreement between Arthur Morgan and Lilienthal, while Harcourt Morgan continued to support the latter. Roosevelt did little to outline his own preferences or resolve this tension. Instead, the board divided the three TVA machines among its three members. Arthur Morgan, an engineer with experience in building dams, took charge of the river machine, while working to make regional planning a central element of the TVA project. Agronomist Harcourt Morgan focused on developing the land machine, working though regional institutions. This left the power machine for Lilienthal, a lawyer by training—a task he was both eager and well-qualified to lead. With time, however, this division of tasks was not enough; the burgeoning outright feud between Arthur Morgan and Lilienthal was finally resolved in 1938 when the president dismissed Morgan, allowing Lilienthal to entrench his preferred "grassroots" mythology within the Authority.[34] The move toward efficiency and resource conservation, and especially the production of power, was then intensified by the onset of the preparation for, and eventually the participation in, World War II, not to be reversed at its end.

Creese tracks the fate of Arthur Morgan's regional planning goals in this changing institution and highlights how the legalities limited the more idealistic efforts.[35] He especially decries the move from a "philanthropic enterprise to an eminently pragmatic one in an extremely short time."[36] This pragmatism was the hallmark of the engineering approach, which focused on maximizing resources and letting the garden take care of itself. Ultimately, Creese argues, the reality of the TVA's achievements—a series of small efforts—belies its original vision. This study begins with Creese's observation but does not equate the garden with comprehensive regional planning. Instead, it follows the planners, architects, and landscape architects as they negotiated between their commitment to social reform and the machine, the garden, democratic action, and their own changing professional mores. Such negotiations led, unsurprisingly, away from a single vision and toward a wide range of designs, plans, and policies. In pursuing these goals, they worked together and often in opposition to the larger institution; even as they worked to create a physical garden in a machine, they also operated as one. The utopian and plural approach they adopted mirrored professional attitudes toward architecture and design during the

Great Depression and into World War II, making the TVA an illustration of wider trends. As James Marston Fitch commented in 1965: "One of the great virtues of this decade . . . was its absorbing interest in theory—especially utopian theory."[37]

In his discussion of the "pastoral ideal," Marx distinguishes between two literary approaches. The first, which he calls the sentimental, "manifests itself in our leisure-time activities, in the piety toward the out-of-doors expressed in the wilderness cult, and in our devotion to camping, hunting, fishing, picnicking, gardening, and so on."[38] In this version the natural landscape is conceived as being in stark opposition to signs of technology. The garden is a place to escape the artificial, the utilitarian, and the industrial. In the second literary approach, the opposition between the garden and the machine is used to order "meaning" and clarify "our situation."[39] Literary works in this category, Marx argues, do not allow us to "come away with anything like the simple, affirmative attitude we adopt toward pleasing rural scenery." Instead, they "bring irony to bear against the illusion of peace and harmony in a green pasture."[40] The literary approaches Marx identifies have architectural and landscape counterparts in the work discussed here. Using both picturesque gardens and mountain homes as models, the TVA designers fashioned many landscapes that directly evoke the "pastoral ideal" (fig. 2). Torben H. Larsen examines this legacy as the "Enduring Pastoral" of the Tennessee Valley.[41] Working within the TVA machine, however, planners and architects did not rely on symbolism alone. Many of their designs do not *look* pastoral but do function—or at least could function—as "ordering devices" in a rapidly changing situation.

The first ordering device was the rural landscape of small, dispersed communities promoted by Arthur Morgan. He created a Land Planning and Housing Division (LP&H) even before the board met for the first time, and appointed Earle S. Draper, a regional planner, to direct it. Draper and his staff collaborated on reimagining the area surrounding the first dam built by the TVA, Norris Dam (named for Senator Norris). The model region they produced included not only a "garden-city" dotted with community buildings and model homes but also a "freeway"—a scenic route connecting the dam with nearby highways—as well as parks for recreation, public forests, and an area designated for wilderness conservation. Christine Macy and Sarah Bonnemaison rightly celebrate this region as one of the most comprehensive demonstrations of regional planning in the United States.[42] The garden as regional planning and the ways in which it was shaped by the TVA

**Figure 2.** The Gunter family cabin in Fontana Village, North Carolina. Built in the late nineteenth century, this structure predated the TVA housing by several decades but was preserved as a museum to document the "primitive" life in the region. The cabin's plan is simple: two connected rooms, each with a fireplace, access to an attic, and wide porches on either side.

machine—the institution and the landscape—are the topics of chapter 1, "Regional Planning."

Chapter 2, "A Planning Region," examines the implications of Harcourt Morgan's and Lilienthal's grassroots approach for the practice of regional planning and architecture. The LP&H was directed to adhere to the language of the TVA Act and produce "surveys of and general plans" rather than detailed master plans. The assumption was that the scientific foundation of this work—referred to as research and demonstration—would be enough to convince Valley residents to adopt the plans and designs and the social order they implied. This insistence was registered in a preference for the term "land-planning" over "regional planning" and a shift, in late 1930s, when the LP&H was replaced with the Department of Regional Studies (DRS), without "planning" in its title. Research and demonstration were central to the operation of the power machine, and Lilienthal's engagement with this aspect of the TVA project further entrenched his conviction that grassroots planning was *democratic* planning. He captured this polemic in his seminal book *TVA: Democ-*

*racy on the March,* published during World War II.[43] The demonstration efforts were rooted, for the most part, in Arthur Morgan's regional planning, but they also yielded substantially different results. The development of industry in the Tennessee Valley is a telling example. In the regional vision, following the Norris model, industry was to be spread across the region in small communities. Lilienthal, on the other hand, supported communities in the Tennessee Valley, especially the portion in Northern Alabama, in their quest to develop a robust industrial base on the newly controlled river. The TVA architects and landscape architects were thus enrolled in city planning projects in which they sought environmental harmony by planning both for industry and for opportunities for outdoor recreation and wildlife preservation. This emphasis, born of the garden ideal, was then presented as professional expertise.

The interest in planning and research did not displace design as a symbolic and aesthetic pursuit. On the contrary, as Tim Culvahouse and his colleagues show, persuasion, or the visualization of ideals, came to play a significant role in the story of the TVA.[44] This effort was led by Roland A. Wank, whom Morgan and Draper had appointed as head architect and who was given a wide range to explore multiple projects. Wank soon set about making the three machines visible in the landscape, revealing the promise of a renewed garden to a wide audience. These demonstrations appealed to human emotions, and especially the sense of community engendered by sublime conditions—in this case the technological sublime.[45] Wank began with the river machine. While the engineers were still developing the plans for Norris Dam, he convinced all three members of the board to allow him a say in the aesthetics of the dam and powerhouse. As I discuss in chapter 3, "Public Architecture," this design was the start of a sustained process in which every aspect of these buildings was designed to appeal to the ever-expanding number of visitors. This architecture clearly signaled, as Todd Smith explains, that "only with the strong hand of science and government could the true beauty (i.e., God's beauty) of the Tennessee Valley be made evident. Nature alone was no longer enough."[46] The power machine was also given aesthetic treatment, first in a masterful delineation of the interiors of the powerhouses, which were open to visitors until the 1990s, and then in the design of rural cooperatives, which delivered the power to the region's residents. Wank also directed efforts by the landscape architects to mold the areas around the dams into scenic, picturesque designs. Here the relationships between machine and garden were given literal form. Each dam was located in a sliver of the modified garden, and together these slices of the land machine nestle within the technological infrastructure of the river machine.

Chapters 4 and 5 turn to the gargantuan task of housing thousands of TVA employees across more than six hundred miles and twenty years. This project was the central preoccupation of most of the TVA architects and landscape architects and required a coordinated effort of planning, design, and project management. Even as they engaged in this task, however, members of the LP&H and later the DRS saw it as an opportunity to further their utopian visions. The first ideal was the importance of community for social and individual welfare. Using the garden city community at Norris as an example, the TVA staff evolved this typology as they sited and designed construction camp after construction camp. Though temporary, these camps represented a unique opportunity to design communities from scratch. Their interest in building spaces for community engagement only expanded after the United States entered World War II and was evident in the attention given to community buildings both within and around the TVA camps. Libraries, which were tasked with boosting morale, played an important role in this effort. As the war came to an end, the TVA staff worked to promulgate the knowledge they had amassed in the previous decades. Some ideas were circulated as "best practices" and others as speculative proposals; the architects also engaged in the design of specific civic centers and libraries for the region. These efforts were severely limited by local preferences, but they represented the garden ideal as an underlying order for the Tennessee Valley.

Most TVA laborers were housed in dormitories that were segregated by gender and race, but each of the construction camps also included a village of single-family homes, which TVA employees could rent during and after the construction of the dams. For the LP&H staff these houses were another vehicle through which to propagate models of the garden. Houses, especially what they considered to be modern houses, represented miniature utopias in which "individual dreams would take ideal physical forms, with rational societal perfection to follow in their wake."[47] This investigation began in Norris, Tennessee, where more than two hundred permanent houses were carefully sited to offer inhabitants the advantages of both shelter and a connection to nature. The designs also utilized the most advanced construction and electrical technologies, even though they were clothed in traditional materials to signal their symbolic role. These houses also formed the basis for a string of research projects—cost effectiveness, prefabrication, and electric heating—led by Carroll A. Towne. True to the notion of research, the TVA architects collated their knowledge so they could disseminate it to residents of the Valley and beyond. This work is the topic of chapter 5, "Modern Houses."

The final chapter of this study, "Regional Development," examines how the TVA designers harnessed the power of the TVA machine to achieve the environmental harmony they sought. Forestation is a central practice in resource conservation and played a seminal role in the TVA project. The goal was twofold: to protect the emerging reservoirs from erosion and to provide a basis for a regional (rather than national) timber industry. Draper and his staff proposed another industry—recreation—and proceeded to develop it in the Valley. Sites of recreation, they reasoned, would allow Americans to connect with nature as they gathered in relaxed situations. Working within the grassroots model, they began with surveys and studies but soon developed a series of demonstration parks, now state parks, in Tennessee. In the postwar period, when tourism and travel expanded exponentially, the architects designed model cabins, second homes, and boat docks and planned parks and subdivisions, while the regional planners actively supported the development of the tourist industry by writing laws securing public access to the reservoirs. In this process the river machine was recast as a chain of lakes and was dotted with gardens of varying sizes, which still play a seminal role in how residents and visitors experience the Tennessee Valley.

Collaboration was a central element in both the garden *and* the TVA's organizational myths, and none of the planners or designers worked alone. Wank worked with Mario Bianculli and Seth Harrison Gurnee on the designs for the dams; and the projects could not have been constructed without the participation of Harry B. Tour and his team of architects, who worked out of the Department of Engineering. Wank's evolving role, moreover, was less as the manager of an architectural office than as a roving intellectual. In the late 1930s and early 1940s, he was often away from the Authority, on loan to other government agencies such as the Rural Electrification Administration. Housing and community planning remained within the original unit but was directed by Carroll A. Towne, working with Louis Grandgent, George L. Richardson, and Woodruff Purnell. Their story, in turn, must recognize the seminal contributions of landscape architects in Osborne H. Graves's division—particularly Otto J. Priebe, Harold Frincke, and Herbert S. Conover. Robert M. Howes, also trained as a landscape architect, was central to the development of the TVA recreation program. The work of these architects, moreover, relied on the ideas shared by the many planners with whom they collaborated—particularly Draper and Benton MacKaye, as well as Tracy B. Augur, Raymond F. Leonard, and Aelred "Flash" Gray. Architect Alfred Clauss, assigned to the Office of Information, contributed representational and architectural ideas from that office. When Draper left the authority in 1940, he was replaced by planner Howard K. Menhinick, who brought with him a wealth of information from Harvard University. Many other individuals joined the group for a portion of those two decades of the TVA's development, forming close connections with other professionals within and outside the TVA, including social and economic researchers, geographers, and, of course, engineers.

The individuals involved in the various dimensions of regional planning were in constant—and often fruitful—contact, and they shared a passionate (and at time quixotic) belief in the garden in the machine. Their goal was not merely to convince the residents of the Tennessee Valley in the veracity of their ideals but also to promulgate them as professional standards. They imagined a world in which the reform goals of regional planning, and the derivative practice they themselves were developing, would be widely adopted by architects, landscape architects, and city and regional planners. They assumed this responsibility because of their adherence to the garden ideal in their ideology and in their practice. And here the term "atelier" becomes useful. Borrowed by architects from artists in the nineteenth century, the atelier was the defining feature of the education offered at the École des Beaux Arts in Paris. In this system, students studied the theoretical aspects of their chosen profession at the École itself and then practiced their application in the private offices run by their professors. The atelier was thus a hybrid institution: its members divided their efforts between theory and practice. In addition, atelier members were often content to subsume their individual professional identities in return for comradery and collaboration within the group. The TVA architects followed a similar practice, rarely attaching their names to specific projects. Wank, in fact, expected this to become the norm, arguing that the architects working for the government were "probably destined to swap independent achievement for contributions to a greater whole."[48] In architectural discourse, moreover, the term "atelier" is often used to refer to a group working on the cutting edge of architectural practice. As members of the largest and most stable New Deal agency, which retained its importance during the war, the TVA staff did just that.

As the following chapters will show, the atelier's risk taking was rewarded. The design work produced by Wank and his team won accolades in the architectural press, as did the research undertaken by Towne and his colleagues. The physical manifestations of the atelier's work, especially the scenic areas around the dams and the recreational parks, are still visited by thousands of tourists each year, forming an important backbone of the region's identity and economy. My interpretation of the TVA's design work as a garden indeed developed from my own experience of being immersed in the TVA landscape for over a decade. Gardens, always the source of much pleasure, rarely offer unalloyed escape from the artificial, the utilitarian, and the industrial. Observing the sometimes conflicting characteristics of TVA landscapes was a central impetus for this study. It also has roots in my own deep fascination with professional practice, its stated goals, and its many vagaries. The TVA staff, as part and parcel of their insistence on good administration, kept absurdly detailed records of their work: their numerous reports, memos, and architectural drawings are now kept primarily by the National Archives at Atlanta (NAA). I hope that by using these sources in tandem—the observed landscape and the preserved record—I have been able to respect both the machine and the garden aspects of the atelier's work.

# 1

# REGIONAL PLANNING

## A Model Garden

In 1933 Benton MacKaye published a short essay in *Graphic Survey* about the newly established Tennessee Valley Authority (TVA). MacKaye's tone was triumphant as he declared that, in creating the TVA, President Roosevelt had introduced regional planning to the nation; he had now "sown the seed of that 'national planning' [he had] announced in his inauguration speech."[1] Though the popularity of regional planning among progressive reformers was still relatively new, MacKaye was well qualified to make this declaration: his own career had traversed the multiple discourses the field had attracted. Trained as a forester and employed by the United States Forest Service, MacKaye had participated in field surveys in New Hampshire that formed the basis for the creation of the White Mountain National Forest. At the same time, he advised farmers and other landowners on wood lot management, and he saw forestry as a promising industry to provide meaningful jobs for Americans. Combining his scientific and social interests, MacKaye proposed a new form of homesteading that he referred to as "colonization." Members of these new communities would settle on public land, holding resources in joint ownership and manage functions such as education and marketing through democratic processes. These householders would benefit from the continuity and stability of successful homesteading—preparing themselves for a productive life, they would be spared the fate of so many disintegrating American families. MacKaye believed the power of efficiency, planning, and technical expertise must be dedicated to the goal of social reform rather than business development and resource exploitation.

The year 1921 was pivotal for MacKaye. Following the death of his wife, Betty, MacKaye absorbed himself in his work and expanded his intellectual circle to include a diverse group of progressive planners and architects, and along with them he soon established the Regional Planning Association of America (RPAA).[2] The RPAA was, in part, an extension of discussions in the Committee on Community Planning of the American Institute of Architects (AIA). This committee made a concerted effort to introduce regional planning to architects as a progressive alternative to the more militant modernism debated in Europe.[3] They connected architects' focus on buildings with the wider environment, arguing that "we cannot have good buildings unless we have good cities—that is, unless we have well planned cities. . . . We cannot have functioning well planned cities unless we relate them to the surrounding country—the farms and forests and great recreation grounds." Their goal was to convince architects to seize the opportunity, expand their practice, and develop new technical skills to "serve the community."[4] Clarence Stein, the chair of this committee in 1921, was also among the founders of the RPAA. He used his position as an associate editor of the journal of the AIA to showcase the RPAA's vision. Each issue included a section devoted to community and regional planning in which these ideas were discussed explicitly.[5]

"Democracy" was a key term in the RPAA discussions. Lewis Mumford, who articulated this goal most clearly, was well versed in pragmatist thinking and especially the work of John Dewey. As Ben A. Minteer shows, this philosophical foundation was evident in Mumford's description of the four-part planning process. It was to begin, Mumford argued, with a public survey compiled through a combination of on-site exploration and rigorous data gathering. The second stage was to outline the social ideal and purposes as a way of identifying needs and activities. In the third stage, planners were expected to formulate a new vision for the region, which would then be absorbed by the community and, in the fourth stage, translated into actionable policies and decisions through political action.[6] These steps recall both Dewey's method of inquiry and his emphasis on a balance between professional action and social participation, which he saw as the key to democratic engagement.[7]

The RPAA also drew significantly from Scottish biologist Patrick Geddes, who distinguished between the "paleotechnic" and "neotechnic" approaches.[8] The paleotechnic approach, he argued, had produced the industrial cities of the nineteenth century, in which people could not lead fulfilling lives—what he called *living.* His goal was to create a better world, which he called the neotechnic. In the ancient Neolithic period, he argued, humans were able to live a gentle, agricultural life, devoting considerable time to beauty and the arts, which he saw as the hallmarks of vitality.[9] The claim that agricultural societies are superior to others is an article of faith in his theory, as (he asserted) "every anthropologist knows."[10] Like MacKaye, Geddes looked to a world in which both resources and populations would be dedicated to the bettering of humans and their environment, making possible the pursuit of art and philosophy rather than the mere accumulation of capital.

Geddes identifies as the key to achieving his vision the discipline of town planning, which he describes as a "master-art; vaster than that of street planning, it is *landscape making.*"[11] The RPAA embraced the central implication of Geddes's ideas: the imperative that planners ensure that people could escape the sprawling cities to small, self-contained settlements, in which they could cooperate rather than compete with their neighbors, forming a community. They found a blueprint for this idea in the work of Ebenezer Howard, who in 1902 published *Garden Cities of To-morrow,* based on his earlier work, *To-morrow: A Peaceful Path to Real Reform.*[12] Howard described a region of towns protected by "greenbelts," which he referred to as "garden cities."[13] Such cities, Howard and his followers maintained, would offer people the benefits of stable community together with the spiritual connection to nature.[14] The RPAA members expanded Geddes's and Howard's ideas with an American emphasis on ecological balance and the conservation of natural resources, envisioning what Peter Hall calls an "*urbs in rure.*"[15]

The comprehensive nature of regional planning was mirrored in the collaborative approach adopted by the RPAA members.[16] Members pursued multiple interests even as they contributed to the group discussions. Lewis Mumford developed a vision of a regional future, which he describes as the "fourth migration" in his book *The Culture of Cities* (1938).[17] Catherine Bauer, after a research trip in Europe, wrote of *Modern Housing.*[18] Their work extended the neotechnic ideal to include single-family homes and neighborhood environments. The "adequate equipment of houses, gardens and recreation grounds," they maintained, "will ensure a healthy and stimulating environment."[19] MacKaye, for his part, developed a proposal for a hiking trail following the ridge line, which he named the Appalachian Trail. Here, he combined the goal of dispersing people, agriculture, and industry across a region by means of a new element: recreation—camping, hunting, fishing, and hiking. This proposal was first published in the *Journal of the American Institute of Architects* as "A Project in Regional Planning."[20] MacKaye also developed a utopian definition of regional planning: "Regional planning is a comprehensive ordering or visualizing of possible movement, activity, or flow (from source onward) of water, products, and population, within a defined area or sphere, for the purpose of laying therein the physical basis for extending that range of choice which amounts to the good life or optimum human living."[21]

G. Donald Hudson, a geographer who worked for the TVA, elaborated on this definition using unpublished memorandums by MacKaye. First, he explains, the planning process must have a clear purpose, which is agreed upon at the start of the process. Commitment to this goal, he adds, must be steadfast, even if the process itself changes course in response to new conditions. Hudson also describes planning as visualization: "Planning discovers what nature renders possible. It does not build nature. It builds upon nature. Planning does not produce rainfall or forest growth. It does not contrive. Its beginning is in discovery of visualizing."[22] Finally, Hudson highlights MacKaye's choice of the word "flow" in his definition of regional planning, explaining that determining the movement of water, of commodities (which will enable a balanced agricultural-industrial economy), and of populations is key to creating a livable and desirable environment. MacKaye tied these ideas together in the essay in *Graphic Survey.* It includes several roughly drawn diagrams, and one captions reads: "How population flow might be controlled in the Appalachian valleys. The big dots are principal cities—sources of the 'backflow' of population. The arrows show the trend, via highway. The means of control are A, a townless highway to connect the valleys, B, highwayless towns, C, wilderness area to be reserved on the slopes."[23]

MacKaye's high hopes for the TVA as a planning authority were based primarily on two sections of the TVA Act, numbers 22 and 23. Indeed, he repeatedly declared them to be the "the Magna Carta of American big-scale regional planning."[24] Authority staff who tracked the history of these sections highlighted the persuasive work that was required to secure even these meager allusions.[25] They traced the sections to Fredrick A. Gutheim, a friend of MacKaye's, and planner John Nolen Jr. According to their account, Gutheim had worked behind the scenes with Sen. George Norris, the author of the act, to slip the sections into the version that was approved by Congress.[26] Gutheim's own career offers an example of the zeal that characterized the porous field of environmental planning during the early twentieth century in the United States. While still in college Gutheim met architect Frank Lloyd Wright, edited his papers, and developed a lifelong friendship with him. He also tried his hand at planning a relocation village for Native American in California. Following his work on the TVA Act, Gutheim held public posts in the planning and housing fields. He devoted the bulk of his career to the Washington, DC, area and was seminal to the creation of Washington's metrorail system, the Pennsylvania Avenue Redevelopment Plan, and the new town of Reston.[27]

Reviewing these findings, planner Howard K. Menhinick concluded that this legislative coup owed its success to Roosevelt's personal interest in regional planning: the "idea was basically the President's own, [and] it was he who introduced it to the Tennessee Valley legislation."[28] Roosevelt's fascination owed much to his admiration for professional city planners, including his uncle Frederic Delano. His interpretation of the term "regional," however, focused on transcending legal boundaries and preparing comprehensive visions; he still expected politicians to implement such plans.[29] Indeed, sections 22 and 23 did not direct the TVA to engage in the entire planning process but only authorized the president to request that the Authority engage in the preliminary visualization and the production of surveys and general plans.[30] This broad authorization fell short of the full vision outlined by MacKaye, which would have included the authority to move people and protect wilderness, but even he recognized it as an unprecedented step toward these goals.

Arthur E. Morgan, the first TVA director appointed by the president, read this directive as a mandate to engage in regional planning at both the spiritual and physical levels. Working as a young man in his father's surveying firm in Minnesota had given Morgan a hands-on education in engineering, and by the age of thirty he had earned a reputation as one of the country's best field engineers. After the Miami River flood of 1913, the government of Ohio hired Morgan to design and construct a series of dams for flood control. Perhaps channeling his mother's "evangelical piety," he turned his energy for social reform to the development of homes and small communities for farmers in the region.[31] At the center of these communities were public buildings, surrounded by small cottages equipped with running water, electricity, and sanitation facilities.[32] Following this successful enterprise, Morgan was appointed the president of Antioch College, a position that allowed him to more fully develop his deeply interwoven moral and political stance. He held the job until Roosevelt appointed him to head the TVA in 1933. Morgan's eclectic understanding of reform resembled Roosevelt's, and he shared the president's excitement at the new challenges. He was also convinced that he himself best understood how to translate these goals into actionable plans.[33] He declared: "A common end is to be promoted. It is that the whole people shall have life and have it more abundantly; that young men and women shall find adventure, opportunity and interest, and not despair; that the earth shall yield its toll of crops and minerals and power for the general good, and not chiefly for the favor of a few; that we shall have regard for posterity, and work for the good of tomorrow as well as for today; that industrial development is good only so far as it increases opportunity and health and happiness for the whole people."[34]

Morgan's approach was rooted in his faith, shared by the RPAA, in the moral superiority of trained professionals. In 1934 he described a government led by people who exhibit not only technical knowledge but also a "professional spirit" dedicated to public service as "a regime that would be far superior to universal collectivism." This spirit, he argued, would "dominate the field so that any able business man who did not live by it would be beneath contempt."[35] Morgan believed the ability to plan and execute complex processes was nothing less than the sign of civilization.[36] This belief shaped his managerial style—he set the goals but delegated responsibility for achieving them—which was intended to promote creativity and collaboration. He shied away from establishing clear institutional hierarchies, preferring to surround himself with people he admired and allowing them to develop the projects he would outline. In this worldview, which would come to dominate professional life after World War II, organization and technical expertise were the basis for creativity rather than its death knell. It was a creativity assigned, however, only to a small group of actors—mainly newcomers—in the Tennessee Valley.

## A Model Region

One of Morgan's first actions as TVA director was to establish the Land Planning and Housing Division (LP&H) and place Earle S. Draper at its helm. The new director had graduated from the Massachusetts Agricultural College in 1915 with a Bachelor of Science degree in landscape architecture. He then worked in Massachusetts with the preeminent planner John Nolen. Two years later he moved to Charlotte, North Carolina, to supervise one of Nolen's projects and soon decided to remain in the South. Draper focused on textile mill towns; the program for these towns was a quintessential machine-in-the-garden project. Textile mills needed swift rivers to operate and thus were located in the undeveloped foothills of the Appalachian Mountains. They also needed an efficient and reliable workforce, but the workers in these mills were, for the most part, small-scale farmers who came looking for better incomes. Most of these employees brought their families with them; indeed, entire families would work in the mills together. This cheap but untrained workforce required (from the owners' point of view) constant supervision. Building company towns near the textile mills was one way to achieve this control. Draper, who was hired by the owners, was thus tasked with creating a machine environment for people who were far more familiar with agricultural and pastoral landscapes.

Draper did not question the mill owners' requirement for planned housing to support the efficient functioning of their mills. He insisted, however, that these towns also meet what he saw as minimum standards of light, water, electricity, and other infrastructure, at least for some residents: Black workers were segregated to the margins, and their dwellings were cruder than those built for the white population. At the same time, his designs celebrated the rural origins of the residents rather than the industrial environment in which they now found themselves. As Margaret Crawford shows, this preference was a sympathetic reading of their cultural heritage, even if it did not amount to a radical challenge of their condition.[37] In the course of his practice Draper developed a series of trademark designs to support this goal. These included surrounding the town with greenbelts, constructing winding roads, and building a town center composed of a school and commercial area. He also retained as many wooded areas in and around the towns as he could, weaving them into a system of recreation spaces and parkland. These designs drew heavily on the designs of Fredrick Law Olmsted and allowed the workers to return to "a microcosm of the *Piedmont* landscape" after a long day in the machine.[38]

Draper assumed his new position with the TVA in a double bedroom in the Washington Hotel and then moved to an office in the "old Interior Building" in Washington, DC.[39] He was able to attract talent, especially since the TVA was actively recruiting in government agencies, professional societies, and universities.[40] He would later appoint Tracy B. Augur as his assistant. Augur was a 1917 graduate of Cornell University. In 1921 he completed Harvard's Master of Landscape Architecture program, where he wrote a thesis titled "Industrial Growth in America and the Garden City."[41] Augur described himself as a regional planner and criticized any proposal for garden cities that did not acknowledge the wider regional vision.[42] Before joining the TVA he worked in city planning, including as a consultant to the Detroit City Plan Commission (in connection with their slum clearance project) and the federal Public Works Administration (Housing Division).

The TVA Act specified Muscle Shoals, Alabama, as the official headquarters of the TVA, but the eventual headquarters of the LP&H division was in downtown Knoxville, Tennessee. Arthur Morgan had decided that the organization needed a presence in the center of the area, "from the human standpoint and from the standpoint of low income [people who] needed the help that might come from TVA."[43] In Knoxville the LP&H occupied offices in the Sprankle Building, which also housed the TVA's board of directors, the Office of Information, and, later, the general manager.[44] This proximity allowed them to work collaboratively through multiple opportunities to discuss ideas and comment on work.[45]

In 1934 Draper proposed that the LP&H engage in Project R.P.1: Tennessee Valley Section of the National Plan—a comprehensive scheme that would address architecture and housing, parks and recreation, highways and parkways, general land use, planning legislation, colonization, public relations, and cartography. The primary goal was to identify the areas in the region suitable for settlement, ultimately allowing the TVA to direct settlers to them. At the same time, the plan would assure that industry could be properly and efficiently decentralized across the region. Once the project was approved, Draper set about hiring MacKaye, in the process bidding against the TVA's division of forestry. Draper was successful, and MacKaye joined the LP&H in April 1934. MacKaye's ideas were by then well formulated. He wholeheartedly supported Arthur Morgan's utopian ideas and was seen by some in the agency as a "super-idealist."[46] MacKaye threw himself into the planning project; he produced diagrams and charts to advance the full menu of design tasks under the plan, describing the ideal flow of people and goods across the region.[47] He also discussed extending the TVA's "sphere of influence" over the entire region, to direct its development towards the common good.[48] He would later publish these ideas as part of a discussion of regional planning as human ecology, or the "search for the optimum relation to environment."[49]

The energetic MacKaye failed to convince the TVA administration to adopt his plans, and he eventually lost Arthur Morgan's support, who wondered whether the diagrams and charts were worth the paper they were written on.[50] MacKaye was much more successful at influencing and inspiring his colleagues in the LP&H and infusing their work with the pioneer spirit typical of architectural ateliers (as described in the introduction). He attracted a group of planners, architects, and landscape architects who enjoyed discussing the interconnected elements of regional planning. Dubbed the Philosophers Club, this group included geographers Hudson and Allen Twitchell as well as landscape architects Carroll A. Towne and Robert M. Howes. Daniel Schaffer captures the group's quixotic character: "These TVAers never reached positions of high power within the agency; rather, they would carry the dim torch of regionalism and environmentalism into an era of TVA history marked by overriding concerns for low-cost and economic growth."[51] MacKaye's subsequent departure from the TVA in July 1936 owed something to his own personality and his inability to work within an institution. By all accounts an "eccentric and hardheaded man," he clashed with Draper, who became exasperated by his utopian approach and, especially, by his leading young colleagues into an "immature cynicism."[52]

Draper and the LP&H were much more successful in implementing Morgan's more specific directive: to create a model region in the area surrounding the first TVA dam, built on the Clinch River (a tributary of the Tennessee) in Cove Creek, Tennessee. The dam was later named Norris Dam after Sen. George Norris, who had spearheaded the legislation that established the TVA. This project was possible because the river machine, which was under Arthur Morgan's direct supervision, required the appropriation of land. The TVA could legally buy, or take by eminent domain, the parcels required for building the dam and filling the reservoir. This meant a dramatic change in land ownership and, of course, the displacement of thousands of individuals. Many in the TVA advocated that the Authority buy only what was necessary for construction, but Arthur Morgan insisted that the TVA think ahead and plan the region after the dam was completed. He was especially cognizant that in creating a reservoir the TVA was inundating the river valleys—the best farmland. He insisted that the TVA buy entire farms, not just the portions in the valley, so that families would not be left with only the less productive part of their farms. He also advocated buying "marginal" land and converting it to public use.[53]

Morgan's land-purchasing policy was used liberally at Norris, where he directed the LP&H planners and landscape architects (rather than the engineers) to establish the full extent of the "taking lines" for the reservoir. The purchase includes, for example, a peninsula that was never expected to be covered by water, but its residents would have needed new, and expensive, access bridges across the reservoir. By including it in the reservoir "taking lines," the TVA displaced sixteen families. W. H. Droze recounts: "Some became dam builders. Others left the farm for non-farm jobs. Still others became part-time farmers. Some relocated and became full-time small acreage farmers who dominate the rural population of the eastern part of the Valley."[54] This land is known today as the Chuck Swan Wildlife Management Area and offers visitors access to the undeveloped banks of the reservoir, where the water level fluctuates dramatically with the changing seasons (fig. 3).

The land amassed at Norris was surveyed and studied, and visions for its reorganization were drawn and discussed within the TVA. The planning process did not, however, follow the fourth step described by Mumford; this step had been preempted when the previous landowners had relocated to new homes. More importantly, Arthur Morgan wanted to demonstrate how a planned region might look, not the process of planning itself. Indeed, the land amassed at Norris was refashioned as MacKaye's vision in miniature. It includes the dam itself and its demesne and an adjacent demonstration (now state) park, which we will return to in chapters 3 and 6. The core of the model region, however, is the highwayless town, townless highway, and wilderness areas MacKaye identified in his 1933 essay in *Graphic Survey*.[55]

The town, as the beacon of a renewed citizenry, was at the center of the project, and in October 1933 it too was named Norris.[56] Like earlier garden city models—and drawing especially on the design of Radburn, New Jersey—it is surrounded by a protective greenbelt, and its generously sized sidewalks are separated from the roads

**Figure 3.** The undeveloped banks of the reservoir behind Norris Dam. The TVA controls the water level and adjusts it to prevent floods and maximize power production. These rocky banks were once the most productive farms in the region but are now marginal land supporting the smooth functioning of the TVA river machine.

intended for vehicular traffic. Special attention was given to the town's community spaces, particularly the centrally located school and the large commons in front of it, designed to offer a picturesque setting for individual and community recreation (fig. 4). Draper and his staff designed a small commercial area that included a space for the display and sale of local agricultural products.[57] Arthur Morgan hoped Norris would develop into a hub of small-scale industry for the surrounding rural region. Ceramics manufacture was selected as promising direction, and Norris also houses service buildings, warehouses, and a ceramics laboratory, which was eventually turned over to the United States Bureau of Mines (fig. 5). One of the first plates the ceramics factory produced featured a map of the TVA region surrounded by rough sketches of the projects it was engaged in, a signal to Arthur Morgan's commitment to regional planning as a holistic enterprise.[58]

Norris, Tennessee, is connected to its closest neighbors (Knoxville and Coal Creek, now named Rocky Top) by another element of the model region—the Norris Freeway (fig. 6).[59] Draper described this design in glowing tones, comparing

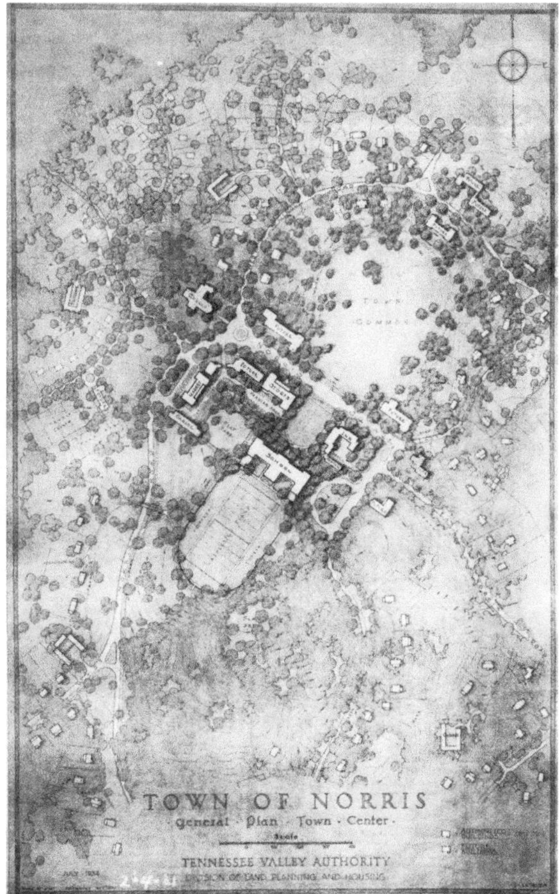


**Figure 4.** A landscape plan for the town center at Norris, Tennessee, drawn and rendered in crayon by Osborne H. Graves and dated July 1934. In an attached note Graves comments that the plan was based on his own studies and on "consultation with the Architecture Section." The buildings marked "School" and "Market," as well as the houses and shared garages, were completed according to this plan.

it favorably to both state and federal highways and to conventional parkways and boulevards: "A freeway, as planned by the Authority, will be simply a wide rural roadway, designed in regard for landscape beauty, safety, land use and highway utility."[60] He also extolled the aesthetics of the road, commenting that "the freeway has been designed as a natural development, rather than a gashed line of communication between two points. Literally, it has been molded into the earth—a man-made

**Figure 5.** The industrial center in Norris, Tennessee. Arthur E. Morgan envisioned the production of porcelain from the rich Kaolin clay deposits in the region. The building is used today by the TVA Norris Engineering Lab.

structure treated as a natural formation."[61] Draper directed that the freeway be planted with local shrubs and trees, which would harmonize the new form with its surroundings. This work was completed between April 1934 and November 1935, when two Civilian Conservation Corps (CCC) camps were engaged in seeding and sodding, bank sloping, grading, ditching, planting, and building wayside picnic areas, all overseen by the LP&H staff.[62] The Norris Freeway represents a built example of what MacKaye called the "townless highway." Such roads, he posited, would support the regional vision by offering drivers a pleasant, perhaps even recreational, drive between destinations, encouraging them to support the regional model (fig. 7).

Surrounding both town and freeway is another element of MacKaye's vision: a publicly managed forest, known as Norris Lake Forest, then Norris Reservoir Area, and now the Norris Watershed. The land had been purchased primarily to protect the reservoir through erosion control, but by 1935 it was designated as a demonstration unit for the forestry and farming development envisioned by MacKaye.[63] The

**Figure 6.** Photograph captioned "Surfacing Freeway Between Halls Cross Roads and Norris Dam," dated May 31, 1934. This image was included in a report on the relocation of roads and highways traversing the area flooded by the Norris Reservoir.

TVA prepared a detailed management plan to show how the region could be developed as an "integrated economic unit," combining watershed protection, timber production, and forest recreation, including housing for the forestry workers.[64] This forest included areas for demonstrating the advantages and methods of "good" rather than exploitive silviculture: "The application of practical methods of forest management on a sustained yield basis," to use the TVA description.[65] The Watershed still offers recreational activities, including hiking trails, to residents and tourists and opportunities to enjoy natural surroundings individually or as a group (fig. 8).

Working on the Norris region, the LP&H planners, architects, and landscape architects were encouraged to "approach the design problem from a fresh point of view and to make a complete reappraisal of essential and nonessential points in

**Figure 7.** The Norris Freeway and the Clinch River between Norris Dam and the town of Norris. This is a popular location for fishing enthusiasts—the TVA built a small weir dam to oxygenate the water and encourage fish breeding.

housing and town planning."[66] They also experimented with new techniques, such as plotting the location of the Norris Freeway using a low-flying airplane.[67] They worked collaboratively—and anonymously: none of the elements in the Norris model region were attributed to a single individual. Augur, who consulted on the plan for the town before he joined the LP&H as Draper's deputy, described this aspect in glowing terms: "In its planning Norris truly exemplified the collaborative effort needed for success in modern community planning. Architects, landscape architects, engineers and town planners comprising the staff of the TVA Division of Land Planning and Housing, under the guiding hand of Earle S. Draper, Director, pooled their efforts and their skills to produce the blueprint for a living community."[68]

The LP&H was as diverse as Augur described. Draper was continually recruiting new talent, and the TVA project attracted professionals who shared a progressive commitment to its mission. The lack of a clear hierarchy allowed individuals scope

**Figure 8.** Norris Dam as viewed from the Norris Watershed. This observation point was designed by the TVA landscape architects and constructed by members of a Civilian Conservation Corps camp stationed at Norris Dam in the 1930s.

to innovate and to shine in numerous ways. This was especially true of the Town and Site Planning Section within the division, which was responsible for the design and construction at Norris. This section was composed of landscape architects by training, or by choice, and was directed by Carroll A. Towne. Towne had graduated in 1923 from the University of Massachusetts (then the Massachusetts State College); he joined the TVA a decade later and remained on its staff for more than twenty years. He enthusiastically embraced the TVA's goals and methods: "There is a great deal of detail that I could go into with regard to the adventures involved in locating and designing and subsequently observing the construction of these communities."[69]

Another stalwart member of the Town and Site Planning Section was Osborne H. Graves—who was known as "Bib"—an architect by training (and a Syracuse University graduate) whose interest in city planning had taken root in college. After working for a while as an architect, he wandered into the office of a landscape architect in Providence, Rhode Island, and discovered an interest in site and landscape planning. Switching professions, he worked with Thomas Sears from 1915 to 1933, managing a staff of twenty-five until the Great Depression curtailed their work. When Graves approached Draper, he was invited to join the LP&H for a modest salary; at around age forty-three, he was older than most of his new colleagues. He first moved without his family to Muscle Shoals, Alabama, to work with landscape architect Sam Brewster on recreation projects in the area. After just three months, his work was noticed in Knoxville; Graves was invited to join the team working on the plans for Norris.[70]

Harold C. Frincke, also a landscape architect, had trained at Cornell and had worked for the Westchester County Park Commission (under Gilmore D. Clark) and at a variety of other public agencies. In the 1930s Frincke joined the CCC and moved to Gatlinburg, Tennessee, to oversee work on the newly created Great Smoky Mountains National Park. Preferring the valley to the mountains, he applied for a job at the TVA and was hired in September 1933, while the LP&H was still unorganized. Frincke was committed to public work: "When I came to the understanding that I wasn't going to be a world-renowned landscape architect—I was just going to be a TVA landscape architect—I wanted to be their best one."[71] One of his new colleagues was Herbert S. Conover, also fresh from the CCC, who provided "planning from a horticultural point of view."[72] Conover had won recognition as a student at Pennsylvania State College for his design of "a landscape setting . . . portraying a paved terrace with a modern garden termination feature, a fountain, and an enclosure of clipped hedges, beyond which was a naturalistic background planting."[73] The TVA work—larger in scale, scope, and purpose—presented a very different kind of challenge.

## A Model House

In April 1935 Carroll and Emily S. Towne moved from Knoxville to Norris and settled in a four-room house at 85 Pine Road (fig. 9). The house, surrounded by the well-tended garden, was similar in plan to nineteen other houses in the town, all built to the specifications of Type 41E. In the original design the house was entered on center, with a small porch covering the front door, opening directly to a spacious living room equipped with a fireplace. Those continuing into the house discovered a small hallway leading to a kitchen on one side and to two bedrooms and access to

**Figure 9.** The permanent residence at 85 Pine Road, Norris, Tennessee. This house was home to Carroll and Emily Towne in the 1930s. Emily Towne was involved in many of the town's social and landscaping initiatives. Carroll Towne was a central figure in the Land Planning and Housing Division and later the TVA's Department of Regional Studies.

the attic on the other. The single bathroom—a detail that Emily Towne attributed Lucy Morgan's penurious opposition to "luxuries"—was centrally located off the hall as well.[74] Both the kitchen and one of the bedrooms had access to large, screened porches, separated by a dedicated laundry room. The porch connected to the bedroom was specifically labeled as a sleeping porch, and these interior/exterior spaces added about 30 percent to the 1,820-square-foot footprint of the house. Constructed of pine boards with an oak floor (produced locally) and Celotex walls and ceilings, the house was made of the same combination of local and new materials used to construct all the homes in the town. It was equipped with electric hot water, a range and refrigerator, and portable heating: the TVA had spent $7,242,72 building it.[75] TVA director David E. Lilienthal and his family lived in a home with the same layout, though its dimensions were slightly larger.

The houses in Norris played a significant role in the garden rhetoric: each house represented a building block of a model community, a base that would support individual growth and family life, preparing citizens to engage democratically in public.

From the designers' perspective, the Norris houses provided the necessary comforts and convenience. The solid and well-built structure was mechanically heated, offering a haven in the cold winters, while the screened porches extended the house in the hot summer months. As to efficiency, they would have pointed proudly to the carefully laid out and well-equipped kitchens, which relied on electric power and offered considerable storage space. These kitchens, they would have argued, followed Patrick Geddes's dictum that a "housewife" should have the opportunity to develop her skills in "home-building" with the help of modern conveniences and hygiene.[76] Geddes maintained that such kitchens could serve as the basis for women becoming full citizens, able to inspire social uplift and cultural advances. TVA personnel, however, did not challenge social norms about race or gender, and they did not mention the role of women while discussing the homes they had designed and in which several planners, including the Townes, lived.

The importance of the design of the Norris houses was registered in the creation of a section dedicated to this task. Draper first recruited Roland A. Wank—whom he described as "one of the most gifted architects that I have ever met"—to direct this section.[77] Born in Budapest, Wank was a 1903 Beaux Arts student at the Royal Technical University in Budapest and later studied in Brunn and Vienna. He worked designing factories, bridges, and power plants before emigrating to the United States in 1924. He began his American career in New York, working for a firm named Springsteen and Goldhammer to design housing for the Amalgamated Clothing Workers—the first project for which he claimed credit.[78] His most important project in the United States was the design of the Cincinnati Union Terminal, with the firm Fellheimer & Wagner. Wank was eager for the role in the federal agency. He would later contribute to *Technical America,* the journal of the left-leaning Federation of Architects, Engineers, Chemists, and Technicians, writing about being employed by the public, which, he argued was the "architect's special obligation."[79]

Wank's interests were wide ranging, and he soon turned his attention to a very different kind of work—the design of the dams and powerhouses (work I will discuss in chapter 3). Draper then recruited a Knoxville architect, Charles I. Barber, to direct the Norris project. Barber was the son of George F. Barber, an architect who specialized in residential architecture and published his designs for houses to wide acclaim. Charles Barber studied Beaux Arts design at the University of Pennsylvania under Paul Cret and later cofounded an award-winning, nationally recognized firm, Barber & McMurry, which still operates today. Barber's knowledge of houses and of local materials was instrumental in the design of permanent houses at the Norris, Wheeler, and Pickwick Landing Dams, but he did not remain long with TVA, preferring to return to private practice. At that point, Louis Grandgent took on much of the design responsibility for Norris. Grandgent was an MIT graduate with a Beaux Arts education who had served as architectural director at Antioch College in Illinois, where Arthur Morgan had been president.[80] Among his early designs were the award-winning "Pavilion in a Ark for Orchestral Concerts" and "Interior Design of a Monumental Window in the Waiting-Room of a Great Railroad Terminal."[81] Grandgent was also interested in technical issues: he filed a patent application for a garage door that a driver could operate without exiting the vehicle (granted in 1934).[82]

The design and construction of the Norris houses provide an example of how the atelier negotiated the intersection between their utopian ideals—the garden—and the realities of the TVA machine. The schedule for design and construction of the houses at Norris was brutal. Preliminary surveys were begun in August 1933, and working drawings for the houses were ready three months later in November. Construction began in January 1934, and by September of the same year 150 houses were in use.[83] To meet this goal the Architecture Section applied machine logic to the task. The houses were based on thirty types, allowing the architects in the LP&H to standardize their own design work and then the houses' construction (fig. 10). The section documented its work meticulously and continued to gather data after the houses were complete (fig. 11). The houses were built to high standards (for the region) and equipped with running water and other utilities; most were also connected to the electric grid. Notably, however, none of these houses were occupied by African American families. Morgan and other officials had argued that creating a "section" for Black families would have cost more than the project could afford—a textbook example of cloaking prejudice in the language of efficiency while ignoring the severe historic implications of excluding a disadvantaged population from the utopian vision.[84]

The outward appearance of the finished houses belies their mechanical construction. Wank, whose progressive approach to architecture had been honed in Europe, was sincerely committed to "honesty" and "authenticity" and argued for a modernist

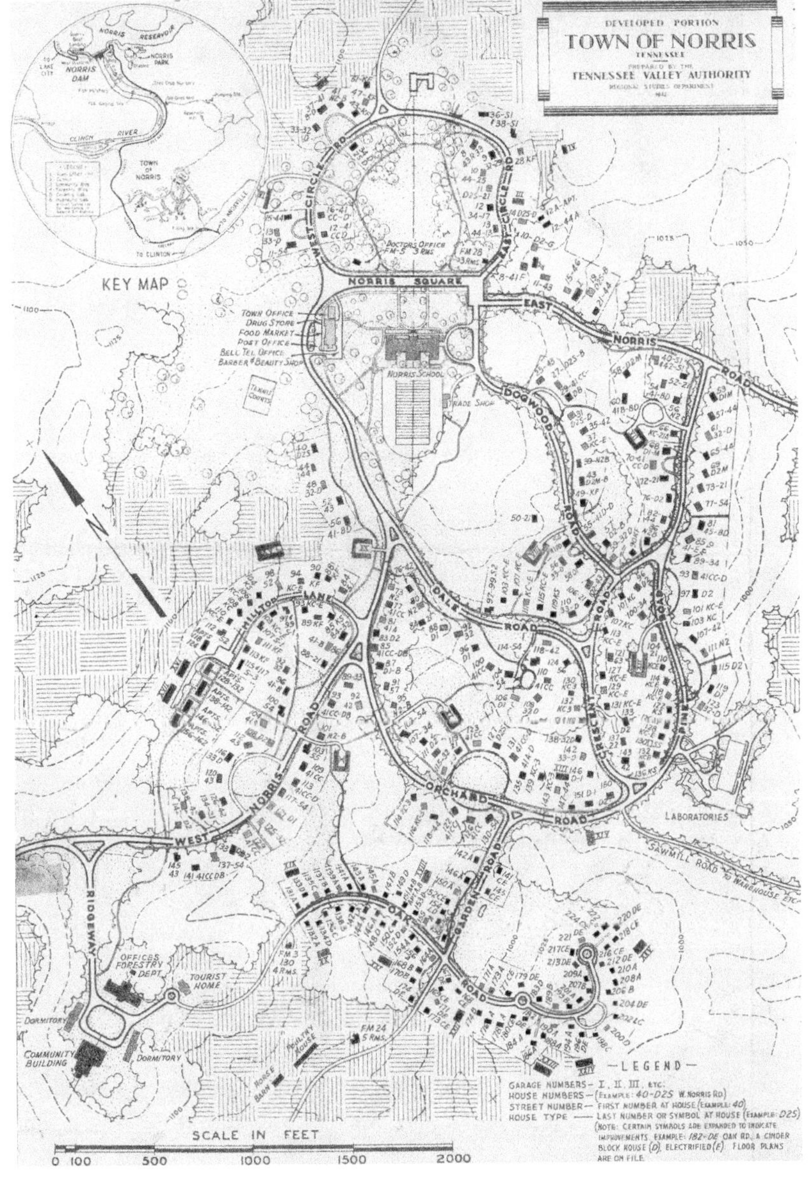


**Figure 10.** A map showing *The Developed Portion, Town of Norris, Tennessee*, prepared by TVA's Department of Regional Studies in 1942. The plan documents not only the location of the houses but also their type and any added improvements (e.g., a connection to electricity). The cluster of large buildings in the bottom left-hand corner is the construction camp built for the employees building the dam. By 1942 they had been converted to community use.

TVA 406
TENNESSEE VALLEY AUTHORITY

STRUCTURAL DETAIL SHEET

LOCATION Norris, Tennessee
TYPE 21
BUILDING NO 119 Orchard Road
REFER TO PLANS attached

PLACE Norris, Tennessee
DESIGNATION OF BUILDING Permanent residence CAPACITY 3 rooms & bath
TOTAL COST $ 5,008.25 DATE COMPLETED June 16, 1934
MATERIALS: WALLS Brick veneer FOUNDATION Brick
ROOF Hand rived oak shingles FLOORS T&G oak
TOTAL FLOOR AREA ABOVE BASEMENT, SQUARE FEET 825
SIZE MAIN BUILDING 38'-0" x 22'-6" WINGS None BASEMENT None
HEIGHT OF FIRST FLOOR ABOVE GROUND Varies with grade
HOW LIGHTED Electric
WATER CONNECTIONS Yes
SEWER CONNECTIONS Yes
GAS CONNECTIONS No

| HEATERS | |
|---|---|
| TYPE | TVA NO |
| Electric hot water | 24161 |
| Portable electric | 40035 |
| " " | 40001 |
| Electric range | 24262 |

| REFRIGERATOR | |
|---|---|
| TYPE | TVA NO |
| Electric | 24962 |

| METERS | | |
|---|---|---|
| TYPE | LINE | SERIAL NO |

ADDITIONS AND INSTALL
(Below enter chronologically all modifications, additions, introducti

K-71-D

K-84-B

INSTRUCTIONS—"a" State whether heated from central heating or by individual heating plants, stoves, furnaces, or fireplaces.
"b" State whether steam, vapor, hot water, hot air, or electric.
"c" State whether gas, coal, oil, or central heating plant.

See reverse

**Figure 11.** "Structural Detail Sheet" prepared in February 1936 by the TVA architects for a permanent residence in Norris, completed a year and half earlier. Built to the plans of Type 21, this is one of the smaller houses, extended with a screened porch. As part of the experiments with building materials conducted at Norris, this specific house was fitted with a copper gutter.

articulation of the facades.[85] He would have seen such aesthetics as a way to clarify and order the situation in the new town. Arthur Morgan and Draper took what Leo Marx might call the sentimental approach.[86] They directed the architects to study local homes as "aids for building designs."[87] Following these investigations the designers incorporated local materials and methods, including wood shakes, hand-split wooden shingles, and stone foundations and chimneys. This was in part an economic choice—the TVA paid local residents for this work in the winter months. More importantly, however, it was a symbolic move: combining local traditions and modern techniques into one architectural element was a romantic gesture. It tied regional planning, and specifically garden cities, to a widely held image of Appalachian people as the lost frontiersmen.[88]

The houses at Norris are each markedly different, despite their shared plans. Draper, in fact, boasted: "There is no monotony in Norris Houses."[89] This is due, in part, to Draper's expertise in site development; as Phoebe Cutler notes, "Open space supersedes architecture."[90] Under his direction the garden city diagram was carefully adapted to each site to take advantage of its topography. The lots, which Draper laid out in the field rather than on a plan, are generous, and each house was individually sited in its specific plot. The product of this lengthy process is evident in each of the homes, which boast either views, generous gardens, or both. The careful site planning also allows residents to make good use of the porches, which are mostly shielded from neighborly intrusion by trees. The town of Norris represents all the principles Draper developed in the Piedmont and is an exemplar of Geddes's vision of "*landscape making*."[91] As such, it is a literal interpretation of *garden* in the *machine*.

The TVA promoted the Norris model widely; Draper prepared descriptive press releases. The atelier also employed professional magazines; in August 1939 the *Architectural Forum* included plans of the Towne house type (together with other models and photographs of interiors) in a lengthy article devoted to all aspects of the TVA project.[92] Detailed information on the houses, including architectural drawings, was publicly available for fifty cents per set.[93] In 1936 Draper reported that the LP&H had addressed neighborhood groups to encourage home improvement and had collaborated with the regional extension service on a "mimeographed booklet on rural home building, landscaping, etc."[94] The TVA persisted in this project and in 1950 was able to report that twenty different agencies—including national, state, and local organizations (clubs, lodges, churches)—had participated in their educational effort.[95] Information was also disseminated indirectly: in 1938 the Knoxville Small House Bureau published a brochure of small house designs, a number of which were the work of the firm Barber & McMurry.

The TVA promotional material was based on the assumption that the Norris houses were superior to the regional building stock. This was an easy argument to make; readers most likely compared them to their image of mountain homes (see fig. 2). These cabins were indeed dramatically different than the Norris houses. They were almost invariably built by the homeowners themselves or by members of their community, using traditional building methods, some of which dated back to the European colonization of the region in the early nineteenth century. Simple and makeshift, these houses were inefficient, offering not much more than basic shelter. The TVA circulated images of such cabins taken by photographer Lewis W. Hine in October 1933 in the area to be inundated after Norris was complete.[96] Residents are pictured working in the fields around the house or gathered as a family on the porch or by the fireplace. The caption of one of these images reads, for example: "Family group of Fletcher Carden, Route #1, Andersonville, Tennessee, a night-watchman at the bunkhouses at Norris Dam. His home is on the townsite of Norris and will be moved. Carden has 12 children. He is shown here repairing shoes at the fireside."[97]

The mountain cabins, however, represented only a fraction of the homes in the Tennessee Valley. In fact, even as the LP&H was transforming the Norris region, colleagues in the Social and Economic Division, which would later be merged with Draper's unit, were conducting studies of the local population in which they assumed that the residents of the valleys (the more fertile land) were representative of the rural population in the region. Their houses were of much higher quality than the mountain cabins, both sturdier and better insulated. In fact, the Town and Site Planning Section preserved and reused such houses in Norris (fig. 12). The most important difference between the local farmhouses and the Norris houses was their plan. Farmhouses included multiple rooms, but these were usually multifunctional and opened onto each other rather than a shared hallway. Such arrangements were expansions of nineteenth-century working-class homes, which were usually divided between a kitchen and a workspace, with residents sleeping in the main room or in small additions or attics.[98] Such layouts, the TVA staff assumed, offered little or privacy.[99]

The Norris houses, by comparison, followed what Thomas C. Hubka and Judith T. Kenny call the "Progressive Era Plan."[100] By the 1930s, they explain, nine specific rooms and domestic amenities had come to be regarded as the basis for comfortable housing: a dedicated bathroom with three fixtures (sink, toilet and bath); a kitchen with appliances and other "housework improvements"; a room dedicated to dining; private bedrooms; a front porch; a garage to house the family car; ample storage; and a connection to public utilities, including electricity.[101] These were all features of the Norris houses, except the private garage; residents were expected to use shared parking structures as part of the TVAs insistence on community (fig. 13). These nine elements were also the topics of a set of circulars prepared by the architect Max H. Falkner of the Tennessee Extension Service, whose work was financed by the TVA. Falkner's circulars discussed myriad topics—estimates and costs, foundations, fram-

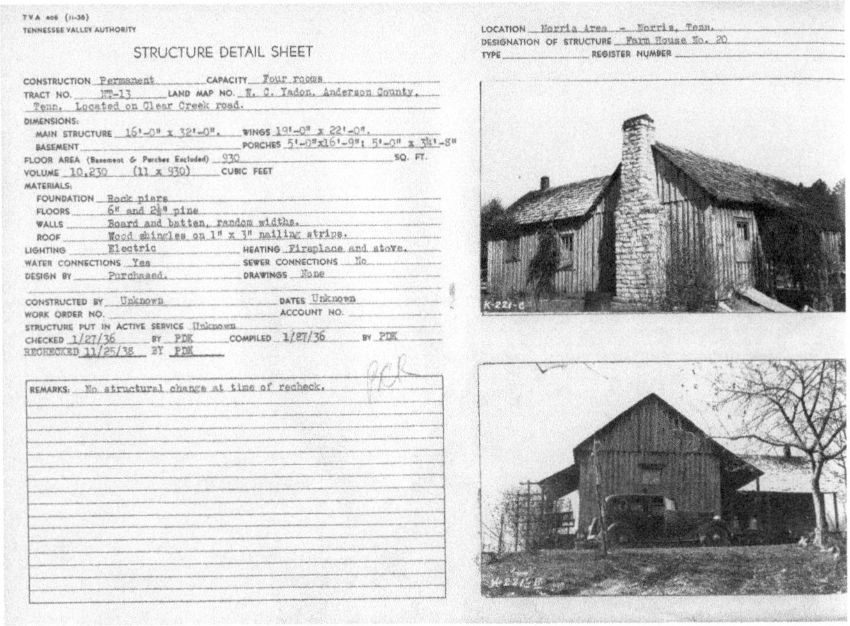

TVA 406 (11-36)
TENNESSEE VALLEY AUTHORITY

STRUCTURE DETAIL SHEET

CONSTRUCTION Permanent CAPACITY Four rooms
TRACT NO. NT-13 LAND MAP NO. W. C. Yadon, Anderson County, Tenn. Located on Clear Creek road.
DIMENSIONS:
MAIN STRUCTURE 16'-0" x 32'-0". WINGS 19'-0" x 22'-0".
BASEMENT PORCHES 5'-0"x16'-9"; 5'-0" x 34'-8"
FLOOR AREA (Basement & Porches Excluded) 930 SQ. FT.
VOLUME 10,230 (11 x 930) CUBIC FEET
MATERIALS:
FOUNDATION Rock piers
FLOORS 6" and 2½" pine
WALLS Board and batten, random widths.
ROOF Wood shingles on 1" x 3" nailing strips.
LIGHTING Electric HEATING Fireplace and stove.
WATER CONNECTIONS Yes SEWER CONNECTIONS No
DESIGN BY Purchased. DRAWINGS None
CONSTRUCTED BY Unknown DATES Unknown
WORK ORDER NO. ACCOUNT NO.
STRUCTURE PUT IN ACTIVE SERVICE Unknown
CHECKED 1/27/36 BY PDK COMPILED 1/27/36 BY PDK
RECHECKED 11/25/38 BY PDK
REMARKS: No structural change at time of recheck.

LOCATION Norris Area - Norris, Tenn.
DESIGNATION OF STRUCTURE Farm House No. 20
TYPE REGISTER NUMBER

K-221-C

K-221-B

**Figure 12.** "Structural Detail Sheet" prepared in February 1936 by the TVA architects for the W. C. Yadon farmhouse, which had been incorporated into the Norris community. Built of board and batten with a wood-shingle roof, the house was connected to water and electricity but was heated with woodburning fireplaces and stoves.

ing, interior walls and ceilings, insulation, ventilation, and termite protection—all as part of the "proper" design of houses. Falkner also emphasized the importance of the site: "The location of the house is important but cannot be done on paper. . . . Prevailing winds, vistas and views, the location of other farm buildings and of drives and highways, all have their influence."[102]

The Norris houses, and their paper derivatives, took the ambiguous language in the TVA Act—"fostering an orderly and proper physical, economic, and social development"—and translated it into detailed design.[103] Private rooms, the LP&H staff assumed, allowed family members to develop individual interests and prepared them to participate in family and social life as active contributors rather than as subjects. They thus made a connection between the design of houses and the utopian goals they espoused as regional planners. The presentation of this connection, however, was shaped by the institution in which they practiced; the political argument

**Figure 13.** Photograph of community parking garage no. 11 in Norris. This garage was in the center of town, adjacent to the house featured in figure 11. It had twenty-seven stalls and cost nearly $5,000 to construct.

is masked by the language of resource conservation. This argument was more easily accepted, even though it was not necessarily true. Tennessee Valley native Paul K. Conkin, who went on to write important histories of the TVA, undermines it:

> The farm was confining because of the care of livestock, but the work was usually leisurely. As a matter of strict religious principles, no one worked on Sunday except for necessary chores and the cooking of meals. Laundry on Monday was hard work, but the amount was slight by contemporary standards (one set of sheets per bed, two or three towels, and only one set of soiled clothes for each person). A broom was used for most housecleaning. Children usually washed and dried the dishes. My mother, despite all she accomplished, always took an hour after lunch for a nap. My father never worked, or required me to work, beyond noon on Saturday, except during the harvest.[104]

Conkin does, however, recognize how electricity changed his village, explaining: "When people first gained electricity (beginning in 1940), they referred to their electric bills as their light bills (some still do)."[105] He describes the many ways electricity did indeed substantially decrease time needed for chores, especially washing clothes, and extended the active hours. The TVA rhetoric thus conflated a preferred social layout with technological changes—especially electric appliances—that Tennessee Valley residents were adopting, supported by the TVA power machine. This conflation would shape the atelier's efforts in the housing field in the next two decades (see chapter 5.) The preference for technical over political arguments became the hallmark of the professional language of architecture, landscape architecture and planning, and will still be familiar to practitioners and their clients today.

The atelier submitted to the institutional structure of the TVA, and especially its legal substrate, in another way as well. Among the Tennessee Valley residents was one group who would have objectively benefited from the design and construction of new houses: the families, including those photographed by Hine, whose homes would be flooded by the rising reservoirs.[106] The efforts to support this group, however, were highly circumscribed. TVA personnel were legally limited to assisting displaced residents only in locating real estate and providing advice about future homes. Michael J. McDonald and John Muldowney lament that despite Roosevelt's rhetoric about the "forgotten Americans," the TVA allowed its legal department to curtail its actions in the region.[107] In practice this meant that TVA staff had to refer residents to national and state relief agencies, as well as to local citizens and businesses, for direct support. This practice limited the data and knowledge they produced that might have been helpful in improving economic opportunities more generally.[108]

Most displaced residents had many months before a dam was completed, which was considered time enough to identify a new location to either build or refurbish a house.[109] The Tennessee Extension Service took the lead in working with individuals on their particular challenges, but Draper and the LP&H undertook an extension role of their own, reporting in 1936 that "much of the rural architects' time was spent in the field rendering individual service to displaced families requiring special assistance in working out their building problems."[110] This work was time-consuming: in 1936 eighty-one families were furnished with detailed house plans and another thousand with plans for kitchens. Here, too, African American families were discriminated against. None of the field agents were Black, and they tended to assume that "black families were not being uprooted from settled communities and that poor farmers were eager to leave farming."[111] The TVA also accepted direct financial responsibility, reimbursing other agencies for their extra expenses involved in supporting those dispossessed by the TVA projects.[112] After the 1937 reorganization of the TVA, this quasi-extension work was coordinated by the Department of Reservoir Property Management rather than the Department of Regional Studies, and the atelier focused on other challenges.

The Norris demonstration region achieved its goal; it is the physical manifestation of what was until then only an idea. It also provided an opportunity for members of the newly formed LP&H to form the atelier spirit that characterized their work. Noted economist Stuart Chase, who was also a member of the RPAA, described the TVA in a four-part essay in *The Nation* in 1936, claiming it as the "New Deal's Greatest Asset." [113] A copy, belonging to Chase, of an early organizational chart for the Authority outlines not only the mandated river, land, and power machines but also the development of elements of the regional demonstration. These include housing and resettlement projects, new highways and industries, and the revival of local arts and crafts. A column titled "new resource base" refers to the development of tourism and includes a long list of recreational facilities such as new parks, swimming beaches, campsites, summer cottages, speedboats, and fisheries.[114] This list outlines the scope of project the TVA architects, landscape architects, and regional planners strove to achieve in the following two decades.

# 2

# A PLANNING REGION

## Land Planning

Arthur E. Morgan represented the idealistic thinker on the Tennessee Valley Authority (TVA) board of directors.[1] It was he who championed the utopian goal of wholesale regional planning. Focused on social and individual improvement, he could not imagine falling short of the full garden. Harcourt A. Morgan, his fellow director, shared these concerns but believed in resource conservation as the vehicle for change. An early ecologist, he maintained that people and nature were interdependent, a relationship that created meaning in human life: "Man has a need for "a reason for being"—a purpose in life beyond that of immediate personal gain and satisfaction—a common mooring to help him understand his importance and his responsibilities in the eternal plan of life. He must realize that he alone of all living creatures has the urge to inquire, discover, and use the results; the ability to unravel the universal laws of nature, and the intelligence to become her cooperating partner."[2]

The key to this "common mooring" was the soil. Maintaining good soil cover was both an end in itself and the basis for the garden; only by cultivating the soil could people cultivate their lives and minds. Stuart Chase described Harcourt

Morgan talking about soil "ablaze with excitement" and full of "passion and tenderness."[3] James Dahir emphasized that this focus was "a conviction bordering on an obsession . . . a moral issue."[4] Harcourt Morgan was thus the TVA representative of a central focus in progressive circles—soil conservation was a national concern in the 1930s, following the devastating dust storms in the plains. Special attention was given to the South, which had always suffered from water erosion; for many Americans the Tennessee Valley was the most dramatic example of this problem.[5] The Department of the Interior had a Soil Erosion Service (a research and demonstration agency), and Franklin D. Roosevelt commissioned a national survey to map the dangers to the nation's soil resources. As Neil M. Maher explains, worries about the health of the environment had a long history in American culture, in which "nature, not humans, made landscapes sick, while human labor such as agriculture transformed such places into more healthy spaces."[6] Harnessing the TVA machine toward soil conservation was thus yet another way to connect the enterprise with a hallowed past.

In the Tennessee Valley, saving the soil required changing farming practices from a reliance on row crops such as cotton, corn, and tobacco to farming legumes such as clover and lespedeza, augmented with fruit trees and animal husbandry. Such a change, Harcourt Morgan argued, would require the use of fertilizers, which would help produce and fix nitrate in the ground, turning exploited land into fertile soil. Congress had recognized this task when it assigned the TVA the responsibility for the nitrate factories at Muscle Shoals, Alabama. These were converted to the production of fertilizers, using new synthetic processes that had been perfected in Germany (fig. 14).[7] Fertilizers appear, alongside power and forestation, in early outlines for the Authority's units, and Harcourt Morgan oversaw the development of a robust research program in Northern Alabama, which augmented the research and development programs of the Department of Agriculture.[8] The TVA also produced fertilizers and distributed them to residents of the Tennessee Valley. This system, which was based on the principle that "the benefits of federal projects should go to small operators who would prosper through the application of their own energy," challenged Arthur Morgan's centralized planning efforts most clearly.[9]

Harcourt Morgan's professional experience was rooted in agriculture. A Canadian, by 1933 he had become an honorary Tennessean. He first arrived in the region as an agronomist, helping farmers combat several severe pest infestations: the boll

**Figure 14.** A photograph taken by architect George L. Richardson (or one of his associates) in the 1930s. The original caption identifies the location as the "Grounds at Main Office, Fertilizer Works."

weevil, the gypsy moth, and the cattle tick. He combined laboratory research with onsite field tutorials, first developing agricultural remedies and then convincing and training farmers to use them. He visited one county after another, talking with thousands of farmers and gaining their trust. Harcourt Morgan was also an experienced administrator, having served as dean of the University of Tennessee College of Agriculture and then, after 1919, as president of the university, where he oversaw a significant transformation in the institution's health and status.[10] In the late 1920s he also served as president of the Association of Land Grant Colleges and Universities. People in the Tennessee Valley, he argued, would not take directions from an unfamiliar, federally imposed agency. Without regional support the Authority and its programs would "be disregarded and cast aside."[11] Harcourt Morgan believed the TVA's path forward lay in delegating authority to institutions that had already gained regional trust—the land-grant colleges (such as the one he had presided over) and their established extension services. These agencies "extended" academic research into the field, informing farmers about new technologies and demonstrating their usefulness through a small army of field agents armed with flyers, circulars, and displays.

The land machine was thus inherently different from the river machine. The project of building the dams had clear boundaries, schedules, and methods. The rising reservoirs would inevitably replace local social traditions and political ties. Working on the land, in contrast, required direct and ongoing interaction with the citizens of the Valley, incorporating "ideas which are basic in democracy, such as voluntary participation and local initiative."[12] Harcourt Morgan proceeded to develop such a system, based on demonstration farms. Farmers who volunteered to be part of the program would allow agents from the university extension service to survey and inventory the farm and propose changes; they then signed an agreement, promising to follow the prescribed methods and record the results. In return, they received fertilizers developed by the TVA's chemical engineers, paying only for shipping and handling.[13] This system put planning and execution firmly in the hands of individual farmers, who benefitted from expert knowledge and scientific research.[14] Harry B. William, a county agent, called it a responsibility to make "scientific information understandable, meaningful, and motivating to people who can use it to help themselves."[15] W. H. Droze describes this as a "three-way arrangement combining the farmer's lands, the knowledge of the agricultural scientists and extension workers of the land-grant universities, and the fertilizer and funds of the TVA."[16] This system, TVA personnel argued, meant that different aspects of the work were undertaken by the "organization best fitted for the job."[17]

David E. Lilienthal, the third member of the board, was also committed to demonstration farms and enjoyed traveling with Harcourt Morgan and meeting with farmers, calling this a "refreshing experience."[18] Lilienthal recognized the deep bond between the fertilizer distribution component of the land machine and social change. Harold V. Miller, a member of the Land Planning and Housing Division (LP&H) staff, recalled taking foreign guests to see the Norris demonstration area and then joining them for lunch with Lilienthal in Knoxville, Tennessee. One of the visitors challenged Lilienthal to explain why he still saw evidence of soil erosion, even though the TVA had been in operation for five years:

> Lilienthal was completely unruffled. He sat back and in a gentle and almost leisurely manner he pointed out to the visitors that in those frantic and desper-

ate and dark days when TVA was created, if TVA had embarked on a course of action giving number one priority to bulldozing and scattering grass seed on every gullied area of the Tennessee Valley, that they probably could have brought in enough bulldozers and recruited enough people under those emergency conditions that they could have from one end of the valley to the other in 30 days doing this remedial work on the land, and they could have then stood off at the end of the valley and said, "Look, the greatest piece of real estate on the face of the earth without a single gully in it." "But," he continued saying, "If we had done that, there would be far more gullies in the Tennessee Valley than there are today, because in that process we would have violated every farmer's concept of the ownership of land and responsibility for land. We would have infuriated enough people that they would practically have been praying for the rains to come and wash out the handiwork of this crew that had come through and so brutally invaded our home places and messed up our fields."[19]

Broadly speaking, the demonstration farms worked: the TVA oversaw a sea change in farming practice in the Valley. Paul K. Conkin notes that the fertilizer program was effective in his village and that as land was turned over to pasture the landscape became greener. He also notes that this was part of a larger change: "Life on the farm in 1930 was closer to that of 1830 than 1960, so rapid were the changes already under way."[20] As it became more verdant the region also came to resemble the sentimental images of the "pastoral ideal."[21] But the system also exhibited drawbacks. Most of the farmers did not keep the records the TVA required, so it was difficult to measure specific successes and make revisions as necessary. Even more serious were the biases built into the system: few tenant farmers took part in the extension project. Even among farm owners, the system favored those who were in a secure enough financial position to risk making changes; farmers with extensive acreage could experiment on portions of their land while earning income from the rest of it. The system also favored those who could develop a personal relationship with the field agents, none of whom were Black. In fact, none of the Black agricultural colleges were included in the project.[22] It seems that by the time Harcourt Morgan joined the TVA, he had accepted Jim Crow as part of the landscape. These glaring inequities were the basis for Philip Selznick's postwar study of the TVA, which concluded that the public agency had been coopted by local and regional interests.[23] Nancy L. Grant shows, further, how the TVA engaged in "Planning for the Status Quo."[24]

Harcourt Morgan's demonstration farm system had far-reaching consequences. For a range of reasons, the TVA in those years was under constant threat of being abolished. By making the Authority acceptable to residents of the Tennessee Valley, he very likely saved the institution.[25] Following this success, Harcourt Morgan insisted that all the TVA programs that were not clearly outlined in the TVA Act would be managed through on-the-ground collaboration.[26] This attitude, which Lilienthal whole-heartedly supported, placed immense institutional pressure on the work of the LP&H, which had been organized under the assumption that a cadre of scientifically trained professionals would direct public projects according to a specific spatial vision. Harcourt Morgan and Lilienthal also enshrined the value of private land ownership over public regulation and interference. They did not rule out public ownership completely—the river machine itself was most definitely public—but they did limit regulation. Arthur Morgan and his colleagues never advocated fully public land ownership, but their ideas went furthest in that direction; and in an institution consistently attacked as "socialist," they became a vulnerability. These tensions were amplified by the personality conflicts of the early TVA; Harcourt Morgan and Lilienthal objected to some proposals simply because they originated in the LP&H, which they considered Arthur Morgan's "bailiwick."[27] The result was continual infighting—between engineers and the legal team, between forestry and agriculture, and between the LP&H and other divisions.[28] Squabbles persisted until Arthur Morgan left the institution, giving lie to the sanguine view that collaboration would resolve all issues.

Earle S. Draper, as director of the LP&H, was torn between his commitment to comprehensive regional planning and the immediate goal of helping the residents of a suffering region.[29] As he explained: "The Tennessee Valley Authority had two alternatives: (1) It could refrain from active developments for several years in order to survey, study, develop techniques, and formulate objectives concerning the broad aspects of regional planning, or (2) it could go along with the job, and build up to these broader phases gradually. It chose the latter course."[30] Daniel Schaffer describes Draper's approach as "pride in his [own] ability to administer and get things done,"[31] a point made by staff members such as architect Mario Bianculli, who described Draper as "a real executive and very aggressive with his ideas."[32]

Draper defined the role of his division as land planning rather than regional planning: it facilitated "*the arrangement of the land for human use and enjoyment* and the *provision of shelter and the facilities for life on the land*" (emphasis in the original).[33] Draper saw planning not as "idealistic" but rather "orderly, economical and flexible."[34] This meant falling back on the first step in regional planning—surveying and developing public knowledge. It also meant encouraging and supporting the establishment of local and regional government units with the authority to act; in 1933 the Tennessee Valley states did not have planning commissions and within each state, sometimes within each county, the rules differed from location to location. An incorporated city, for example, would be delegated responsibilities that the nearby rural area did not have. As Draper's colleagues Howard K. Menhinick and Lawrence L. Durisch explained: "TVA, in line with an expression of John Dewey, has helped to produce, not a planned region, but a planning region."[35]

The mission to promote planning in the Tennessee Valley was soon evident in the organizational structure of the LP&H. At the core of the unit was the planning staff, composed of Tracy B. Augur, Menhinick, and several other planners, as well as Roland A. Wank (the architect who came to consider himself a planner, and even joined the American Institute of Planners).[36] The Land Classification Section was the largest component of the division, responsible for gathering the knowledge needed to create detailed maps of the entire region—to classify all "Valley land into five categories based on present condition and use."[37] This work was crucial, as there were hardly any maps of the region. Draper remembered that most of surveying had to be done on horseback, since the roads were hardly passable. Land classification work progressed rapidly, and by 1935, based on aerial photographs, mosaics of the entire basin had been constructed and mapping personnel were hired to compile planimetric maps as a basis for the final set of maps. The TVA also gathered statistical material supplemented with detailed field inventories. This knowledge was brought together in the *Atlas of the Tennessee Valley Region,* prepared by geographers G. Donald Hudson, J. S. Gibson, Victor Roterus, and N. B. Guyol. The atlas was distributed in sections, made available to planning departments across the Tennessee Valley.[38] The Land Classification Section also produced a system of modular maps showing data by county; this process included creating puzzle pieces for the counties, to be arranged to illustrate specific information. Their goal was to bring together all aspects of the region into a "comprehensive spatial understanding."[39]

Such a synthesis was considered the "highest skill of the geographer" and, of course, the planner.[40]

Following Harcourt Morgan's dictum, Draper also assigned the LP&H a role in coordinating between TVA departments to avoid duplication. He recognized that physical planning had to be grounded in knowledge of social and economic processes and in the plans developed by the TVA engineers. Draper's staff often worked with members of the TVA's Social and Economic Division, which was separate from the LP&H, and was responsible for studies of the social resources in the region and their use.[41] Their work included studies of regional populations, such as "History and Indigenous Culture of Southern Highlands Region."[42] They documented the relocation of families from the TVA reservoir areas, even if they were constrained from actively assisting them.[43] The LP&H also contributed reports to national efforts, especially the work of the National Resources Committee.[44] One such report was a 1938 document titled "Regional Planning in the Tennessee Valley."[45] This study is indicative of the LP&H's limited role: it presents a picture of the needs of the region and describes the impact of the Authority's many-sided programs, without making specific proposals for regional planning.[46] The division also continued to be involved in delineating the "taking lines" of these reservations.[47] They often advocated land acquisition specifically to prevent "unrestrained private exploitation which might result in the development of rural slums and other detrimental uses of the land."[48]

In June 1937 the TVA appointed its first general manager, John B. Blandford Jr., who was able to bring together the three silos that had developed under the three directors. Along with his appointment, a set of interdepartmental agreements settled some of the disputes that had long plagued the Authority. This reorganization further entrenched Harcourt Morgan and Lilienthal's approach: the Regional Survey and Demonstration Service departments, including the LP&H, were expected to coordinate rather than to plan, and were therefore kept small.[49] The LP&H was consolidated with the Social and Economic Division to create a Department of Regional Planning Studies (DRPS). The name of the new department triggered lengthy discussion. Draper, of course, favored "regional planning," but Gordon R. Clapp, then head of personnel (and a future chairman of the board after World War II), objected that other offices in the TVA were also engaged in planning. Adding the word "studies" resolved this dilemma, clarifying the role of the new department. Within a year, the name was shortened to Department of Regional Studies (DRS). Despite its diminished status—compared to Arthur Morgan's vision—Draper was proud of the department, commenting that "I believe that it is the first time in the history of the country and place in the world that any such wide range of skills have been assembled in one division to tackle a project of this size."[50]

The resolution creating the new department, which was based on Draper's recommendation, recognized the work the LP&H had undertaken.[51] The DRPS was charged with assisting with preliminary investigations about lands to be acquired, including highway and railroad relocations and the readjustments of families and communities in the affected areas. It was also responsible for housing TVA employees and designing facilities for visitors to the dams. More broadly, it was expected to facilitate programs for the "utilization, conservation and development of [the Valley's] natural resources for the welfare of its people."[52] This work was done in collaboration with another newly created entity, the Department of Reservoir Property Management, which architect Louis Grandgent described as the DRS's main "client."[53] This department was responsible not only for assisting the relocated families but also for running all reservations, towns, villages, and construction camps under the control of the Authority—in other words, the land subject to the TVA's planning and design. Draper was the director of the new DRPS, but now he presided over three divisions: Social and Economic Research, headed by Lawrence L. Durisch; Land Planning under Donald Hudson; and Community Planning, for which Carroll A. Towne was responsible.

True to its role as a "field coordinator," the DPRS/DRS actively produced and circulated knowledge.[54] The land classification project continued, and the resulting information was shared with agencies such as the Soil Conservation Service and the Bureau of Agricultural Economics. In collaboration with the Bureau of Public Roads and the Bureau of Air Commerce, the DRS prepared a plan for airways and airports in the Valley, even considering use of the TVA reservoirs for seaplanes. The department also developed a program to promote local planning, zoning, and conservation. The planning staff cemented working relationships with various other government agencies, both within the Valley and beyond, establishing its role as a cutting-edge institution. These partners included not only national, state, and local planning and conservation agencies but also agencies engaged in national relief work, as well as universities, professional societies, citizens' groups, and individuals.[55]

Menhinick was instrumental in this regard, regularly reporting on meetings with the National Resources Planning Board and its interests. These collaborations expanded the DRS's reach beyond the scope of its limited funding.[56] Individual employees were also loaned to other agencies: Wank and Augur, for example, worked for the Resettlement Administration on the design of Greenhills, Ohio.[57] Practicing in this manner did not, and could not, produce a second model region, but it did bolster the TVA staff's claims to professional expertise.

Draper also created a Regional Planning Council composed of representatives from across the TVA. The general manager chaired this council, and Draper, as director of DRS, was the secretary.[58] Draper told congress in 1939: "The council does not function as an administrative department of the Authority, in conflict with other departments. Rather, it keeps actively in touch with important programs and synthesizes them."[59] This grandiose language was belied by a rather minor role. The minutes of these meetings, however, do tell us about the planners' focus and struggles. In January 1938 the council meeting was devoted to three topics: (1) the possibility of a coordinated approach to the "racial problem" in the TVA; (2) the question of whether regional planning should be undertaken by the TVA or by an external agency; and (3) an explanation of the National Resource Committee's program in the Southeast.[60] Unsurprisingly, none of the topics was resolved. In a sign of the times, and of professional biases, however, the discussion of planning expertise commanded significantly more attention than the severe implications of racism and segregation.[61]

## Democratic Planning?

Harcourt Morgan was worried about support for the TVA from people in the Tennessee Valley, but Lilienthal's concern was even broader. For many Americans, planning and resource conservation appeared at odds with long-held beliefs about democracy, and even those who favored centralized public action insisted on clear limits. Reconciling these views—or rather, subsuming them within an overarching and utopian ideal—would be key to the TVA's survival and success. As Brian Black details, the TVA was not alone in these efforts. Teaching the wider public about resource conservation was a dominant theme in many New Deal campaigns, though the TVA project was clearly the grandest experiment of them all.[62] A year after the

TVA Act was passed in Congress, the TVA established an Office of Information (also referred to as the Information Office). Led by journalist W. L. Sturdevant, the office was responsible for preparing and distributing information about the policies and accomplishments of the Authority. Sturdevant's principal writers divided among themselves the reports on agriculture, electricity, and engineering. He was assisted by Harry C. Bauer, who was manager of the Authority's technical library, which supported the regional coordination role the TVA had assigned itself. The office also included a Graphic Arts Service staff, directed by photographer Charles Krutch, which designed educational exhibits, graphic displays, and movies. Krutch remembered architect Roland A. Wank as an "awful good friend" and "a really powerful man."[63]

Lilienthal recognized that many of the projects promoted by the TVA were not new. In fact, southerners had advocated for the control of the river and for rural electrification for several decades before the 1930s. Casey P. Cater describes this support for "electrical democracy" as a step toward the goal of creating a New South, which had been a topic of discussion since the Civil War, when the end of slavery also meant the collapse of the economic system that it had upheld.[64] Lilienthal also recognized that the surest path to people's hearts was an overall raising of their standards of living. Enlarging the opportunities for business entrepreneurship and individual initiative was the most expedient vehicle with which to convince people of the efficacy of the TVA. This project would have the added advantage of providing jobs for Tennessee Valley residents who would not be able to continue to depend on agriculture for their livelihood.[65] As with the discussion of the New South, emphasizing economic growth was yet another way to elide the issue of segregation. Lilienthal believed that economic opportunity would also lead to equal rights for Black southerners. While he did not approve of Jim Crow laws, he saw them as a given and expected them to persist for several generations more. More than anything, he separated his personal opinions from what he saw as necessary evils in the path of securing the future of the TVA.[66]

Lilienthal's first priority was rural electrification and closing the widening technology gap between farms and cities.[67] New Dealers, beginning with President Roosevelt, saw electricity as the key to keeping Americans on the land. Farmers, they assumed, would be less likely to seek work in urban industrial centers if they enjoyed an electrified and mechanized farm. In 1936 Congress passed another bill championed by Sen. George Norris—the Rural Electrification Act—which ratified Roosevelt's creation of the Rural Electrification Administration (REA) by executive order in 1935. A pamphlet produced by this new agency captured the notion that the balance between urban and rural—the very goal of regional planning—was to be achieved through expanding the electric power grid.[68] In one diagram the power station is connected to "cities," "industry," and "farms" through transmission lines and substations (fig. 15). This visual balance between farms and industry was crucial. An REA official, M. M. Samuels, told an architectural audience in 1942: "This concept of farm electrification springs from the realization that the farm is no less a factory engaged in production than it is a place where people live."[69]

The mechanism set up to support rural electrification—the power machine—was, necessarily, the most decentralized of the TVA projects. The dam system itself was constructed as a "unified" whole, a single complex structure directed primarily by engineering concerns. The land machine, as directed by Harcourt A. Morgan, relied on existing institutions—zoning, planning, and extension agencies—as well as on the production of fertilizers at the Muscle Shoals nitrate plant. Lilienthal's electrification program, on the other hand, had to contend with private power companies. These entities had the ability to produce and distribute electricity, but they invariably skirted rural areas in favor of urban areas, which promised higher returns on their investment. The TVA power machine was thus designed as a two-pronged attack. On the one hand, the Authority would augment the supply of power with cheaper (i.e., below market price) electricity. As the same time, it would promote the demand for power in rural regions. This dual approach, Lilienthal argued, would create a new "yardstick": "a standard of performance for evaluating the efficiency of privately owned companies."[70]

Lilienthal was determined to make the TVA politically acceptable from the start, but his battles with the private utilities in the region only deepened his resolve. These utilities at times focused more on their efforts to prevent the implementation of the power machine than on expanding their service.[71] From its inception in 1933 to the end of the decade, the TVA contended with a series of lawsuits, and the Supreme Court did not rule in the Authority's favor until the early 1940s.[72] Richard Lowitt explains the implications of these legal challenges: "TVA was engaged in a series of struggles any one of which could have terminated or drastically changed its status as an independent agency."[73] The lawsuits deferred the production and distri-

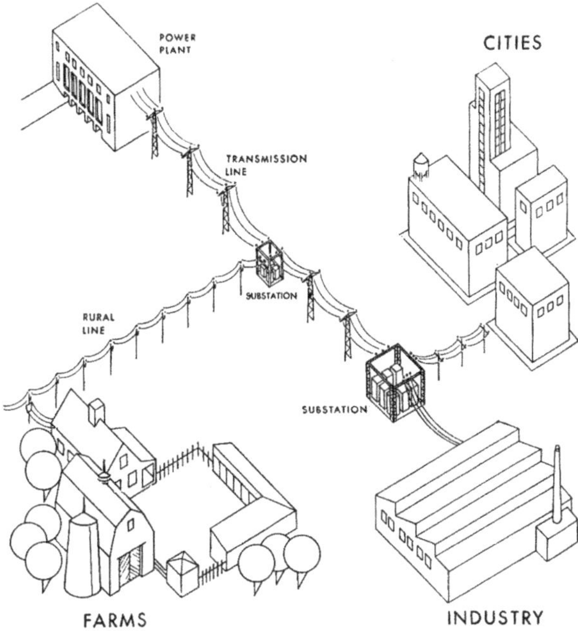


**Figure 15.** A diagram included in a 1930s publication, *Electric Power on the Farm: The Story of Electricity, Its Usefulness on Farms, and the Movement to Electrify Rural America*, edited by David Cushman Coyle for the Rural Electrification Administration (98). The visual balance of "industry" and "farms" echoes the regional planners' insistence on a dispersed pattern of development.

bution of electric power to the Tennessee Valley; they also focused public attention on Lilienthal and the power machine, often without any mention of the river and land machine goals of the TVA.[74] In the process the plaintiffs also categorized the TVA as creeping socialism and an anathema to American democracy and individualism. Many Americans regarded rural electrification as synonymous, for better or worse, with the TVA.

The TVA's ability to establish a yardstick for power rates relied on three stages: producing power, distributing it to the grid, and, finally, delivering power to the end users, the farmers. The production of electric power was relatively straightforward. One legal challenge hinged on whether the dams could be used for power production, but once this was resolved the TVA employed its technical knowledge to install the necessary generators and substations. The second phase, transmitting the power across the region, also depended on a positive legal outcome. When it was able to do so legally, the TVA negotiated piecemeal arrangements with commercial companies to access their systems, gradually extending its service area beyond the Valley into northern Alabama. The TVA also augmented the grid by installing new transmission lines, located according to the land classification project that was undertaken in the LP&H and continued by the DRS.[75] The TVA would have preferred applying a "rational" method to expanding the grid, rather than an approach geared to the political system. The reality incorporated elements of both systems, but Lilienthal celebrated the outcome: "Marching towards every point in the horizon you can see the steel crisscross of electric transmission towers, a twentieth-century tower standing in a cove beside an eighteenth-century mountain cabin, a symbol and a summary of the change."[76]

In 1939 Lilienthal told his audience in Knoxville, Tennessee, that the supply of electricity—that is, the generation and transmission—was centralized but that the distribution was done in a decentralized manner.[77] By this he meant that the TVA divested itself of controlling the third phase of the power machine. Unlike European governments, which undertook rural electrification as a centralized project the federal administration expected farmers to organize cooperatives that would handle this task.[78] These institutions were given "the first right of refusal for federal waterpower."[79] The cooperatives were newly formed nonprofit organizations created with government loans, a system initiated by Lilienthal in 1934 when he helped establish the Alcorn County Electric Cooperative in Corinth, Mississippi.[80] For Lilienthal, this system was an exemplar of democratic action, although, as Erwin C. Hargrove points out, the terms for these cooperatives were strictly outlined by the TVA power department. The arrangement did, however, allow Lilienthal to claim that the Authority was representing the people of the Valley.[81]

REA and TVA loans were issued to newly formed cooperatives on the assumption that the organizations would be repaid from the proceeds of selling electricity. This meant that producing and transmitting power was not enough; unless it was used by people in the region, the entire system fell apart. Residents of the Valley had to learn to rely on electric appliances, preferably large ones such as threshers, corn huskers, and pumps on the farm and refrigerators, ranges, and washing machines in the home. In pursuing this goal Lilienthal adopted Harcourt Morgan's "three-way arrangement."[82] The TVA would supply power and knowledge, extension workers information, and farmers the farm-factory.[83] This approach had an added advantage: it made the impact of the environmental efforts, and the interconnectedness of the river, land, and power machines, evident in people's homes. In 1936 the TVA prepared a proposal for electric farm demonstrations that would "not only demonstrate the mechanics of electrical installation but also the economic and social results of their use."[84] The proposal called for farms that were reasonably accessible, typical of the region, and well managed. It listed specific electric requirements for different types of farms: dairy, poultry, and so on. It also described the demonstration home, taking the Progressive Era house layout (discussed in chapter 1) and adding outlets in each room, good lighting, running water, and a "range, radio, electric iron, at least one of the following: refrigerator, washing machine, water heater. And three more smaller appliances such as a fan, electric clock or ice cream freezer."[85]

Lilienthal focused on the development and distribution of appliances. In 1934 he oversaw the creation of the Electric Home and Farm Authority as a sister agency to the TVA. He used this agency to work with the manufacturers of electric appliances to develop low-cost versions of their products that Valley residents could afford.[86] As Barry M. Katz points out, design played a central role in making these appliances attractive to valley residents.[87] In 1938 the Office of Information prepared a pamphlet explaining how "cheap electricity pays its way."[88] Information was also distributed through the universities' extension services. One publication, *Wiring and Lighting the Farmstead: A Combined Text and Laboratory Manual,* covers a range of topics, including specific recommendations for the Tennessee Valley.[89] Such texts were yet another part of the "battle" with the private utilities, since they suggested that "commercial publications could not be trusted" and that "scientific" knowledge originating in the TVA was superior.[90]

The rural electrification efforts conformed to traditional expectations of gender roles. In 1941 Carroll A. Towne coauthored an article with George DeWitt Munger (who directed the Division of Electrical Development in the TVA's Department of Power Utilization) and another TVA staff member, in which they describe courses on the "proper preparation of food on electric ranges" for "farm girls of high-school age."[91] Such courses were organized by the Domestic Electric Service program, directed by Eloise Davison. A former associate professor of home economics at Iowa State University, Davison had also worked as an adviser for the National Electric Light Association, a trade association.[92] Moving into the public sector, Davison had a staff of five home economists, and together they not only taught courses at colleges and high schools but also organized public demonstrations of electric appliances and published yet more informative pamphlets. As Michelle Mock points out, however, their work was directed primarily at white women and "largely neglected African American households."[93]

Lilienthal's efforts to embed the power machine in regional action were slow, but they achieved his main goal: "easing the authority's political situation."[94] His correlation between democracy, economic development, and homegrown expertise, however, locked him in a fierce disagreement with Arthur Morgan, although they would have probably clashed even without this substantive difference.[95] Each was accused of wanting to mold the TVA in his own image, which was at least partially true. The details of the feud have been well documented and are not relevant here; what is important is that their dispute went public. Arthur Morgan eventually accused his colleagues of corruption and abuse of power, though when asked to substantiate these allegations he declined to do so. Roosevelt had been wavering between him and Lilienthal for a while, and he dismissed Morgan on March 23, 1938. Arthur Morgan then brought his charges to Congress, which conducted a lengthy investigation into the TVA in 1939 but took no action.

Following Arthur Morgan's departure, Lilienthal enshrined his organizational vision in the TVA. As Hargrove notes, this narrative had three parts. First, the TVA had to be independent from central (federal) control to be able to focus on its regional objectives. Second, the people of the Valley—as represented by their state and local governments and by private enterprise—had to be engaged with and committed to the TVA's program.[96] Finally, the role of the Authority included coordinating the work of federal, state, and local agencies as what he called a "field coordinator."[97] This coordination would encompass not only social and environmental programs but also stimulate industry, ultimately bringing back the entrepreneurial—one might say, pioneering—spirit.[98] Lilienthal referred to this three-part ideology as "grass-roots democracy."[99]

The administrative changes within the TVA were not the only ones to impact its function. In the early 1930s many assumed that the Tennessee Valley was the new frontier.[100] By the end of the decade, however, national focus turned to a military frontier in Europe. The Roosevelt administration had maintained a strict neutrality, but in 1938 it had begun to prepare for war. One result was an unaccustomed alliance between the federal government and American businesses, which had often been at odds during the New Deal.[101] Lilienthal, still worried about the Authority's future as an independent agency and fearing that Roosevelt seemed to have lost interest in supporting its work, wrote to the president proposing that the TVA would support the national emergency by producing electric power and manufacturing nitrates. Lilienthal's offer thus shifted the TVA's priorities from the independent regeneration of an underdeveloped region to its "integration with the national economy."[102] He also put power and industry at the center of the TVA's function, moving away from the unified ideals that underpinned the enterprise and materially changing its focus from the original purpose outlined in the TVA Act.[103]

The preparations for war and the engagement in World War II amplified, rather than diminished the rhetoric on democracy, now seen as bulwark against totalitarian regimes.[104] Roosevelt, moreover, went to some lengths to develop what Walter Creese calls "conspicuous emblems of peace."[105] Lilienthal, accordingly, now declared that the TVA experiment was geared not toward regional development but to saving democracy from death.[106] In 1944 he summarized these ideas in a book, *TVA: Democracy on the March.*[107] It was written with the help of TVA staff, who were asked to submit stories to illustrate the book's main topics, including examples of "new faith in people in themselves."[108] In *Democracy on the March* Lilienthal referred to the TVA as a pioneer in "modern democratic planning."[109] This formulation took hold; it was adopted by visitors from abroad, including Englishman Julian Huxley, who described the TVA as an "adventure in planning."[110] After Lilienthal left the TVA in 1946, the idea of democratic planning helped define the TVA's role on the international stage, even as it came to serve more as a power company than as a planning agency responsible for regional development and resource conservation.[111] Thus the utopian aspirations persisted, despite substantial changes in focus and organization.

Members of the atelier also adopted the rhetoric of democratic planning and popularized it in their professional circles. In 1942 Wank published an essay in the journal *Pencil Points* titled, "Time to Choose Our Destiny: Planning or Disintergration?" He too cited the TVA as the "nation's original contribution to democratic planning" and stressed that planning was not a policy but a tool that could be adopted by any form of government.[112] With the war as a backdrop, Wank even called for a reorganization of land ownership, concluding that "someday, perhaps soon, we may find out that security can dwell henceforth only in dynamic, planned, unfettered expansion; we may also discover that in contemporary affairs, the individual's lone quest for economic advantage is as sterile as it can be catastrophic to society, and our boundless power to create great and good works can be unleashed only by collectively planned action."[113]

## City Planning

In Arthur Morgan's regional vision, industry in the Tennessee Valley would be limited to light industries, such as ceramics, spread across "democratic communities" in the Norris model. As Lilienthal's vision replaced Morgan's, this aspiration was set aside as well. Having made the power machine the center of the TVA's public face, and having promoted the grassroots approach, Lilienthal supported the industrial and commercial aspirations of communities in the Valley, especially in Northern Alabama.[114] This support was in line with the powers unleashed by the TVA river machine. The system of multipurpose dams along the Tennessee River and storage dams on its tributaries was essential for flood control and power production, but it also created the basis for a navigable waterway between Knoxville, Tennessee, and Paducah, Kentucky, where the Tennessee flows into the Ohio. The Ohio then pours the Mississippi about sixty miles further west. In fact, shipping boosters and other entrepreneurs in the Valley had been calling for the construction of such access since the early twentieth century.[115] In Florence, Alabama, the chamber of commerce celebrated the TVA as the resolution to this agitation.[116]

The TVA committed to building or clearing a nine-foot channel along the river, a process that included dragging the river and also involved considerable construction along its banks. Work on this channel was slow but steady, and it was mostly completed by the end of World War II. The Army Corps of Engineers installed locks in all the river dams and still operates them today. The TVA also invested in public-use barge terminals at Knoxville and Chattanooga, Tennessee, and Guntersville and Decatur, Alabama, which in turn promoted private investment. Freight travel along the channel—really a chain of reservoirs—expanded exponentially after 1945 and included cargo from a wide range of industries, including mills (flour, timber, and paper) and factories producing inorganic and organic chemicals, plastics, fertilizers and metals, refrigeration machinery, and parts for shipbuilding and repairs

**Figure 16.** A 1940s photograph of a crane unloading pulpwood at the Bowater Southern Paper Corporation pulp and paper mill at Calhoun, Tennessee. The mill, located on the Hiwassee River, a tributary of the Tennessee, still operates today under the name Resolute Forest Products.

(fig. 16).[117] These changes dramatically altered both the economy and landscape of the cities in which they were located.

The unexpected move toward industrial development opened a new realm for the TVA architects and landscape architects, here referred to as the atelier. Being true to the garden ideal while also supporting industrial development indicated, to the LP&H staff, a need to emphasize good city planning. Such planning would, on the one hand, create conditions to attract companies to cities in the Tennessee Valley and allow them to benefit from the navigation and power the new environment provided.[118] At the same time, these plans were expected to help safeguard the quality of life for the residents and assure them access to the natural and outdoor amenities needed for individual and social rejuvenation. Inserting open spaces and recreational areas in zones that would otherwise be industrial thus became another manifestation of the garden in the TVA machine. Here land planning—specifically the determination of "the best use of land of all types for all purposes, to prevent waste such as the building of expensive improvements in the sites of future reservoirs, and to furnish guidance for both public and private use of land"—was crucial.[119] The LP&H went further, however, and engaged in demonstration planning and design, using specific communities as opportunities to exhibit what they considered good planning to the region. Thus, an important thrust of the atelier's work was shifted from the design of new towns to mimic Norris, Tennessee, to supporting planning efforts in existing cities.

Building on his institutional acumen, Draper set up a section dedicated to these efforts, guided by Raymond F. Leonard and Aelred J. "Flash" Gray. The latter, a proponent of regional planning, later argued that the "TVA could have been more effective in its planning and development, and might well have achieved more, had the enabling legislation been clearer, and had the ideas of the visionary Arthur Morgan continued to guide the Authority."[120] Still, he was able to work within the institutional framework that emerged and remained with the Authority throughout a long career. When Leonard and Gray began their work, they acted as liaisons between the LP&H and the social scientists in the Economic and Social Division.[121] In 1937 they formed a new unit within the DRS, at first named Assistance to Communities. Leonard directed this effort until 1941, when Gray took responsibility (under the supervision of Towne, who also oversaw the architectural and site-planning sections). As with other endeavors, atelier members often participated; Mario Bianculli later remembered those tasks involving contact with officials and residents for planning purposes as among the most enjoyable (fig. 17).[122]

True to their conception of professional practice, the atelier began by assessing the situation through surveys and research. One of the tasks it set itself was to create an index of all the town and city names within the Valley and adjoining area, which was deposited in the TVA's technical library.[123] Regional planners and landscape architects also worked to better understand the Tennessee Valley region from the perspective of community building. In 1934 Towne completed a study of "Comparative Cost of Utilities in Rural and Urban Communities," which was distributed to TVA divisions as well as selected outside planning bodies.[124] Industry and

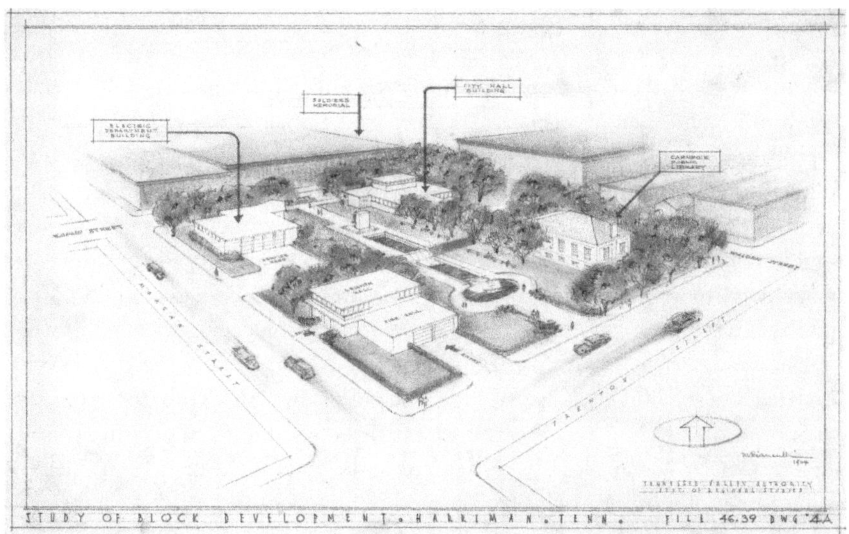


**Figure 17.** A drawing of a "Study of Block Development" for Harriman, Tennessee, signed by Mario Bianculli and dated 1944. The plan represents the TVA planners' and designers' attention to the siting of city halls, electric cooperatives and departments, libraries, and community buildings. The building labeled "Carnegie Public Library" is still in this location today, but the Roane Street side of the block is occupied by the Harriman fire station.

employment were central topics of a study in 1936—including, especially, the task of developing metrics to describe and compare industries.[125] Atelier members also developed methods for forecasting population growth and identifying new centers of economic activity. These methods were limited, however, by the fact that in the grassroots approach the decision to engage in industrial and commercial activity lay in the hands of private developers, who were not beholden to the TVA's planning.[126] In 1939 Draper also authorized a general study of county organization and administration across the Tennessee Valley; a study based on the resulting data was published in the same year, in cooperation with the University of Tennessee—an example of the TVA's contribution to the study of both political science and planning in regional institutions.[127] The social scientists also studied Norris, Tennessee, hoping to gain insight from the commercial activities there.[128]

City planning, especially the collaboration of designers and social scientists, was a new field. In fact, a definitive study of this body of knowledge had been completed just a few years prior, with the contribution of their colleague Howard Menhinick. A graduate of the landscape architecture program at Michigan State University, Menhinick continued his education and earned a dual degree in Landscape and City Planning at Harvard University; there he taught courses in city planning and founded the *Planners' Journal*.[129] He then collaborated with Harvard University faculty members Theodora Kimball and Henry V. Hubbard on a survey of city planning in the United States. The goal of the book was to identify the most promising subjects of research and "to furnish ammunition immediately usable in the fight against congestion, against unbalanced distribution of urban population and unwholesome urban environment."[130] Here was a progressive preoccupation that predated, but had not been displaced by, the obsession with soil conservation. The book itself is a product of a selective survey that was conducted over five months across 120 cities. Menhinick was recognized in the book as the main researcher and an important contributor who had studied "zoning, control of land subdivision, major street systems, mass transportation, rail, water, and air terminals, park and recreation areas, aspects of the city's appearance, with the legal and administrative means of effecting city and regional planning."[131] Menhinick's travels for this study had also brought him to Knoxville, which he analyzed as "an interesting example of a city, with a one-street business district, opening a new thoroughfare at great cost and expansion [of] the business district over five or six blocks wide."[132] Eight years later, in 1937, he moved to Knoxville and joined the TVA.

In northern Alabama, Leonard and Gray, with Lilienthal's backing, worked primarily with two urban communities: Decatur and Guntersville. Their efforts illustrate the many layers that planning assumed in an institution devoted to grassroots action. Decatur was the largest city in the region and had been hit badly by the Depression; by 1933 all the industries in its town limits had closed. Located near the construction site of Wheeler Dam, the town was in the position to benefit from surplus power, but it also had to contend with a large percentage of displaced farmers.[133] Here work began with institution building: the TVA arranged for a city planning commission to be organized under a state agency, the Alabama Planning Commission. The new commission, with the TVA's support, began its work by studying the city's finances, a move that surprised Decatur's mayor. Based on this study, the TVA staff recommended that the city *not* refinance their bonds, as private bond companies were urging it to do. They helped the city develop a "proper" record-keeping system and find alternate ways to increase their revenues.[134] Lilienthal believed this work represented the best of grassroots action, since it strengthened the community's leadership and helped change their approach to planning.[135] Draper, too, considered these proposals "elements of Decatur's own local improvement program."[136]

Having laid the groundwork, the community assistance team adopted a dual focus on industry and wildlife conservation. Menhinick later credited this work for Decatur's proud, emerging identity as "the heart of the inland empire."[137] For example, the TVA planners provided the city with a survey of eight specific sites and calculated the estimated cost of improvements needed to prepare them for industrial use.[138] This effort bore fruit; after the war divisions of two national companies, Hecla Consolidated Copper Company and the Chemstrand Corporation, relocated to Decatur (fig. 18).[139] Close to the new manufacturing plants was another product of the TVA community building effort: the Wheeler Wildlife Refuge. This reserve, located within the city limits, offers a safe habitat for wildlife but also provides opportunities for recreation and relaxation—a garden in the machine (fig. 19). In the 1960s Gray would point to Decatur as a successful example of planning with a wildlife in mind.[140] The long-term fate of the city, however, was tied directly to the challenges of World War II, when the federal government located massive defense industries in nearby Huntsville, Alabama, including a headquarters for the National Aeronautics and Space Administration. Huntsville then eclipsed Decatur in its economic growth and is the larger and more prosperous city today.[141]

Guntersville, Alabama, was the city planning effort most celebrated by TVA personnel, but it also illustrates the murky complexity of community building in the Valley. The project had several origins. The Land Classification Section first explored the "Tributary Trade Area of Guntersville," and in 1936 the LP&H authored a report titled "Recommendations for Shore Line Adjustment, Guntersville, Alabama."[142] In November 1936 the Construction Engineering Division proposed building a dike around the eastern side of the city, basically transforming it into a peninsula in the planned Guntersville reservoir. When local government and the public accepted this proposal, the Family Removal Section asked the LP&H to provide advice on this process. Further studies indicated the need to relocate railroad beds. Meanwhile, the LP&H was engaged in institution building, persuading the city to pass a set of planning and zoning ordinances and other regulations

**Figure 18.** Aerial view of the Chemstrand Corporation in Decatur, Alabama, while under construction in December 1951. The TVA planners prepared the surveys and advised on the zoning that made Decatur attractive to companies such as Chemstrand.

and to create a city planning commission.[143] These ordinances were drafted with the help of the Alabama Planning Commission and were later used in other municipalities as well.[144] The TVA funded much of this work while also providing needed technical assistance.[145]

As in Decatur, the spatial proposal for Guntersville focused on a balance between industry and recreation. The city's location on the reservoir connected it, through the emerging navigation channel, to large commercial and industrial centers. In an interview Menhinick later highlighted the development of both a petroleum depot and a terminal where shipments of cars could be unloaded from barges, to be delivered throughout the region.[146] These constructions were paired with a "municipal boat-park harbor."[147] The TVA architects contributed to this wide-ranging planning effort with a design for a proposed concession building at the boat harbor, devel-

**Figure 19.** One of the entrances to the Wheeler National Wildlife Refuge in Decatur, Alabama, established by President Franklin D. Roosevelt on July 7, 1938. The TVA planners and landscape architects promoted this project as a way to add provisions for migratory fowl to the rising Wheeler Reservoir. The refuge still supports a wide range of wildlife and is a popular destination for recreation.

oped in 1942 (fig. 20). Lilienthal described the Guntersville experience as a success, not only of engineering but of community building as well: "What at first seemed a calamity was turned into an opportunity, and a community sense of direction has resulted that continues to bear fruit."[148] He was especially pleased with Guntersville's transition from agriculture to industry and recreation.[149]

As the TVA planners and architects engaged in institution building and advisory planning, they developed professional practices that could be repeated in location after location, as well as being shared more widely in their disciplinary circles. In this discourse Norris, Tennessee, and Guntersville, Alabama, could be presented as part of the same drive toward a garden in a machine—different in degree but not in kind. But the tension between planning and democracy remained. The trend toward technical proficiency raised serious, and still unanswered, questions: If the TVA planning staff was instrumental in achieving goals, could this still be called grassroots action? What was the more important consideration—an orderly and planned development or the self-determination of each community, whatever its

**Figure 20.** Drawing of a proposed concession building for the boat harbor in Guntersville, Alabama. Drawn by Seth Harrison Gurnee and approved by Mario Bianculli, this was one way in which the TVA Department of Regional Studies supported local (Guntersville city) and state (Alabama) planning commissions while also developing standards for city planners.

preferences? As planners became more professional, they became invested in their careers, which, in turn, depended on their command of technical knowledge—knowledge that might at times be in tension with local priorities. Draper, despite his efforts toward professionalization, signaled his commitment to his utopian goals in 1940 when he wrote an essay titled "Urban Development in the Southeast: What of the Future?" "It is not enough that plans be technically sound. In these precarious times we are forcibly reminded that the ultimate decision and execution of any plan, whether it be confined to a minor parking ordinance or include consideration of a wide range of civic problems, must rest with the community itself."[150] The atelier's resolution of this dilemma is the topic of chapter 4.

# 3

# PUBLIC ARCHITECTURE

## The River Machine

The Tennessee Valley Authority's plan for its first dam—initially named Cove Creek, later renamed for Sen. George Norris—did not include an architectural treatment of the dam itself. This omission is not surprising. Engineering firms that designed dams for private companies did not engage architects; even the federal Bureau of Reclamation, which was assisting the TVA with detailing the construction, only consulted architects after the engineering work was done. Of course, those architects could not—nor were they expected to—contribute much to the design beyond superficial adornments, such as coping, cornices, or windows on the powerhouse.[1] At Cove Creek, moreover, the TVA and bureau engineers were working from a proposal for the dam's layout prepared by the Army Corps of Engineers in 1928, a design they then adjusted to accommodate the data from geological surveys in the field. The main structural elements of the dam—the spillway, powerhouse, and substation—were shown grouped haphazardly around the main dam structure. The powerhouse, as the element most resembling a building, was to be finished with classical architectural flourishes.

The TVA, however, was an exceptional institution: created at the height of the Great Depression, it readily attracted remarkable professionals in every field.

Roland A. Wank, appointed as head architect by the first director, Arthur E. Morgan, challenged the prevailing assumptions about the role of architects in engineering by presenting an alternative design that reconfigured the dam itself. Wank's proposal created visual drama by applying core architectural practices to this novel project. First, he rearranged the structural elements of the dam to produce a harmonious composition without undermining functionality. By locating the spillway in the center of the dam rather than on its eastern slope, he gave the dramatic waterway a central position in the view of visitors, while breaking the mass of the dam into a more complex, but still weighty, structure. The spillway still is the main feature of the dam; whenever it is in use, either before or after a heavy rain, the simple slope of concrete is transformed into a waterfall, drawing visitors from across the region. Wank's second architectural decision was to separate the substation from the powerhouse, elements that had been stacked in the original design. By locating the substation on the east bank (in place of the spillway), Wank created a compositional balance between the machine, in the form of the electric towers and connectors, and one element of the sentimental "pastoral ideal," a verdant slope abutting the dam to the west.[2]

Moving the substation also allowed Wank to redesign the exterior of the powerhouse, eliminating all ornament and giving it a sleek modernist form. He scaled the windows of the building to mask rather than highlight the great bulk of the powerhouse and also to avoid "dating" the building.[3] He further distinguished the structure by adding a tower above it, housing the elevator shaft and the flagpole. In its new form, the powerhouse enhances rather than detracts from the sculptural beauty of the dam. In a second set of architectural decisions, Wank accommodated human-scale functional elements, weaving them into his bold design with careful detailing. The Norris Freeway crosses the Clinch River on top of the dam, emerging from it on either side of the river as a coherent extension of the dam structure. The design of the highway railings and the lighting serve to unify the mass and form. The road is flanked by pedestrian sidewalks that widen into overlooks above the central spillway. Pedestrians can observe the fine detailing on the tower door and the connection of the flagpole to the concrete (fig. 21).

Wank's proposal has usually been analyzed as a stylistic choice and a signal of his modernist training in Europe. The redesigned Norris Dam also resembles other dams of this period and thus serves as a register of shifts in American architec-

**Figure 21.** Norris Dam, the first TVA dam to be completed, in an aerial view from October 14, 1950. The Norris Freeway crosses the dam above the spillway and powerhouse and connects between two overlooks. In the upper left-hand corner of the image is the quarry from which aggregate was excavated during the construction of the dam.

ture.[4] Wank and his colleagues were well aware of these changes, as Mario Bianculli recalled: "We designing architects were inspired by the feelings in the TVA that something momentous was taking place. Something momentous that would last for decades and that would leave an imprint in the life of America. Therefore, we were very serious and careful in not missing the opportunity to arrange things in such a way, and I mean organically and functionally and aesthetically, so as to not only express itself, but to also last forever as a part of American life."[5]

More important than style, however, is the relationship between Wank's design and the allegorical nature of the TVA. The river machine was, at its core, an engineering project, usually described in scientific and technological language—as in the TVA's 1938 annual report to Congress: "Stream flow data are applied to determine the greatest flood which should be designed for, the amount of power which can be generated, and the number of generating units to be provided."[6] As Linda Nash points out, such language removed the human subject experiencing the river and conveyed little to the public.[7] Wank's architecture in effect returned the dam to the realm of human comprehension. It transmuted an element of the TVA machine into an environment people could experience and appreciate. More specifically, the design drew on human interpretations of the sublime, in this case the technological sublime. As David E. Nye argues, humans have an innate need to invest landscapes with "transcendent significance" and "moral value."[8] When experiencing these emotions, moreover, they often overlook divisions between themselves and others in society. Wank's striking design thus invested the dam with the social role of building community, transforming it into an element of the utopian garden. It also placed architectural design on par with other TVA efforts to make resource conservation and regional planning acceptable to a wide audience.

The TVA circulated images of Norris Dam taken by Charles Krutch, an accomplished photographer who had joined the Office of Information. One such set was included in a 1937 edition of the *Knoxville News-Sentinel* magazine with the title "Power & Beauty."[9] These images were accompanied by text extolling the ways in which the architects and engineers united their talents in the design of the dam.[10] The same newspaper also published photographs by readers, including a five-minute exposure taken on a misty, moonlit night.[11] In another nighttime photo, available from the Library of Congress, a couple stands in the shadows, lit from behind by the floodlights of the dam and the illumination emitted from the windows of the powerhouse.[12] The caption attached to this photograph contains factual information about lighting and shrinkage cracks, but, as Todd Smith explains, the image recalls a honeymoon scene at Niagara Falls. The comparison seems to say: "For a couple at Niagara, their union has been ordained by the forces of nature and God; for our friends at Norris, however, their union is blessed by nature, science, and the government."[13] Smith's interpretation is but one example of what Tim Culvahouse and his colleagues refer to as the TVA's enrollment of design in its project of persuasion.[14]

At Norris, TVA employees were surprised by the number of visitors who came to see the dam while it was still under construction. The *Knoxville News-Sentinel* reported in May 1934 that "huge crowds" had been allowed to use a temporary road between the west abutment and a bridge over the Clinch River. W. L. Sturdevant, director of TVA's Office of Information, counted forty-one cars using this road in

**Figure 22.** Photograph of the temporary observation building at Norris Dam, built in January 1936. The TVA spent $1,000 to provide this simple amenity to the thousands of visitors who arrived to see the dam being completed.

an eleven-minute span, calculating that this number indicated an average of 224 cars per hour.[15] Exactly four months later the *Knoxville Journal* proudly reported that the number of visitors to Norris Dam was four times as many as those visiting the Boulder Dam construction site.[16] The TVA count even distinguished between local and out-of-state cars and visitors.[17] By January 1936 (a few months before the dam was completed), the TVA built a small visitor building as a temporary measure to accommodate the influx of visitors. It was little more than a shed, but it did boast a porch overlooking the construction site where visitors could enjoy the vista of the nearly finished dam (fig. 22).

Wank's design proposal also instigated institutional changes. Earle S. Draper, director of the Land Planning and Housing Division (LP&H), supported Wank in this venture and joined him when he presented his sketches to the TVA board of directors. Arthur Morgan strongly supported Wank's proposed changes; indeed, it is quite possible that Morgan had appointed Wank as head architect with just such a transformational design in mind.[18] Morgan then devised an interesting administrative anomaly: he assigned Wank the specific task of designing the dams and powerhouses but made no change in his institutional position. Wank remained in the LP&H, nominally under Draper's supervision, but in practice functioning with almost full independence.[19] The responsibility for developing and executing Wank's design sat in a separate department, with a new group of architects hired by the engineering division for the new dam. By keeping design and development in different departments, Arthur Morgan assured that any differences of opinion would be brought to the general manager and ultimately the board of directors for arbitration. This bifurcation proved successful, as Howard K. Menhinick recalled: "Many such hearings were held, and the architects were never overruled."[20] Draper saw in this unique situation a clear indication of Arthur Morgan's expansive approach: "He wanted to get as many presentations as he could. He didn't want to leave any avenue unexplored. And that gave us the toe-hold in the door to get in."[21]

Wank's counterpart on the engineering side was Harry B. Tour, who was assisted by Hiram H. Ostrander and Troy B. Minton, among others.[22] Trained as an architectural engineer at the University of Illinois, Tour had worked for a decade and a half—first for the Toledo (Ohio) Board of Education, designing schools, and then for the Consumers Power Company at Jackson, Michigan, where he joined a new program to design steam and hydroelectric plants. He started work at the TVA in the fall of 1935 as resident architect for Norris Dam, drawn by the challenge of the job as well as the opportunity to live in Norris, Tennessee. At first, the Authority promised him only a year and half of work, but his promotion to senior architect was rapid, and by 1937 he was earning a yearly salary of $5,000.[23] By this time the TVA had organized a single Design Department for all projects (they had been handled separately before), and Tour became responsible for the Architectural Section in this unit, where he remained until his retirement in 1965. With his architectural engineering background, Tour found engineers "very easy to get along with," appreciating their straightforward approach.[24] He even joined the American Society of Civil Engineers, in addition to being a member of the American Institute of Architects, where he served as president of his chapter in the 1940s.[25]

In his role as head architect, Wank gathered around him a small coterie of four or five architects, chief among whom was Bianculli. An immigrant like Wank, Bianculli was an Italian and a veteran of World War I. He completed a doctorate in Engineering and Architecture at the University of Naples and then came to the United States on a fellowship, where he was hired by the Foundation Company of New York as a young engineer.[26] He later designed power plants for the Electric Bond & Share Company of New York, but he soon decided to devote his time to architecture rather than engineering. He specialized in housing, working for the firm of Andrew J. Thomas in New York, maintaining a steady flow of work until the 1929 stock market crash. He later opened an office with Piero Ghiani, as Bianculli and Ghiani, Architects, New York. The firm focused on recreation buildings, such as movie houses, built as "demountable" (potentially temporary) structures. The venture was successful, but Bianculli was attracted to the TVA by its mission, its government status, and its importance to the United States; he joined the Authority in January 1936.[27] Wank and Bianculli together were responsible for "preliminary studies, sketches, renderings, and three dimensional drawings with only enough attention to working details to insure that the necessary architectural effect will be achieved."[28] This work required not only bold sketches but also careful attention to detail. Marian Moffett describes the slight but critical differences between two "immense" drawings of Hiwassee Dam, which represented possible designs for the top of the spillway.[29]

By 1936 design work for the engineering department consumed the largest portion of the atelier's time. In March the TVA board submitted another report to Congress on the "Unified Development of the Tennessee River System."[30] This report became the master plan for the design and construction of dams into the 1950s. It included both a statement of policy and a list of projects illustrated with plans and photographs.[31] In their continued design work, Wank and Bianculli followed the direction of this multipart report. Using Norris as a template, they developed a "language" that was flexible enough to apply to the entire river machine, from the powerhouses of the large river dams such as Kentucky Dam, to the storage dams on the tributaries, to elements of much smaller, earth-built dams in the mountains, including Chatuge Dam (figs. 23, 24). They also designed standalone powerhouses, such as the one built with the Ocoee No. 3 Dam (fig. 25). This language, they argued, was derived from the process of taking engineering elements and "making them into

**Figure 23.** Kentucky Dam visitor center and office building. This dam is the longest and lowest on the Tennessee River, located close to its confluence with the Ohio River.

a 'grammar' for architecture."[32] It was then used freely in every location. At Guntersville, for example, they chose to face the powerhouse in brick, since they were unhappy with the concrete work in previous buildings (fig. 26).[33] At Chickamauga Dam, however, they were concerned about water conditions below the dam and returned to the concrete finish (fig. 27).

By most accounts Tour and Wank made a good team, harnessing the architectural perspective to the engineering requirements. Menhinick remembered Tour as "very sympathetic to the good architecture that Roland Wank was proposing."[34] In 1938, for example, Tour argued that transferring Bianculli to the engineering department would result in lower cost and greater efficiency, but this decision was overruled in favor of the more complex, architecturally beneficial arrangement.[35] Tour himself celebrated their collaboration in a letter to the editor of *Civil Engineering,* which he titled "Engineers and Architects Cooperate on TVA Projects."[36] This collaborative relationship allowed Wank to have a hand in many different projects. In 1940 the TVA recognized him for "progressive and sustained excellence in the

**Figure 24.** Chatuge Dam, located high in the mountains of North Carolina. The dam itself is a simple earth dam, but the water gauge is identified with the distinctive TVA typography.

**Figure 25.** The Ocoee No. 3 powerhouse. This building houses turbines powered by water brought by tunnel from the Ocoee No. 3 Dam, about four miles away. The design of the building, especially the large entrance, is similar to the architectural treatment of all buildings in the TVA system.

**Figure 26.** The powerhouse at Guntersville Dam, Alabama, seen from one of the (open) dam gates. Unlike other powerhouses, this one is faced in brick, which was then painted a warm cream color. The gate was opened to allow dam operators to conduct repairs on the dam.

architectural design of the Authority's dams and power houses, the progressiveness and uniqueness of which have been recognized by the architectural profession and have been reported upon in professional journals with great credit to the Authority."[37] His salary was raised to $6,400, the maximum in his pay grade.

In 1940 Menhinick, as the new director of the Department of Regional Studies (DRS), circulated a memo comparing the TVA's in-house design work to the role of a "private architectural firm." He referred to their work on the dams, powerhouses, and other major engineering structures as the "special assignment." He affirmed that Wank, Bianculli, and Seth Harrison Gurnee were in charge of this assignment, though they could call on other architects in the department for special assistance. All contact with Tour and the other engineers was Wank's responsibility. In her detailed study, Christine Macy aptly describes this situation as Wank's "consulting service" out of the LP&H and, later, the DRS.[38]

The TVA "consulting service" designed unprecedented architecture; it also preserved professional norms and preconceptions. Bianculli, despite (or perhaps

**Figure 27.** Architectural details of the Chickamauga Dam powerhouse, north of Chattanooga, Tennessee. Chickamauga was designed after Guntersville was completed and the architects had time to evaluate the use of brick veneer and prefer the more durable concrete (see fig. 26).

because of) his background as an engineer, made a clear distinction between "design" architects and others in the field, and he considered the work on the dams and powerhouses as the most "architectural" of the atelier's undertakings. Landscape architect Osborne H. Graves called Bianculli an "artist at sketching" and described him spontaneously drawing "a picture of the action" at Fontana Dam, even as "rocks were blasted in their direction."[39] Indeed, most of the beautiful presentation drawings of the dams and other elements of the river machine bear his signature. Bianculli judged skill at drawing as a measure of architectural acumen. He respected an architect's opinions if they could *draw* their ideas, and he disparaged those he referred to as "bureaucratic expeditors," who were, he judged, "really not architects"—a group in which he included Tour.[40] He was especially protective of authorship: he insisted that, as part of the design and consulting unit, he would have (together with Wank) the final say on all design issues and that the work of the unit should therefore be credited to the two of them. Nevertheless, a photograph published in *Architectural Forum* in 1939 depicts Draper, Tour, Wank, and Chief Engineer

Theodore B. Parker on equal footing. Bianculli's remarks might therefore reflect his experience as the assistant and stand-in to a head architect who was involved in many other projects, including designs for the other TVA machines—power and land.

## The Power Machine

Wank's proposal for Norris Dam was not limited to a redesign of the dam itself; it also included a sequence of spaces that allowed visitors to observe the production of electric energy. The sequence, which was open until the 1990s, begins at the base of the dam. The entrance pathway offered visitors an impressive vista that comprehended the dam, the powerhouse, and the electric substation. Coming closer, they could admire the imposing aluminum door scaled to the size of the careful concrete work. Mardges Bacon notes the impact this approach had on one illustrious visitor, the architect Le Corbusier.[41] Visitors then entered a reception room and experienced a dramatic shift in scale. This was intentional; Wank argued that people might not recognize a feat of engineering, but they would recognize a good building. Bianculli described this work as paying proper attention to the "flow lines of the various functions of the project, especially as they related to the human activities and relationships therein, and the human 'presence.'"[42] Once inside the center, visitors were greeted by trained docents, "employed to insure the safety of visitors and to provide accurate information."[43] These docents would have directed attention to the colorful mural on the wall, which explained the function of the dam and related it to the larger "unified" system.[44]

The most exciting part of the tour was entering the powerhouse itself, a carefully orchestrated spectacle. Visitors walking past the turbines could imagine the power of the water as it rushed through them; this was the location where, as Benton MacKaye remarked in 1933, the flow of the river was "converted into electric juice."[45] They could look into the control room and admire the work of the operators of the dam. And throughout, they experienced an unprecedented architectural space. The massive windows—whose scale masked the size of the powerhouse for outside viewers—from the interior presented, undisguised, an almost completely transparent wall that dwarfed any human figure standing near it (fig. 28). Wank and his team had even specified the color schemes, furnishings, and materials for this space, all

**Figure 28.** Interior of the powerhouse at Norris Dam, looking toward the large entrance door. The photograph was taken during the eighty-year celebration of the dam, during which the TVA allowed the public to once again experience the visitor route designed by Roland A. Wank and his collaborators in the 1930s.

of which came together to amplify its impact.[46] The tour then took visitors to an outdoor balcony poised mere feet above the spillway, where they could sense the dramatic change in temperature while gazing at the sheer face of the dam towering above (fig. 29).

The visitor sequence at Norris inspired continuous iterations at the subsequent dams. The architects experimented with different color schemes and roofing systems for the enormous generator halls. Their goal was to combine "functional expression" with a dramatic and arresting look.[47] Talbot F. Hamlin reported appreciatively on Pickwick Landing: he described the powerhouse as "simple pylon, almost Egyptian in its quiet strength. The interior of the powerhouse is a definite step ahead. The light is more perfectly distributed, and the whole system of walls has become cleaner, simpler, more direct." (fig. 30.)[48] The sequence at Chickamauga Dam, which is located near the city of Chattanooga, Tennessee, was given special attention. Beginning at the parking lot the visitor walks past the switchyard before entering a large and well-lit reception room, finished with Campagna Rose marble from the

**Figure 29.** View of Norris Dam from the balcony to the west of the powerhouse. The TVA architects and landscape architects orchestrated a unique visitor experience that included this unusual, and exciting, view.

hills of Tennessee and reddish-brown terrazzo.[49] The dedication reads, "1936—Built for the People of the United States of America—1940" and adapted versions are standard to all TVA dams. The generator room can be seen through the windows below the dedication, while the reservoir is visible from apertures to the right. An elevator takes visitors down to the control room and the observation gallery beside it, and then to the generator room floor. The spectacular design of the hall can thus be experienced from three different points of view. Here, too, the architects combined an ingenious roof system, made of prefabricated lightweight concrete slabs, with refactors directing light to the floor. The hall itself is finished in a striking display of green ceramic tiles and the generators with green paint and bands of aluminum. The stairs that access the generator room are the only human-scaled elements in the hall. The gradation of color, growing lighter above, creates a shimmering, otherworldly space, a full experience of the technological sublime (fig. 31).

The tours of the generator rooms introduced visitors to the first stage of the power machine—the production of electricity—but the next phase, transmission, was on

**Figure 30.** The interior of the Pickwick Landing Dam powerhouse. The TVA opened the powerhouses to visitors to give them a glimpse of how the energy of the river was transformed into electric power. The architects enhanced this experience by design: the roof trusses are painted white, the wall a cream color, and the turbines a combination of green and white.

display as well. Tourists could not, of course, enter the substation, where the electric current is adjusted and distributed to the existing power grid, but they could appreciate these awe-inspiring structures as they approached, and when they left, the dams themselves (fig. 32). When the TVA, during World War II, added steam plants to its arsenal, they too were given an architectural treatment.[50] *Progressive Architecture,* for example, celebrated the opportunities that power production and

**Figure 31.** Interior of the powerhouse at Chickamauga Dam, viewed from the visitor gallery outside the control room. The roof system, made of prefabricated concrete slabs, includes light refractors, which enhance the effect of the tile and paint finishes—all in shades of green.

distribution offered "open-minded" architects and described the New Johnsonville, Tennessee, steam plant, located on TVA's Kentucky reservoir. These included the TVA architects' thoughts on the design, showing how the postwar (and unidentified) team continued the work that Wank had pioneered in the 1930s: "The lake serves as a mammoth reflecting pool and brings the buildings into a position of prominence seldom found in a grouping of this magnitude. . . . This called for a design that would symbolize the machine-like character of a modern industrial plant and which, at the same time, would embody bold masses of shape and color to present a striking outline at a distance of some 5000 feet from the highway. Bringing

**Figure 32.** The powerhouse and electric substation at Guntersville Dam—this is the view that greets visitors arriving at the site. The pool of water is temporary, a product of a month of continuous and heavy rain.

gigantic building elements into human scale as visitors approach the plant became one of the most interesting architectural problems."[51]

The powerhouses and substations are the most formidable elements of the power machine; they are also those that were kept under the TVA's tight control. Having established the "consulting office," Wank and his team had direct input into the experience that would greet visitors to these sites. The complete power machine, however, included a third stage: the local and regional cooperatives organized to distribute electricity to rural consumers (see chapter 2). The TVA supported these cooperatives but did not own them. Wank and Bianculli, however, sought to highlight their role in rural electrification through architectural design—to create a visual continuity between the powerhouses and the cooperatives. They proposed identifying the offices of these organizations, initially merely rented storefronts, with distinctive signage (fig. 33). These minor proposals reflected TVA director David E. Lilienthal's insistence on grassroots action; it was he, after all, who was responsible for the power machine. The offices were also an indication of the attitude

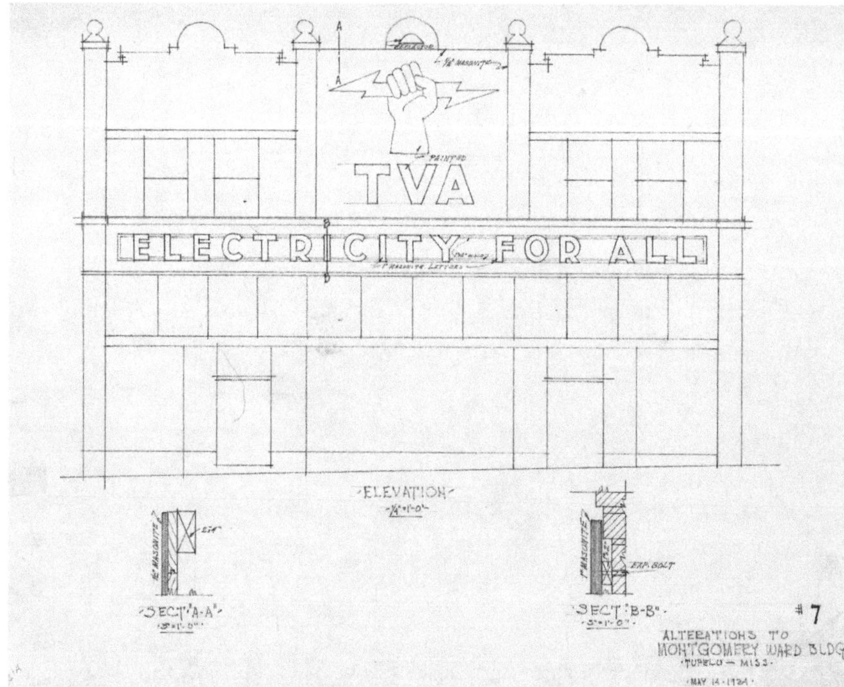


**Figure 33.** A sketch for "alterations" for the façade of the Montgomery Ward Building in Tupelo, Mississippi, dated May 14, 1934. The addition of the TVA logo and the motto "Electricity for All" in Masonite letters was part of the designers' contribution to the TVA's public relations program directed by David E. Lilienthal.

adopted by the administrators of another federal agency involved in supporting the cooperatives—the Rural Electrification Administration (REA). In the early 1930s, as Sarah K. Rovang relates, the agency's first two administrators regarded any funding for building construction as superfluous to the primary goal of the agency: bringing power to rural people. Even when the REA did eventually establish a program for standardizing signage, the then-director stated that he "regarded money spent constructing buildings and buying real estate as money that might have been more profitably spent constructing power lines."[52]

In the late 1930s electric cooperatives outgrew the rented storefronts and began searching for more office and warehouse space. In this context a preliminary building program did emerge, creating the prototypes for all future buildings. By this time the TVA's profile had enlarged as well, with news coverage in large national newspapers. In November 1938 the TVA loaned Wank as a consultant to the REA, having established his ability to give form to engineered machines as well as his willingness to work within complex institutions.[53] His absence from the TVA, however, soon became problematic, and the arrangement was terminated.[54] The REA then established its own in-house architectural office. Wank was retained in a supervisory role, visiting the REA headquarters in Washington, DC, on a regular basis. This arrangement continued until 1942, when defense-related duties took precedence for both the REA and TVA.[55]

Working with the REA, Wank gave form to a new building type: the rural cooperative headquarters. These buildings provided both offices and public space; some were located adjacent to the power plant. A 1943 article in *Architectural Forum* describes their program. The buildings required a lobby and reception room to welcome cooperative members when they arrived to pay bills or attend meetings; this area included a large display of electrical appliances and farm equipment as part of the REA's educational program. The building also housed an office and an assembly room for the monthly meeting of the board of directors, as well as toilets and storage. A garage and warehouse area were provided for trucks and for the storage of line equipment and material.[56] Drawing on the designs of the TVA powerhouses, Wank proposed a palette of soft colors: a basic grey accented with terra cotta and powder blue. When possible, he created a direct view into the power plant for the buildings' users, similar to the visitors' route he evolved at the Chickamauga and other powerhouses.[57] The symbolic import of these buildings, however, went far beyond these mundane functions. The REA expected cooperatives to see themselves as "a front-line force to secure for rural America the benefits of modern civilization."[58] Wank agreed. Writing in 1941 in the REA's publicity organ, *Rural Electrification News,* he maintained that "recognized immediately as landmarks, the new headquarters have added greatly to the standing of the cooperatives and to their reputation for competent management and good citizenship."[59]

Wank also advised on the location of these buildings in their communities. His preference, which was shared by the REA, was to place them—especially in small towns—on the outskirts of development.[60] Here, they were expected to "exert an influence on the development of its surroundings, and that this feature should be utilized to guide the growth of rural towns in desirable directions."[61] Bianculli worked with him, employing his sketching skills to dramatizing these designs; many

**Figure 34.** Photograph of the headquarters building of the rural power distribution cooperative at Shelbyville, Tennessee. The design of this building, by Roland A. Wank and Mario Bianculli, highlighted the connection between the cooperative and the production of power at the TVA dams. Indeed, the TVA published this photograph under the heading "Chickamauga Dam and Powerhouse."

of these drawings were published in *Rural Electrification News* issues. Most of the REA buildings designed by Wank and Bianculli lay outside the Tennessee Valley, but those within it were identified as both TVA and REA structures (fig. 34). The TVA included photos of these buildings in its publicity material, highlighting their modern and open design. The *Rural Electrification News* concurred, noting that the buildings had "many new features" and that "Mr. Wank often specifies yard facilities for demonstrations of farm electric equipment, thus making headquarters buildings more useful to members."[62] The TVA continued to be involved in designs for the power machine into the 1940s. In grassroots fashion, however, the Authority prepared only preliminary sketches, which were then made available to local architects. Menhinick reported that not all of the design ideas were realized in the construction drawings, but he considered the "educational value" of this process in line with TVA objectives.[63]

Planning attractive tours that took visitors past substations and into power houses and cooperative headquarters allowed Wank and Bianculli to experiment with designs intended to engender sublime experiences. An unexpected stream of visitors also opened the door to didactic instruction. By 1939, only three years after the TVA built the little visitors' shed at Norris Dam, more than 1.5 million people visited the Valley, including school groups, conventions, prominent writers, and visitors from foreign countries. Lilienthal would later include a list of the visiting royal, political, and professional leaders as a footnote in his book, *TVA: Democracy on the March*.[64] These visitors were greeted with what *Architectural Forum* described as an innovative form of display: "Large photographic displays of the dams which have been constructed under the TVA are made concretely intelligible to the layman through the medium of a model showing how a lock actually works. Landscapes demonstrating conditions in the vicinity of a controlled river and uncontrolled river are compared in two large models of typical watershed country, while a diorama of an electrified farm illustrates the comfort and efficiency available to the farmer."[65]

The preparation of these graphic displays was undertaken by the Office of Information, and particularly by Alfred Clauss, a member of Charles Krutch's Graphic Arts Service staff. Clauss had studied architecture in his home city of Munich, Germany, before moving to Hamburg. Interested in modernist architecture, Clauss approached Mies van der Rohe and asked to work for him. As part of that studio, he was involved in the design of the German Pavilion for the 1929 Barcelona International Exposition, a benchmark for modernist architects. In 1930 Clauss emigrated to New York and immediately purchased a drafting board—and a car: "Everyone told me that everyone in America has a car. So right away I bought one."[66] He secured a job with Howe and Lescaze and contributed to the PSFS Building in Philadelphia. Here he met George Daub, with whom he collaborated on several projects both before and after World War II. Clauss also worked on designs and models with Louis Skidmore for the 1933 Chicago World's Fair, on the basis of which he was hired by the TVA as an associate architect.

Clauss and other atelier members also experimented with the spatial presentation of these displays. At the Kentucky construction site, for example, they built a simple shed marked with large lettering on both sides. Within the displays were arranged as transparencies, lit by natural illumination during the day and floodlights at night.[67] At Watts Bar Dam the visitors' center was located high above the dam and combined a sublime view with the informative posters. The displays at Watts Bar were destroyed by fire after the visitors' center closed. At Fort Loudon Dam, however, they have been preserved and even restored, including a stylized ceiling, reminiscent of the turbines in the generator room.[68] Here too the spatial arrangement balances between an experiential view of the dam and the didactic displays (fig. 35). These innovative designs became models for other government agencies. Menhinick recalled getting a call from the Vicksburg office of the Army Corps of Engineers; they asked to visit the TVA facilities to adapt the Authority's designs to their own dams: "We felt that was a great compliment."[69]

The TVA architecture team also joined the public relations effort spearheaded by the Office of Information. Images of the dams, powerhouses, and even architectural details—boosted by hyperbolic descriptions—were circulated along with the

**Figure 35.** Interior of the visitor center at Fort Loudon Dam, which combines the spatial acumen Roland A. Wank brought to the TVA architecture and Alfred Clauss's finely developed graphic displays. Visitors could compare the view of the dam (seen through the windows to the left) and the didactic information displayed in the posters.

display material the TVA had prepared. TVA exhibitions traveled to venues such as the California-Pacific International Exposition in 1935–36 and, a year later, to the Paris International Exposition. Tour commented on the exhibits' importance: not everyone would read "a factual article or one that was filled with data or one that has nothing but engineering pictures on it."[70] The architectural achievement became an integral part of the TVA's larger political successes.[71] Wank actively promoted the TVA's modern designs in the architectural press, serving as the principal liaison to architectural journals, competitions, and exhibitions.[72] In 1939 he orchestrated a blitz of publications, with full-issue spreads in *Pencil Points* and *Architectural Forum*. These and many subsequent publications combined laudatory text with photographs, plans, elevations, and detailed drawings of architectural elements.

The TVA architectural work was very well received. The buildings were hailed as some of the first examples of modern architecture in the United States, positioning the atelier nicely within the progressive architectural milieu.[73] In 1957 Norris Dam tied for ninth place in *Architectural Record*'s "100 Years of Significant Building."[74] In the same year, Fredrick A. Gutheim, who had been instrumental in including regional planning in the TVA Act, cited Fontana Dam in a similar publication, *One Hundred Years of Architecture in America, 1857–1957:Celebrating the Centennial of the American Institute of Architects.*[75] This stellar position was formally recognized in 1941 when the Museum of Modern Art (MoMA) in New York hosted an exhibit prepared in collaboration with the TVA staff.[76] The goal of the exhibit, the curators explained in the museum's bulletin, was to show that government architecture could produce fine results; going further, they asserted that these collaborations between architects and engineers displayed "a mutual understanding of each other's skill unmatched since the great utilitarian building campaigns of Imperial Rome."[77] Such accolades surely deepened the architects' commitment to their work at the TVA, proving that they could advance their careers and the Authority's goals at the same time.

The advent of this amalgam of architecture with engineering and—yes—planning conveyed an even wider message. In the 1920 the Regional Planning Association of America argued that the future of architecture as a profession lay in its members' willingness to expand their purview and consider the larger scales of city and environment. Douglas Haskell, writing in *The Nation* in 1949, identified the MoMA exhibit as an opportunity to teach young architects just that: "It's as if Joshua had fit a new battle of Jericho and the walls came tumblin' down. In the forward view that is opened at TVA the walls, even the big ones, have dropped to a minor role. The glimpse that is given is of man working on the *whole* of his environment to put it into habitable, workable, agreeable and friendly shape. As a concept, architecture can today be no less."[78]

## The Land Machine

Lewis Mumford also visited the 1941 MoMA exhibit of the TVA architecture, but he commented on the role of landscape in experiencing it: "The actual buildings, as I saw them recently in their natural setting [*sic*] of hill, woodland and quarry and boat basin and river, are even more breathtaking. These structures are as close to perfection as our age has come. . . . The Pharaohs did not do any better."[79] Marian Moffett and Lawrence Wodehouse relate a similar reaction by British town planner and architect Raymond Unwin, who remarked that the TVA was "fortunate to be able to locate its major installations in such handsome parks."[80] Mumford and Unwin did not recognize, however, the extent to which the landscapes they admired were gardens, in the sense that they had been modified by human intervention (fig. 36). Wank deserves credit for his insistence on making TVA lands surrounding the dams into "handsome parks" and on developing equally compelling visitor facilities. But the landscape development itself was largely the work of the landscape architects under the direction of Osborne Graves, who was a great believer in "teamwork."[81] In 1953 Graves told his colleagues in the American Society of Landscape Architects: "Effective planners must understand and believe in people, and, incidentally, this belief must begin with an understanding and belief in fellow workers. I am very proud of the teamwork that has been developed within our own design organization. Landscape architects, architects, and engineers have learned to work together as one team, coordinating their ideas with others, all interested in the broad valley-wide program."[82]

Once again, Norris, Tennessee, was the testing ground for this design intervention, which was developed as the dam was being built.[83] The landscape architects focused their attention on the construction site itself, identifying areas that could be reimagined as highway approaches, parking areas, and overlooks for the dams. Two enormous towers anchored a huge cable, used to move material to the dam;

**Figure 36.** Norris Dam and the Clinch River, as seen from the access to the Songbird Trail, about five hundred yards below the dam. Even at this short distance the TVA landscaping masks the mechanical aspects of the dam and powerhouse, creating a veritable machine in the garden.

the engineers' plan was to flatten their bases once the dam was complete. But when the towers and machinery had been removed, these areas were instead finished as overlooks, following the landscape architects' plans (fig. 37). The landscape architects also prepared the specifications for the blasting and transport operations in a nearby quarry—the source of the stone needed to produce concrete for the dam. As a result, when the builders' work was finished there remained a well-designed boat dock at the quarry, in what was once Cove Creek (fig. 38). In 1948 TVA personnel discussed placing a crib for swimming lessons in the quarry. Robert M. Howes supported this move, explaining that the operator had been giving lessons for several years in another location, which was not being leased. Graves, however, was concerned that the site was too polluted with discharge from the houseboats and suggested that an agreement could be reached about keeping the crib in the existing location.[84]

On the eastern abutment of the dam the designers used concrete to extend the aesthetic of the dam into the landscape, creating a wide terrace (fig. 39). They also

**Figure 37.** The western overlook at Norris Dam. Behind the dam is Norris Lake and to the right are the powerhouse and substation. The junction between the concrete and the dam and the green glade (here covered in snow) is carefully maintained, part of the presentation of the TVA dams as machines in gardens.

**Figure 38.** The Cove Creek Marina as seen from Norris Dam. The marina is located in what was the quarry that provided the aggregate for the concrete used for the dam's construction. The landscape architects provided specific plans so that the blasting would accommodate recreational use.

**Figure 39.** Concrete details at the eastern overlook at Norris Dam, in front of the permanent visitor center. The sign at the center reads: "Norris Dam, named for George W. Norris, United States Senator from Nebraska, in recognition of his public service. Built for the People of the United States of America, by the Tennessee Valley Authority, under direction of the Congress and the president 1933–1936." A version of this plaque is placed in each of the TVA dams and visitors' centers.

designed a permanent visitors' center constructed of a wood frame with cinder-block veneer and finished with local marble-dust sand to match the nearby concrete work. It contained an information booth, a refreshment and souvenir stand, a salesroom for mountain craft products, and public toilets. (This building has since been replaced with a newer model, which is still staffed by TVA docents during the summer months.) Below the terrace and building and toward the powerhouse, the TVA refilled an area that had been blasted during construction, creating a grassy slope that is still mowed regularly. Visitors could carry their refreshments out to the terrace or down to the picnic area on the glade. The entire installation masterfully integrates the machine scale of the dam with that of a garden—the human scale. Standing on the terrace, one cannot ignore the dam, its purpose, or its builders.

Surrounding the dam, with its terrace and overlooks, is a lush forest—one of the focuses of the land machine—punctuated by the reservoir on one side and the river on the other. A traffic circle just east of the dam serves as a gateway to a state park (described in chapter 6). The river, the forest, and the mowed glade together create the overall effect of a pastoral landscape cradling the sculptural concrete monolith of the dam. As Brian Black argues, this vision was intentional: "This was not a landscape of domination. Instead, the dam's relationship to the land was more cooperative, even organic, and symbolic of a conservation ethic that the New Deal would market to the American people."[85] The pastoral effect was achieved only with great effort. Not only were there deep construction scars to be erased, but the landscape architects had to insist on funds for sodding, mulching, and maintenance.[86] Once these preparations were accomplished, they also oversaw the restoration of disturbed areas by planting grasses, shrubs, and trees. Harold Frincke recalled being "concerned" with this phase of the work.[87] At Norris much of the physical labor was undertaken by a Civilian Conservation Corps (CCC) camp assigned to the TVA and housed nearby. Still, the TVA staff needed to coordinate this work and oversee the delivery of materials and plants.[88]

Compared to the engineering and architecture on display at the TVA dams, the landscape is an unobtrusive element. Draper explained in 1939: "Since simplicity is in harmony with the environment of its projects, the Authority has avoided expensive and overelaborate treatment."[89] It is also a surprisingly straightforward artistic statement; no one familiar with American frontier imagery or with the garden traditions prized in Britain and the United States (as exemplified by the work of Frederick Law Olmsted) can miss the overt allusions to both. As Moffett and Wodehouse comment, the site designers used the "opportunity to create a naturalistic setting in the tradition of the 18th-century English romantic landscape."[90] Looking at the dams from the designed overlooks and viewpoints is, indeed, to encounter a veritable machine in the garden. While Wank's designs for the dams and powerhouses emphasized their newness, the landscape design signals a timeless continuity.

The landscape architects continued to design overlooks, parking lots, and other amenities in the subsequent dams, including access roads envisioned as freeways.[91] However, the postconstruction work to reclaim the landscapes could only occur in spurts and was the first element to be impacted by any budget cuts. During World War II concerns of sabotage meant the dams were surrounded by security fences and visitors were prohibited from entering. In 1943 Otto Priebe, one of Graves's staff, wrote: "None of the dam reservations has even been thoroughly studied as a complete landscape problem or any proportion to its possibilities or importance as a proper setting for its architectural values, its recreational possibilities or value in a public educational program."[92] Still, the atelier took a comprehensive approach and proposed a general policy for future work on dam reservations. This policy took the more elusive symbolic goals and translated them into the language of function and efficiency:

1. To erase scars of construction and to help in erosion control for the protection of the land.
2. To create a natural approach and setting for the dam by bringing the surrounding landscape into harmony with the structure.
3. To create viewpoints for public observation of the dam and adjacent structures by planting to enframe [*sic*] views and by cutting to open vistas.
4. To provide shade at parking spaces and other public areas and reduce the glare of reflected sunlight.
5. To create mass planting of trees on areas suitable for forest cover and incidentally to create interesting approach to the dam.
6. To substitute the mass planting of trees and shrubs for certain grass areas where the maintenance of grass would be extremely difficult.[93]

The design principles expounded by Graves and Priebe are evident in the scenic routes designed around two dams located high in the Appalachian Mountains. The layout of the scenic route at Hiwassee followed the Norris example, though it was more compact and gave visitors an even more intimate connection with the dam. The sequence began at the southwest border of the TVA reservation with a public overlook. The overlook is no longer maintained, and trees obscure the dam, but a photograph shot by George L. Richardson (or one of his associates) on October 9, 1942, shows the dam as seen through the forest—another quintessential machine-in-the-garden view (fig. 40). The current condition of the Hiwassee sequence highlights, unfortunately, another critical aspect of the TVA landscape architects' role—landscape maintenance. This was a constant preoccupation, and it crystallized the career of one member of the atelier. In 1953 Herbert S. Conover, a landscape

**Figure 40.** Photograph of Hiwassee Dam from a TVA overlook, shot by architect George L. Richardson (or an associate) on October 9, 1942. The overlook has not been maintained and is now so overgrown that the view is no longer available.

architect with the site planning section, created a handbook on maintenance that condensed the information amassed by the landscape architects during two decades of overseeing TVA dams.[94] The TVA version was made available to the public, and the book was later reissued commercially. Thinking back on this project, Carroll Towne commented, "I believe he is still very much in demand as a consultant."[95]

From the overlook at Hiwassee Dam, visitors would drive to the dam and cross it to arrive at the visitors' building and picnic area on the other side. The original visitors' building was a simple structure containing a small reception room and two sets of (segregated) bathrooms. Constructed of cinder blocks with steel columns on a base of concrete, the circular building directed the visitors' attention to the lake, while a corresponding circular landscaped area outside offered views of the face of the dam (fig. 41). Visitors could also descend to a picnic area (no longer maintained)

**Figure 41.** Photograph of "Landscape Planting" at the Hiwassee Dam visitors' center, taken by architect George L. Richardson (or an associate) on May 8, 1941. The TVA landscape architects expended considerable energy to turn the engineering sites into public parks.

that would allow them to sit in the shadow of the great structure itself, where they could admire Wank's resolution of the details of the spillway. Visitors proceeding to the base of the dam, where yet another picnic area was prepared, would discover that though similar in design to Norris Dam, the Hiwassee generator room is not enclosed in a powerhouse, allowing the spillway to fall dramatically to the river (fig. 42).

Fontana, the tallest dam in the TVA system, was built during World War II under great duress. Its location, on the Little Tennessee River in western North Carolina, on land owned by the Aluminum Co. of America (ALCOA), had been a matter of dispute in previous years, even figuring in the ongoing feud between Arthur Morgan and Lilienthal, who disagreed about how the TVA should acquire the land. The war brought a resolution: ALCOA and the TVA reached an agreement about the transfer of ownership in return for an indemnity granted to the company for any

**Figure 42.** The scene below Hiwassee Dam. The sign warns visitors to keep out of the water because of dangerous currents and violent surges, but the picnic table invites them to linger.

claims "arising under the Federal Water Power Act for benefits growing out of the receipt of water from Fontana reservoir at the company's downstream plants."[96] The dam was built at record speed. Workers labored twenty-four hours a day, operating at night under floodlights. Even here, however, the atelier was able to argue for fully developed visitor facilities, appealing directly to Gordon R. Clapp, then general manager of the TVA. The project engineers objected to the unnecessary expense of the air-conditioned visitors' facility, served by an inclined cable car carrying visitors to the powerhouse at the base of the dam itself. Menhinick later recalled:

> At the hearing, all of the items, one by one, were approved by Mr. Clapp. At that point, Mr. Clapp asked if anything had been overlooked, and the chief engineer said, "Yes. Nothing has been said about the cost of this project." Mr. Clapp said, "Well, I understand that the visitors' facilities will cost several million dollars on a fifty plus million-dollar project," and the chief engineer said, "Yes, sir, that's right." Mr. Clapp said, "In my opinion, this will be the best

> money that TVA has ever spent. Congress has attacked TVA on many fronts, but they have never once criticized the money that TVA has spent for visitors' facilities."[97]

The engineers prevailed, however, when their concern was not cost but structural integrity. Tour's team, also closely involved in the project, originally proposed an elevator to carry visitors inside the dam itself. The engineers vetoed this suggestion: they were using cooling coils in the concrete to save curing time on a tight schedule, and an elevator shaft might weaken the dam structure.[98] The internal elevator was replaced with an inclined railway, which was in operation between the 1950s and the 1990s, until the TVA could no longer staff it.[99]

Bianculli headed the design at Fontana. The finished project was a stunning success: the visitors' center would receive an award in the Pan America Congress in Havana in 1950. Frincke was especially proud of the close collaboration on this project: as landscape architect he had successfully directed the placement of the various pits and fills to shape a landscape that would long be enjoyed by the visiting public.[100] Indeed, the product of this collaboration is a spectacular sequence, framing close views of the impressive machine within a stunning vista of public forest (fig. 43). The forest is itself another enduring legacy of the TVA, which had transferred part of the land purchased from ALCOA to the National Park Service to augment the Great Smoky Mountains National Park that now borders the dam. The Appalachian Trail—Benton MacKaye's seminal idea—crosses the river on top of the dam, knitting it into the larger region. It is hard to imagine a more sublime demonstration of regional planning.

But this treatment of the landscape does something more. Extending the designed space beyond the dam and powerhouse to the very edges of the TVA's demesne—the entire reservation within the agency's "taking lines"—creates a kind of diorama. These expanded "gardens" offer visitors from near and far the opportunity to engage in sightseeing, picnicking, fishing, boating, and more, all in the shadow of the dams. They also function as nodes for experiencing the larger system and landscape, whether consciously or unconsciously, making the logic of the whole visible and knowable. It is through the landscape and the architecture—the garden in the machine—that visitors learn how the TVA machine functions. This revelatory characteristic reflects the dual nature of architecture: it is at once part of a larger

**Figure 43.** Southwest view from Fontana Dam, encompassing the powerhouse, the substation, and the Cherokee National Forest. Hikers on the Appalachian Trail (proposed by Benton MacKaye) exit the Great Smoky Mountains National Park by crossing the dam. The showers and restrooms provided at the visitor center are known as the "Fontana Hilton."

system—conforming to its abstract, often linear logic—and also a particular, site-specific manifestation that wants to be understood on its own terms. This is especially true when the rivers overflow after heavy rains. It is mesmerizing to watch the water spill over dams, either high in the mountains or along the river. The juxtaposition between the wild fury of the water and the calm landscaping is a stark reminder of why the TVA machine was first conceived.

# 4

# COMMUNITY PLANNING

## Communities for Labor

Arthur E. Morgan, first director of the TVA, established the Land Planning & Housing Division (LP&H) to plan, design and oversee the construction of a model of regional planning—a garden city, modern houses, and a string of recreation areas connected by the Norris Freeway (see chapter 1). This demonstration was intended for several audiences. First, Morgan and his staff hoped that residents of the Tennessee Valley would appreciate how the well-planned town, especially the school, commons, and small commercial area, provided a meaningful community setting. A second audience was the American public, who were to learn the value of orderly planning by competent professionals. Finally, the staff of the LP&H positioned themselves as pioneers in the fields of planning, landscaping, and architecture and took it upon themselves to propagate the principles of regional planning as new standards for practice in their professional areas of expertise. The drive to persuade these three audiences stemmed from the deep commitment to the central goal of the garden-in-the-machine ideology: balancing the monotony of life in a technological world with the harmony provided by community and nature. The fervor of this commitment led the LP&H staff to develop what is here called the atelier spirit—the sense that their work would serve as a standard for society and their professions.

The Norris model region was planned and designed by a small group of planners, architects, and landscape architects who gathered around Earle S. Draper, the director of the LP&H. Committed to exploring new ideas and to collaboration, they shared the work between them with only rudimentary institutional organization. As the atelier took responsibility for the next projects, two conditions became obvious. First, that the investment in the generous "taking lines"—the bedrock of the Norris demonstration—would not be repeated. Harcourt A. Morgan's and David E. Lilienthal's vehement objection to transforming private land into public land, more than was absolutely necessary for the construction of the river machine, would guide the TVA purchasing policies henceforth. This policy effectively ended the possibility of comprehensive regional planning, though the LP&H still had direct impact on land that the TVA did acquire and indirect impact on the wider Tennessee Valley. Second, the planners and designers would have to conform to the managerial style of the TVA, which emphasized specification and specialization as the basis for collaboration rather than the more chaotic atmosphere of the atelier. Draper had designated a Town and Site Planning Section and an Architectural Section, but these titles were fluid. In addition, the clarity of their roles had been upset by the creation of Roland A. Wank's consulting office, which focused on the design of dams, powerhouses, and visitors' centers (see chapter 3). The LP&H, and later the Department of Regional Studies (DRS), were repeatedly reorganized but always with a view toward specificity rather than comprehensive responsibility.

The changing institutional environments did not diminish the atelier's commitment to regional planning, but it did change its focus. The fine design and construction efforts were now directed, primarily, toward the public architecture of the machines as part of the TVA's public persuasion. Wider efforts at community building would have to be embedded in the gargantuan task of housing the thousands of workers building the TVA dams. These projects, temporary by their very nature, would be shaped by demands of the resource conservation approach—expediency and efficiency—and were unlikely to yield distinguished architecture. But this approach, or, more precisely, the grassroots ideology as described by Lilienthal, did offer an alternative path for practice. In this model, the TVA provided knowledge, not direction, allowing citizens in the Valley and beyond to choose the "best" course of action. Wank wrote in 1942 about the atelier's efforts to design "rural architecture": "Buildings incidental to this work have hardly attained much architectural significance—yet; but experience gleaned along the road may yield some interesting and perhaps useful pointers against the time when this nation will turn, as it someday must, from exclusive preoccupation with cities to recasting non-metropolitan areas into the mold of modern civilization."[1]

The shift from centralized design to demonstration was captured, primarily, in the term "research," which transformed designs, at least rhetorically, into knowledge. Research was thus the key to making the people into experts, as Lilienthal described it.[2] It reconciled the TVA's insistence on technical and scientific knowledge with the commitment of democratic action and free choice. At the same time, research carved a role for the professionals within the Authority similar to one assumed by scientists and engineers. Research did not replace planning and design; members of the atelier were still responsible for the spatial arrangement of construction camps and villages and the buildings and landscapes within them. Transforming their ideas into knowledge thus required an extra layer of analysis, documentation, and dissemination. But for the TVA staff, as for other progressive architects and landscape architects, this was the most direct route to serving the community; they seized on the opportunity to expand their professional practice. In the 1930s and 1940s being part of the TVA machine gave them many opportunities to do so. At the same time, the practices they developed were shaped by the institutional biases—toward "scientific" knowledge and middle-class values and away from challenging Jim Crow segregation and other social and political realities.

Arthur Morgan decided to hire laborers directly, through force account, rather than by third-party contract (as did the Army Corps of Engineers), arguing that good labor relations would ensure a smoothly functioning, efficient work environment.[3] Lilienthal continued this practice, seeing it as crucial to the development of the region; income flowed into local communities.[4] The TVA also recognized that "to expect employees to provide their own shelter and abandon it at the end of the job amounts to a deduction of their earning."[5] In addition, the workforce was drawn primarily from the rural population of the Tennessee Valley. The TVA thus provided relief work and training for future jobs to the very people whose conditions inspired the project and whose land was likely to be flooded. These laborers, however, were usually unaccustomed to industrial projects, tight schedules, and hierarchical authority structures.[6] Good housing thus played dual roles: it helped keep an unruly workforce in line, and it also attracted workers who may have been politically opposed to the federally driven project.

The hierarchical nature of the TVA and its progressive bias toward middle-class norms were inscribed in the housing the Authority provided. Tenants also paid rent toward defraying the cost of building the housing, further stratifying the communities. At the top of the scale were quality-built, single-family homes, which were intended first for managers and engineers and then, once the dam was completed, for its operators. These were the houses that formed the core of the demonstration town at Norris, Tennessee. A rung below these quality homes were smaller, and cheaper, single-family homes, which housed semi- and unskilled employees and their families. The task of providing houses at acceptable costs, while also assuring minimum standards of living, became a project in and of itself and is discussed in the next chapter. Unmarried employees lived in dormitories, also designed and built by the TVA staff. Here too the Authority distinguished between professionals, who were offered private rooms, and the dorms for laborers, which were bunkhouses in every sense of the word. Unmarried women, most of whom worked as nurses or cooks, had their own dormitory.

The tiered accommodation provided the basic everyday needs of the TVA laborers and professionals, but the LP&H also worked to offer a "normal community life."[7] This entailed designing and constructing shared buildings such as cafeterias, recreational halls, hospitals, schools, and libraries. The atelier prided itself on the quality of these buildings, as LP&H staff member Louis Grandgent explained in 1937: "Architecture differs from mere building, in that it not only provides for utilitarian needs in the most orderly way possible, but contributes an expression of special fitness for those needs: harmony of form and purpose."[8] The atelier also invested great effort in site planning; the assumption was that an intelligent location would raise the quality of the buildings. This logic was first applied at Norris: Carroll A. Towne and Malcolm Dill toured the area surrounding the proposed dam and Tracy B. Augur—still acting as a consultant—gave them technical direction.[9] The site they located, just over three miles south of the dam, was, of course, owned by individual farmers, but it was soon bought as part of the policy of generous "taking lines." In the southwest part of the newly acquired plot of land was a small, wooded hill, which was designated as the common outdoor space for the construction camp. (See fig. 10 in chapter 1.)

At Norris the community building was placed in the most commanding location on the hill; opposite was the mess hall, which accommodated workers and visitors in cafeteria style. Grouped around these buildings were a staff dorm, a women's dorm, and six workers' dorms. In July 1934 the *Knoxville News-Sentinel* reported on the opportunities for recreation during the leisure hours, calling these activities "Model Night Life."[10] The community building included a large lounge, a refreshment and lunch space, a three-hundred-seat auditorium, lecture halls, barber and beauty shops, and offices. It was later remodeled to house a restaurant, display room, and other features. The restaurant, seating approximately a thousand persons, boasted a fully equipped kitchen and dining room furniture; it was used mainly by the unmarried employees of both genders.[11] After the dam was completed, the building served as a community space for the residents of the permanent garden city until it burned down in the 1970s.[12] The mess hall was converted into offices for the TVA forestry staff, who moved to Norris in 1937, and it still exists today.

The laborers at Norris also had access to a library, which represented the TVA's commitment to self-driven adult education as a supplement to the skills the laborers learned on the job. In keeping with New Deal policy, the construction work was divided among as many people as possible, so the workdays were only five-and-a-half-hours long. Adult education and libraries were intended, in part, to provide educational and recreational opportunities to fill up the remaining hours of the day. In its first years of operation the TVA managed the libraries by itself. By 1938, however, the TVA's chief librarian, Mary U. Rothrock, began cementing relationships with local library boards, paying them to provide the TVA with the services it needed. The TVA continued to support these systems after construction was finished, but the ultimate goal was that the county, or group of counties, would take responsibility for them. The TVA employed a similar method with other community services such as schools and hospitals. This combination of demonstration and support was considered part of the planning region or grassroots approach.

Having established planning principles in their work at Norris, the atelier applied them in their designs for subsequent construction camps, especially in the 1930s before the TVA—along with the rest of the nation—became absorbed in defense and war. Following Patrick Geddes's and Lewis Mumford's dictum on the importance of a preliminary survey, the community planners based their work on data supplied by the Land Classification Section.[13] This information directed the size of the camp and the number of bunkhouses, single-family houses, and community buildings. Following the planning process, the atelier continued to oversee the construction, documenting the work meticulously. In all locations the siting of the camp—especially the community buildings—was of central importance: "The design of such a community begins at the selection of the location. . . . It should be scenically attractive if possible."[14] The planners insisted on the decisive design influence of landscape elements (topographical features, woods and trees, and in some cases shorefront) as well as climate conditions. They preferred that the natural topography take precedence over buildings: "Building should be adapted to natural grades rather than the landscape destroyed by clearing and grading to make way for building."[15] In places where they did reshape the landscape, they were careful to regrade it to make it as convenient as possible.

By 1940 the atelier had provided accommodation for the workers on all the dams built on the Tennessee River: Wheeler in 1933, Pickwick Landing a year later, followed by Guntersville in northern Alabama. At Chickamauga (just north of Chattanooga) and Fort Loudon Dam (located near Knoxville), the TVA relied on local housing options and offered only a minimum camp. In 1936 the LP&H team also developed the Hiwassee workers' camp (on the Hiwassee River in North Carolina)—the first to be located high in the mountains. Adjusting the community buildings, dormitories, and houses to the steep terrain took some ingenuity, but the residents would enjoy the incomparable scenery. Gilbertsville Dam (later renamed Kentucky Dam), located not far from the confluence of the Tennessee and Ohio Rivers, was the longest dam in the system and one of the more complicated engineering projects. It required more than six years to build (from July 1938 to September 1944) and was supported by one of the largest construction villages in the system (figs. 44, 45, 46, and 47). The success of the atelier's work made a point about the importance of the garden; even the engineers, Howard K. Menhinick recalled, eventually came to recognize the importance of these communities for the smooth functioning of their operations.[16]

The atelier's commitment to developing professional expertise was evident in their search for an optimal dormitory structure. At Norris the six worker bunk-

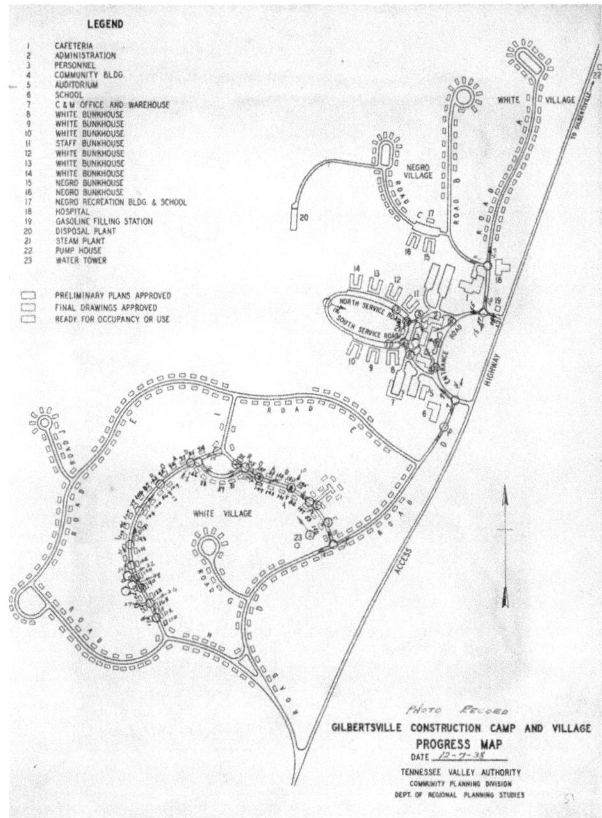


**Figure 44.** Schematic map of the Gilbertsville construction camp and village, used by the TVA staff to document the progress of its construction. The TVA's Department of Regional Planning Studies prepared a series of reports documenting buildings, grading, and planting in the camp and village. These reports illustrate the practical application of the garden-city model in large engineering projects. This specific plan was included in a report dated December 7, 1938.

houses, which accommodated 116 workers each, were roughly constructed, but they had brick foundations to protect against termites. Here the tight site dictated long, narrow, two-story buildings. At Wheeler, where the site was much flatter, the atelier experimented with H-shaped dormitories: the restrooms and showers were physically separated from the sleeping area, which was arranged in open cubicles. This layout was also used at Pickwick Landing, but here each two-man cubicle was heated by an electric heater, framed into the outside wall. The heaters were thermostatically controlled, equipped with a switch regulated by the occupants. The atelier

**Figure 45.** Photograph of the community and the personnel buildings at the Gilbertsville construction camp, taken on August 25th, 1939. Despite the temporary nature of the building, the TVA made every effort to create a convenient environment, at least for the white residents of the camp.

also designed special double-hung, weatherproofed windows; weather-stripping was incorporated in the window construction. Summer ventilation was managed through a transom in each room and ventilators on the roof as well as wide, projecting eaves to protect the walls from the sun. The Pickwick Landing dorm plan was repeated at Guntersville, although the layout slightly refined and the materials upgraded, creating a model that "proved to be about right in every respect."[17] The designers were especially pleased with the decision to move the washroom unit from the center of each dormitory wing to its ends, a move that reduced the noise in the hallways. The compact layout lowered the cost of utilities for the building without sacrificing the views from the dormitory wings—one of their central preoccupations (figs. 48, 49).

In 1938 the team prepared a report on the dormitories they had developed, intended as a convenient reference manual for professionals involved in "power, reclamation, and flood control projects both public and private."[18] This report,

7087-C

Cafeteria from Entrance Road

7087-D

Cafeteria from Entrance Road -- 2 weeks later

**Figure 46.** Two photographs of the cafeteria at the Gilbertsville construction camp, taken two weeks apart. The TVA architects were working under tremendous time constraints but still labored to create a "normal community life." Their goal was to use the temporary camp and village to develop the typology of a "democratic community." This comparison is part of an undated report.

**Figure 47.** Photograph titled "View west from south of house #148 'F' Street," included in a TVA report dated December 7, 1938. These houses are part of the section in the Gilbertsville construction camp designated for white employees and their families.

and others like it, married the surveys of the land planning effort with practical knowledge. A key message was the importance of standards for health and safety and specific examples of how to provide a refreshing environment through the design of window sizes, lighting, heating and ventilation, and sanitary facilities. This research was part of a larger effort to codify such standards nationally. The dormitory report was completed in the same year that the Committee on the Hygiene of Housing of the American Public Health Association published its own preliminary report on minimum requirements for space, light, privacy, and sanitation. Draper was a member of this committee, and his LP&H colleague Allen Twitchell (who had been part of Benton MacKaye's Philosophers Club) was its technical secretary.[19]

The TVA site planners and architects wanted visitors to the dams to see the TVA construction camps as good "specimens of public planning."[20] The reality, however,

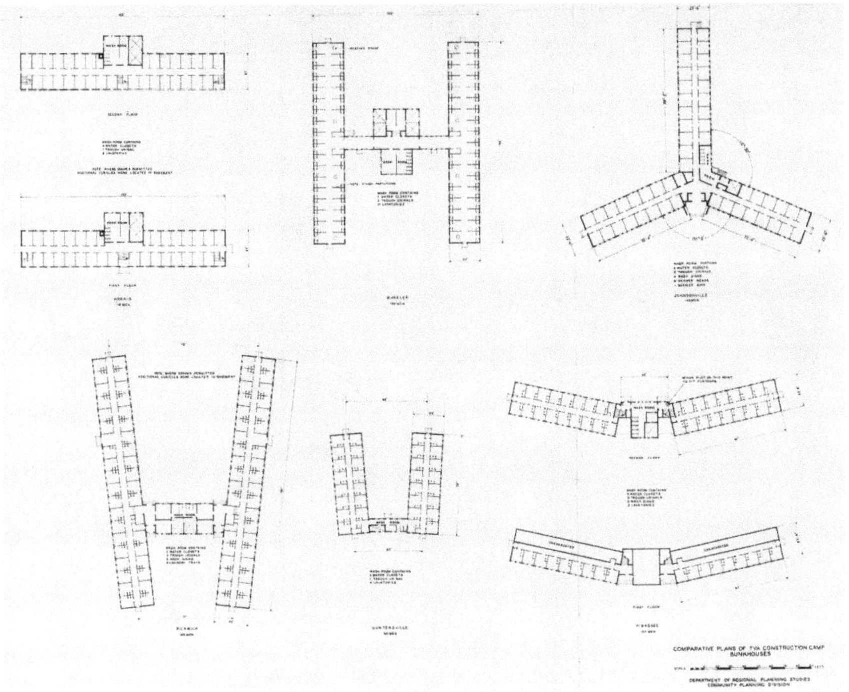


**Figure 48.** Plans of TVA-designed bunkhouses, included in the report "Construction Camp Standards" prepared by the Community Planning Division and completed in January 1938. The plans illustrate the attention the TVA staff gave to perfecting the bunkhouse layout.

was more complicated. The TVA camps were not permanent villages, and neither were their residents permanent; employment numbers fluctuated as the construction of each dam progressed. The dormitories at Norris were not sufficient for the period of peak employment, and the LP&H staff developed the dorms' basement space and erected about a dozen portable huts behind them. These were very basic cabins, but they did provide plumbing, kitchens, and a screened porch.[21] They also had to watch as several of the camps, including Wheeler, Pickwick Landing, Hiwassee, and Guntersville were surrounded by temporary huts and shacks that were not connected to water or sewage.[22] Such shacks, constructed independently by laborers, represented a failure of the rational planning the site planners prided themselves on. They worried that inferior sanitation and a lack of social control would negatively impact the residents of the "official" camp; in addition, the shacks would need to be

**Figure 49.** Photograph of staff bunkhouse (#11) and workmen's bunkhouse (#12) in the Gilbertsville construction camp on October 15, 1938.

removed as the water levels in the reservoir rose.[23] Evidence of these failures was not, of course, included in the reports shared with other entities.

The atelier prided itself on its support for community life, but this too was limited by social and institutional realities. Arthur Morgan, who believed that societies progress through the actions of their elites, had no interest in changing the status of women or African Americans. A firm believer in social Darwinism and interested in eugenics, he also questioned the possibility of such progress.[24] Instead, he advocated that Blacks "focus their attention on vocational training rather than on attaining immediate political and educational equality."[25] The racial policy he instituted reflected this bias: the TVA committed to hiring Black residents in proportion to their percentage in the surrounding population, which gave the agency an excuse at Norris, and later at Hiwassee, to exclude African Americans completely. In addition, local racist practices often deterred potential employees from applying, and those who were hired were deemed qualified only for the low-paying jobs in reservoir clearance and manual labor.[26] Harcourt Morgan and Lilienthal continued the policy, and the TVA made no effort to recruit and train Black residents for the more lucrative positions. By relegating Black citizens to the role of laborers rather than community members, the TVA further entrenched Jim Crow segregation and unequal opportunities.[27]

The TVA policy was protested by the National Association for the Advancement of Colored People (NAACP) in a detailed description of the situation in its journal, *The Crisis.* The NAACP also threatened to sue the TVA on several occasions and later participated in the congressional investigation that followed Arthur Morgan's dismissal.[28] They owed some of their information to Dr. J. Max Bond Sr., who oversaw Black personnel in the TVA. A native Tennessean, Bond earned a master's degree from the University of Pittsburgh and a PhD in sociology and economics from the University of Southern California in 1934. Before joining the TVA, he was the director of an interracial commission in Kentucky for several years. Bond helped develop what was called the Negro Program, which shared all the goals of the larger project—to provide intellectual, recreational, and social amenities; to contribute to an understanding of the TVA; and to "develop morale and efficiency on the job."[29] It was, however, separate from the efforts directed at white employees and Valley residents. Bond left the TVA after four years to become dean at Dillard University in New Orleans and then an administrator at Tuskegee Institute in Alabama.[30]

The segregation between Black and white employees was spatial as well as programmatic, creating "racialized landscapes."[31] At Wheeler, and then at Pickwick Landing, the LP&H staff planned and oversaw the construction of two villages, each with its own housing, community building, and school. For many (but not all) Black workers, this housing did represent a noticeable increase in standards of living.[32] In 1937 Bond wrote in the *Journal of Negro Education* that the efforts to adjust the tenants' lifestyles—including lessons in gardening, homemaking, poultry raising, and furniture building—could be satisfying.[33] The attention to site planning, however, was uneven: the two communities were about half a mile from each other, and the Black village was located farther from the worksite.[34] Soon a squatter village—the very unplanned development the TVA tried to prevent—emerged between the Black village and the worksite. Those living in this village were not part of the TVA, and they threatened Black workers on their way to work.[35] There were also cases of harassment on the part of TVA employees.[36] The villages at Pickwick Landing also revealed the limits of landscape and architectural plans and details;

in 1935 Bond told a family member that, though the "people in Knoxville" might respond to TVA's antisegregation rules, local workers ignored these stipulations and engaged in outright discrimination. He told of a white foreman at Pickwick Landing who refused to continue building the houses intended for Black workers because he was convinced they did not deserve the quality of the architects' designs.[37]

There is no record of the architects' opinion of this segregation, but they did register their concern for maintaining the standards embodied in their designs for houses—and substituting scientific discourse for political rhetoric would only increase among the planning and design professions after World War II.[38] Augur, for example, objected to the TVA's policy of housing two Black families in a house intended as a single-family home, first at Pickwick Landing and later at Gilbertsville. In the latter construction camp, the condition arose after the estimates for the number of married and unmarried workers were skewed and resulted in excess dormitory space and not enough houses in the Black section of the village (fig. 50). In

**Figure 50.** Photograph of houses in the Black section of the Gilbertsville construction camp. The title of this image in the original report reads: "View northwest down 'I' street in from in front of house #105," and it was included in a report dated December 7, 1938. The houses were the same in both sections of the camp and village, but families were crowded in the Black section and the amenities were far fewer.

**Figure 51.** Photograph of the rear of the building used as the school for Black children at the Gilbertsville construction camp, included in a report dated December 21, 1938. In the background is the edge of the "Negro Village." White children studied in a new and modern schoolhouse.

this case the DRS added additional temporary houses. The shared facilities in the Black village, a community center and cafeteria combined in one building, remained meager compared to those in the white village, which included a large auditorium, recreational facilities, and a new school building. The school allotted to the Black children was a farmhouse converted to include two classrooms, coat closets, boys' and girls' toilets, and supply rooms (fig. 51).[39] As Eric L. Rousey summarizes: "The practical effect of the thorough segregation at Kentucky Dam was an almost complete lack of contact between black and white workers."[40] As with the TVA's larger vision, there were limits to its self-proclaimed role as a "socially minded employer."[41]

## Communities at War

The TVA construction camps built in the 1930s were only approximations of the ideal garden city model, but they did offer (to some residents more than to others) a bit of garden in which to cultivate a daily life amidst the roaring machine. As war broke out in Europe, even these approximations became difficult. Even before the United States entered the war in December 1941, the nation had been engaged in an all-consuming defense industry. The TVA reopened one of the nitrate plants in Muscle Shoals and began producing munitions; it would later boast that it had supplied more than 60 percent of the 98,000 tons of elemental phosphorus needed to produce incendiary bombs, tracer bullets, and smokescreens.[42] Tons of war-related cargo were shipped up and down the Tennessee River, now mostly transformed into a navigable series of reservoirs and locks. The TVA also committed to providing military projects with unlimited electricity, including the development of the atom bomb in Oak Ridge, Tennessee—a new town created overnight, lying to the west of Norris and northwest of Knoxville. To reach this goal, the Authority rushed to complete several large storage and electricity-producing dams on tributaries of the Tennessee River, named Apalachia [*sic*], Cherokee, Douglas, and Fontana Dams; these dams were built at record speed. The TVA also designed and constructed a set of smaller dams on the Hiwassee River, located above the large dam completed in 1940. The Authority was now overseeing the construction of as many as twelve dam projects at once. It also proposed, and had approved, a new type of installation: a coal-based steam plant, which was soon constructed near Watts Bar Dam. Steam plants were not mentioned in the TVA Act, but during the war the production of energy had overtaken the TVA's other goals and ideals, including the balance of environment and industry. Unlike the earlier hydroelectric dams, the steam plant was all machine—and no garden.

In 1940 Draper left the TVA and joined the Federal Housing Administration to oversee the construction of wartime housing, in part because he realized that he had achieved as much of his original goals as he could.[43] The Regional Planning Council rarely convened without Draper, and it was eventually abolished in 1943. His role as director of the DRS was filled by Menhinick, who was even more invested than Draper had been in the technical professionalization of planning and design. Within a year Menhinick was overseeing a newly reorganized—and seriously strained—atelier. TVA staff members, while pursuing their own work, were also filling in for their colleagues who had joined the armed forces. Architect Mario Bianculli recalled spending years working twelve hours a day.[44]

Menhinick combined the sections for Site Planning and Architecture under the

Division of Recreation and Public Grounds. He expected that Towne, as chief of this unit, would "perform the functions of an office manager in a private architectural firm," that is, be responsible for the administration of planning and design on TVA lands. He then designated landscape architect Osborne H. Graves as Towne's assistant; he knew Graves would not only emphasize the central role of site planning in community planning but would also reinforce the collaborative spirit that had developed in the group. Otto Priebe assumed a position of leadership in the Site Planning Section, where he worked with Harold Frincke, Bernard Krauter, and newcomer Raphael Saraceni (who replaced Herbert Conover, who had been drafted).[45] Menhinick placed George L. Richardson in charge of the architecture team. A Rhode Island native, Richardson was a graduate of the University of Michigan who had served in the US Navy during World War I. He had also practiced as an architect in Memphis, Tennessee, and Jackson, Mississippi. Richardson supervised the preparation of all drawings and specifications and distributed them for review; he also decided when and whether to take drawings to Wank for consultation on the architectural design or to other professionals for technical support.[46] Richardson was also in charge of the photographic documentation of the atelier's work, collecting (and probably taking) images of all stages of their task. Seth Harrison Gurnee continued to be involved in these projects, as were Woodruff H. Purnell and Max H. Wiese.

Housing remained a central preoccupation: the war efforts all required laborers, who in turn needed lodging. The wartime labor force was more complex than the one the designers programmed for in the 1930s. As men left to join the armed forces, women took over many of their jobs, slightly shifting the gender balance in the villages and requiring more women's dormitories. Importantly, the TVA changed its policy and dropped any intention of providing permanent housing, specifying that, unless required by TVA personnel or for use in another TVA location, all housing had to be repurposed or dismantled for salvage.[47] The most stark example was the camp built near Cherokee Dam (on the Holston River, northeast of Knoxville), which was later moved to the banks of the South Broad River, where Douglas Dam was being built. Some of these same buildings were later sold to the University of Tennessee, Knoxville.[48] (Cherokee and Douglas are also the only two dams in the system that have the same spillway and powerhouse design.)

The focus on temporary rather than permanent housing did not catch the atelier unprepared; they had been experimenting with moving complete houses for several years. A substantial number of the houses at Gilbertsville were first constructed at the Pickwick Landing village. This experiment was actually in accord with the garden ideal: if the houses were a means, not an end, then there was no reason not to use them more than once. Towne later recalled that "the idea of moving houses from one construction project to another has always been a favorite topic of discussion in TVA."[49] The actual process of moving the houses was surprisingly simple. They were removed from their foundations in one piece, towed with tractors, and then loaded complete onto barges, to be floated 184 miles down the Tennessee River (fig. 52). At their destination they were dragged into place, again by tractor, and then reset on new foundations (fig. 53). As in other locations, these foundations had been carefully planned, and the landscape architects provided instructions for grading and seeding of the new site (fig. 54). Theodore B. Parker, chief engineer for the TVA, reported

**Figure 52.** A 1938 photograph of houses from the Pickwick Landing camp and village floating on a barge down the Tennessee River to be reused at the Gilbertsville Dam (later renamed Kentucky Dam) construction site. The houses had been removed from their foundations and towed to the river with tractors.

**Figure 53.** Photograph of one of the houses from the Pickwick Landing camp arriving at the Gilbertsville construction camp in October 1938. The TVA architects used this photograph to illustrate a "Detail of House Moving Equipment."

in April 1939 that the savings were even greater than he had anticipated—$37,140 rather than the estimated $30,000.[50] The TVA was not the only agency to employ this method. A photo of houses on barges, similar to the TVA image, was published in the *Architectural Forum* in April 1944, and the caption explained: "Last month 120 houses floated slowly down the Ohio river, are now being re-erected to house civilian workers at Camp Breckinridge, Ky."[51]

Moving whole houses was possible, but it was an inelegant process; the atelier sought to standardize—that is, professionalize—it. In 1943 Menhinick described a more complex dismantling method to the TVA's general manager, Gordon R. Clapp. It involved cutting the houses into sections of about eight feet wide. The roof was then removed and the open sides braced with wood trusses. The parts were trucked to the new location, where the process was reversed and the roof rebuilt.[52] Menhinick was specifically describing the reuse of houses left vacant at

**Figure 54.** Photograph of a house from Pickwick Landing after it had been relocated to Lexington Road in the Gilbertsville construction camp. The TVA planners selected this image to document the temporary paths fashioned to protect the seeding of the landscape.

the Guntersville construction camp, which had been approved for construction by Bianculli several years before.[53] Purnell, who was in charge of this project, developed a budget, solicited bids, and consulted with Harry B. Tour, the chief liaison between TVA architects and engineers.[54] The houses were eventually moved to the site of Ocoee No. 3, one of the dams designed and developed on the Hiwassee River as part of the wartime effort.[55]

The architects also explored a range of prefabricated construction techniques; their goal was to move the process of construction from the site to a dedicated plant. (This system is discussed in more detail in chapter 5.) Their central innovation was similar to the method Menhinick described for the houses at Guntersville. It was based on a sectional unit that could be moved by truck and attached to other such units to form the skeleton of a house or dormitory (fig. 55). As the magazine

**Figure 55.** Photograph of the delivery process of prefabricated sectional units. The TVA architects preferred dividing structures into sections—and not panels—arguing that this approach emphasized mechanical, factory-based processes over construction on site.

*American Building* reported, each section was in essence a slice of a building that was assembled in a plant and then towed into place; the sections could be detached and reused as needed.[56] At Farner, Tennessee, for example, dormitories were built to support the construction of several dams, primarily the medium-sized storage dam named Apalachia. Some of these dormitories, including the nurses' housing, were later moved to Fontana, North Carolina, where the TVA was building the tallest dam in the system (fig. 56).[57]

At another site, Smith Creek, the atelier experimented with building demountable houses that were constructed on the site itself (fig. 57). Smith Creek was built for a very specific purpose: housing the operators and safety personnel of the Apalachia powerhouse from September 1942 to February 1946. This powerhouse is located at a distance not only from the dam but also from any housing, and—with the wartime rationing of rubber and other materials—a daily commute was unaffordable. Wank

**Figure 56.** Photograph of a "Demountable Bunkhouse at Fontana, April 26, 1945." The TVA architects, under the direction of Carroll A. Towne, developed a system for building structures in sections, which were then combined to create single-family homes, bunkhouses, and community buildings. In 1945 these bunkhouses would have served their purpose in Fontana and would have been readied to be moved to another TVA location.

described these houses in *Pencil Points* in 1944, and they were included in an *Architectural Forum* compilation of "well planned, inexpensive houses."[58] The design for Smith Creek also included a community building containing the food market, the village school, the post office, the recreation room, an office, and a large open terrace (fig. 58).[59] In 1946 Smith Creek was dismantled and the buildings were moved to Muscle Shoals, but it is easy to imagine sitting on a house porch or on the community terrace and enjoying the surrounding landscape; Smith Creek was a direct descendent of Norris, Tennessee, and yet another manifestation of the garden in the machine.

The Fontana Dam construction site was the Authority's largest and most complex undertaking during the war; it is also an example of the range of projects with which

**Figure 57.** Photograph of a house at Smith Creek. This temporary camp was built during World War II to house the operators of the Apalachia Dam powerhouse between September 1942 and February 1946. This house was built on site but was designed to be "demountable"—when it had served its purpose it was moved, in sections, to Muscle Shoals, Alabama.

the atelier engaged in these tumultuous years. Work on the dam began the day after it was authorized by Congress, thus eliminating the opportunity for the rigorous collection of data and the preparation of detailed plans. In addition, its location, high amid steep and remote mountains in southwest North Carolina, presented special challenges and the schedule was hectic, with workers laboring around the clock. The Fontana housing requirements were enormous; when the work force was at its peak—3,826 employees—the total TVA population was over 6,000, which exceeded the entire population of Graham County three years before.[60] In response to this situation, the TVA set aside its standard expectations and repeatedly enlarged and expanded the housing offered. The first iteration, Camp No. 1, was composed of thirteen four-person tents and several simple frame buildings which served as community buildings. This camp was later expanded to 103 tents before being aban-

**Figure 58.** Photograph of the community building containing a food market, post office, recreation room office, and school at Smith Creek. The site was planned for temporary occupation, but the TVA architects designed a large, open terrace from which the residents could enjoy the view of the surrounding forest.

doned as a better campsite took form near the dam. The tents were then moved to another location, Camp No. 2, which also included a section for Black employees (fig. 59). The TVA did not abandon its racial segregation practices, but it did make a more concerted effort to employ Black workers, to protect them from violent injury, and to prevent the buildings assigned to them from being burned.[61] The tents in both sections were supported by washhouses, some located in buildings that had been used for other purposes before (including a jail) and some constructed in the prefabricated sectional system the atelier had developed.

The TVA also invested in trailers, and over one hundred were allotted to the Fontana site. The first group arrived in April 1942 and were placed in the parking areas of the central camp that was being developed near the dam, based on plans and designs from previous construction sites. In this original site the trailers accommodated two men each (fig. 60). The TVA also used trailers at other locations; at Douglas they allowed workers to bring their own privately owned structures in addition to those bought by the Authority or leased from the Farm Security Administration. Similar mobile homes, provided by the Division of Defense Housing Coordination

**Figure 59.** Photograph of a tent camp at the Fontana construction site. Fontana Dam was authorized by Congress after the United States entered World War II and construction began the next day. Here the TVA architects scrambled to provide laborers with basic accommodation. Each tent housed four people, who also shared a washhouse and community buildings.

in Washington, DC, were placed in Hiwassee village.[62] Despite these efforts, the atelier was unable to eliminate the need for informal housing. Fontana, like previous construction sites, was surrounded by makeshift shacks that highlighted the limits of professional planning in emergency conditions (fig. 61). Still, Towne did take the knowledge his staff had amassed working on these projects with him to a conference in Washington, DC, convened to discuss policies and standards for dormitories and

**Figure 60.** Photograph of trailers purchased by the TVA and parked at the Fontana Dam construction site. The trailers accommodated two single men each at first but were later moved to Fontana village, where they housed entire families.

trailer camps.[63] He also participated in a "Discussion of Community Facilities for Isolated Communities" organized by the National Housing Agency, Federal Public Housing Authority (FPHA) in Washington.[64]

The atelier was proud of its ability to meet the ever-changing challenges at Fontana, but they did not lose sight of their larger goals. As construction progressed, the TVA developed one more housing location in a small valley named Welch Cove. This area, which was known as the Fontana village, was reserved for families of employees who expected to stay in the region: that is, skilled workers and professionals.[65] The preparation of plans for this location had begun in 1936, when the TVA identified the location of the dam as required for its unified system. Towne then evaluated each site based on ease of access to the worksite at the dam, topography, water supply and sewage disposal, and, importantly, its scenic and salvage value.[66] Once work on the dam actually began, Aelred "Flash" Gray, Frincke, and Saraceni again toured the remote region, identified a more suitable location, and

**Figure 61.** Photograph of shacks built on the outskirts of the Fontana camp and village. The TVA architects did what they could to accommodate all workers in designed housing but were unable to stem the need for temporary structures.

developed a site plan for it.[67] This plan was based on the atelier's early ideal; by carefully siting the main roads along valleys and ridges, the planners were able to demarcate individual plots that maintained a connection to the community buildings and to the surrounding landscape. The dwellings—for more than 3,000 individuals and 920 families—were of every conceivable quality. The TVA built a number of permanent homes, but there were also some low-cost temporary versions and prefabricated houses. They even reused the trailers that had accommodated single workers near the dam, which were now designated as homes for families.

In many ways the Fontana village resembled the town of Norris—a community hub for the entire project. The atelier located the important community buildings here, including recreation facilities, two schools, and a library. The employees working in these centers were charged with sustaining morale in the village to energize the residents to contribute to winning the war.[68] The library staff organized an exhibit, for example, on food rationing in France.[69] They also produced a news-

**Figure 62.** Photograph of a model prepared by the TVA architects for a mountain resort to be named Fontana Village. Even as they were overseeing the construction of temporary and prefabricated houses, the TVA architects were preparing for the end of World War II. This model is but one component of the visual material the architects used to promote the village to potential resort operators. The efforts were successful, and the village is still open to vacationers, albeit without the swimming pool.

letter, and one issue, which described an evening spent with a first grader, highlights how doggedly the TVA employees sought the garden ideal: "The mountains themselves were outlined against the sky giving one of these sharp contrasts that come with the setting sun. As we walked along it was hard to realize that out there somewhere there is strife and struggle and turmoil and suffering and horror. Here in Fontana were peace and industry and contentment. Women finishing the evening dishes, men working in their gardens, and children playing ball or chasing one another up and down hills."[70] The description continues with the child showing the visitors the garden (up the mountainside) and animals he found. The essay concludes thus: "It was getting dark and time first graders were in bed so we said 'good-night' and went home feeling the satisfaction one gets from pleasant conversation with people who find simple everyday living exciting."[71]

The atelier applied all its best practices to build the Fontana village, but it was clear from the start that it would not be designated as a permanent town. It was planned, instead, to be used as a resort after the war. The wartime housing thus became a gateway to recreation in natural surroundings, another important part of the garden ideal, which will be discussed further in chapter 6. By late 1944 Menhinick was collaborating with the Department of Reservoir Property Management to find a suitable company to manage the location, now marketed as the Fontana Village.[72] The architects, for their part, created promotional material, including a stylized map of the village and a model of a possible resort center (fig. 62). The conversion was completed in 1945, and only two years later Loren C. Hastings, writing in *Better Homes and Gardens,* declared it to be a "Top Find in Low Cost Vacations."[73] This was also the eventual fate of the Gilbertsville camp and village, which was used throughout the war and then transferred in the late 1940s to the State of Kentucky to become the Kentucky Dam Village State Resort Park.[74]

## Communities for Living

The TVA planners, landscape architects, and architects worked to make their ideas, and the professional standards they had developed, widely accepted. This goal was occasionally achieved. Even as the atelier was scrambling to direct the housing efforts at Fontana Dam, Augur was loaned to the Federal Public Housing Authority, initially for a three-month span, although his term was extended more than once.[75] Augur relocated to Detroit, Michigan, and joined the team developing the Willow Run housing project.[76] The project was never built, but Augur promoted it in *Architectural Record* as an example of professional expertise.[77] In 1951 TVA ideas made their way to Harvard University. Studio instructors Jean Bodman Fletcher, a founding member of The Architects Collaborative (TAC), and Leonard James Currie, who also practiced in the firm, asked the students in Architecture 2B and Landscape Architecture 2B, 2C, and 4C to design a construction workers' village for the mountainous site, with the requirement that it could be salvaged and reused as a resort. The project brief described the atelier's work at Fontana very precisely, including the types of housing to be constructed and the importance of returning the site to its "natural" state. Segregation is not mentioned.[78]

The atelier's focus remained, however, in the Tennessee Valley. This region was rapidly transforming; the cumulative effects of rapid industrialization, concomitant urbanization, and participation in a defense economy were registered in the landscape. By the end of the 1940s, the Tennessee Valley (and the South more generally) became a large manufacturing belt. At the same time, farms grew larger—minor landowners sold out, first to their neighbors and then to holding companies. Fewer individuals were tenants, but the number of landowners also decreased dramatically.[79] Instead of a clear line demarcating the rural from the urban, most people came to experience "a single labor market, embracing both urban and rural area, accompanied by a complex array of lifestyle choice."[80] Many of the farmers who did remain on the land after World War II could no longer farm full time but continued to supplement their income in manufacturing work with farming as a hobby or a lifestyle. Paul K. Conkin calls this complex urban-rural mix a "rurban" pattern.[81] Leo Marx also describes this condition as "a new kind of decentralized community (if that is not an oxymoron), whose built core may consist of nothing more than a 'strip,' or cluster of shopping malls, and a few services located near a freeway intersection. The regional school and church often are located, more or less randomly, along one of the nearby secondary roads."[82]

Many in the TVA, including its board of directors, accepted these changes as the inevitable outcome of what they called democratic planning or, more specifically, the grassroots approach. This shift was recognized rhetorically when the TVA as a whole came to speak of regional development rather than regional planning.[83] This term focused attention on economic change and further entrenched the resource conservation ideology as the institution's guiding principle. Members of the atelier, however, continued to promote their planning and garden ideals, employing a combination of research and demonstration with outright design. A slim publication, printed in 1941 by the University of Georgia Press, demonstrates the view that judicious and well-researched planning is absolutely necessary to avoid "an urban erosion comparable in seriousness to soil erosion."[84] Its author, Francis Stuart Chapin Jr., had joined the DRS only a year earlier, after graduating from MIT with a bachelor's degree in architecture and a master's degree in city planning. In this modest booklet, titled *Communities for Living,* Chapin especially thanks Menhinick and Raymond F. Leonard, who supervised his work, and Wank, TVA's head architect.

Chapin begins by describing communities as places to live, work, and play, consisting of home neighborhoods, workplaces, shopping centers, and recreation areas. He explores paths and circulation patterns as well as infrastructure such as pipes, wires, and waste systems. The second half the booklet more clearly demonstrates the garden underpinnings of this enterprise. Chapin asks his readers to consider beauty in their community and expands on national scenic resources, site development, and architectural elements. He also examines how the city serves the country, and he outlines the "machinery for [citizen] action," specifically, the official planning agency, zoning, and subdivision control.[85] Most of Chapin's text is unremarkable—similar to other pamphlets produced in those years with similar goals.[86] Indeed, this is exactly why it is interesting. The text refers unthinkingly to segregation, noting without comment that "sometimes a racial group occupies one area of a town and causes another to expand into other areas."[87]

Three topics, however, mark the booklet as distinctly representative of the TVA planning effort (and suggest that Chapin had benefited from discussions in the atelier). First is the interest in electricity and its impact on communities, as well as the hope that southern cities will be able to avoid the congestion and ugliness of larger cities in the North. A second characteristic emphasis is planning for recreation, which, he states, "is good business," a sentiment that was shared and promoted by his colleagues, as we shall see in chapter 6. A third emphasis most clearly places this document in the tradition of regional planning—the balance between rural and urban. "To be communities for living," Chapin tells his readers, "they must be planned to serve the country people as well as the townspeople, for the prosperity of one depends upon the well-being of the other"; "manufacturing and agriculture are two processes in one and the same way of living."[88] Chapin then takes this pronouncement a step further by commending a building type—a centrally located farmers' market to accommodate produce, people, and trucks—which the atelier originally design for Norris, Tennessee.[89]

Chapin's interest in giving the relationship between urban and rural a definite form—so different from the emerging rurban setting—was shared by his colleagues. In 1944 Wank and Bianculli collaborated on a proposal for what they called rural activities centers in the Tennessee Valley, with the hopeful prediction that they will eventually inspire "a more comprehensive program."[90] The proposal, outlined in an essay published in the *Architectural Forum,* begins with the farmers market Chapin describes, and they specifically refer to an existing Farmers' Cooperative Supply Association movement. Wank and Bianculli then go further, incorporating ideas they had developed for the Rural Electrification Administration (REA). They imagine that the rural activities centers would eventually house the headquarters of rural electric power cooperatives. They suggest architectural details for this structure: "The front of the generator hall is made of heat-absorbing glass, and horizontal structural louvers further protect it from overheating by the sun."[91] They also comment on financing and assume the cooperative would use its "accumulated surplus" to purchase land, keeping some parcels for itself but reselling the surplus to processing, marketing, and educational facilities.

Wank and Bianculli develop a proposal for these additional facilities: They imagine a vocational center composed of dormitories, teachers' cottages, an infirmary, and a structure with classrooms and laboratories for instruction. Further developments, including utilities, roads, buildings, and land improvements, they argue, would be financed with public money; the states' departments of education would support the educational center, the library commissions the library. Wank and Bianculli also outlined an updated demonstration farm that showcases what they call "straight-line production." They include descriptions of overhead tracks—to reduce the amount of required manual labor—and the option to expand the farm unit by unit.[92] The culmination of the project, the architects declared, would be a community building. Here, too, they draw directly on the TVA experience, describing a lounge, a flexible assembly hall, a meeting room, manager's office, kitchen, and restrooms. They also recognize the importance of commerce: "At its extreme end is the day nursery, where children may be parked while their mothers shop."[93]

The rural activities center Wank and Bianculli imagine was not the comprehensive and transformative regional planning Benton MacKaye and the Regional Planning Association of America imagined, but it was a translation of that idea, filtered through the reality of the TVA. Compared to the shopping centers that did emerge in the region, the architects' proposal that such locations be built with public money is a progressive, one might even say utopian, proposal. At the same time, it keeps the responsibility for the planning and design of such places in the hands of educated professionals such as themselves, perpetuating the social significance of their pro-

**Figure 63.** Sketch of a proposed power board and municipal building for Tuscumbia, Alabama, drawn by Mario Bianculli and dated February 22, 1944. The design of this building reflects the distinctive modernist style Bianculli and his colleagues developed as members of the TVA staff.

fession. These tensions were not, and could not have been, resolved. They are the inevitable product of the meeting of architects' goals and the institution in which they worked.

Wank and Bianculli's civic vision went unrealized, but the architects continued to work toward it. Bianculli, who remained in Tennessee after quitting the TVA, took these ideas, and even specific projects, into private practice. In this sense the TVA research was successful—Bianculli was instrumental in creating a social context for his own career. Two building types got special attention. First was a civic center combined with a headquarters for a power cooperative. The second, which also drew on the TVA experience, was the rural library. Relieved from Arthur Morgan's and Draper's expectations, the architects gave both building types a modernist treatment.

In 1944 Bianculli prepared a drawing for a building in Tuscumbia, Alabama, part of the Muscle Shoals area (fig. 63). As the marking on the drawing attests, this scheme was abandoned, but the Tuscumbia Utilities Building, which houses

**Figure 64.** Drawing of a "Preliminary Study of the Guntersville Power Board and Municipal Building," by Mario Bianculli, 1945. Prepared by the TVA's Department of Regional Studies as an assistance to the Alabama State Planning Commission, working for the Guntersville Power Board and Guntersville City Planning Commission.

the same functions today, also shares some of its architectural elements. A similar project for Guntersville, Alabama, bridged the public-private divide. When Bianculli first designed it, he was acting as an agent of the state planning commission, which was assisted by the TVA's Department of Regional Studies (fig. 64). The TVA had been instrumental in setting up this planning commission, which was the beneficiary of the preliminary study—the Guntersville City Planning Commission. In 1946, when Bianculli published this very image in the *Architectural Forum,* he had already set up a short-lived firm with Harrison W. Gill in Chattanooga, Tennessee. The proposed building housed offices for the mayor, the city council, and the power board executives and employees. It also provided an auditorium, space for home economics demonstrations, and a public library. The rear of the building was to be devoted to repair and maintenance spaces. All of these functions, the *Architectural Forum* told its readers, were expressed in the "impressive lines" of the building's exterior. "The Gill-Bianculli version of the familiar municipal clock-tower," they added, "provides added height for the auditorium stage."[94]

Bianculli continued to design combined civic and power cooperative buildings with his next firm, a partnership with George Palm Jr. Colleagues from the DRS,

**Figure 65.** The Tullahoma, Alabama, municipal building, designed by Mario Bianculli and completed in the early 1950s. By this time Bianculli was in private practice, but the design clearly draws on his work for the TVA. The building also housed the Tullahoma Power Board until the 1970s and was placed on the National Registry of Historic Places in 2018.

Max Wiese and Woodruff Purnell, were part of this enterprise as well. One of their projects was to complete a community center Bianculli had initially designed with Wank in Clinton, Tennessee. Located north of Knoxville and east of Oak Ridge, the town had seen an influx of population during the war. Building the center was part of a larger effort to rezone the town and build schools with Federal Security Agency funds. The project brief included a gymnasium, bowling alleys, small meeting rooms, and a public library. The Clinton design is another example of a building being used for demonstration as well. The preliminary study (which had been drawn by Seth Harrison Gurnee under Bianculli's supervision) was included in an *Architectural Record* "Building Types Study" devoted to community buildings in May 1946. This study begins with a statement that would have resonated with members of the atelier: a "community building is what a housing development requires to convert it into a neighborhood."[95] Bianculli and his partners' best-known building of this type was completed in Tullahoma, Alabama, in the early 1950s with the help of a grant from TVA (fig. 65). This building was added to the National Registry of

Historic Places in 2018 and still houses the city offices—the power board having moved nearby in the 1970s.[96]

The efforts to establish rural libraries in the counties of the Tennessee Valley offered Wank, Bianculli, and their colleagues another way to promote their social and progressive goals. This project was spearheaded by Rothrock, who had long been worried about the quality of libraries in the region. Tennessee (her home state) did not have centralized library agency, and many of the buildings housing these institutions had been built by outsiders: the Carnegie Corporation of New York and the Julius Rosenwald Fund.[97] Rothrock worried that "the rural library remains much as it was yesterday—an urban institution transplanted into a rural setting."[98] A determined progressive reformer, she argued that the system must be developed in a centralized manner, since "obviously, there is no room here for competitive overlapping library services."[99] The TVA eventually contributed to twelve regional library projects, of which eleven were still in use in 1950 and accounted for almost a third of the regional libraries in the Tennessee Valley.[100] The DRS supported Rothrock's efforts, preparing a map titled "Library Service in Some East Tennessee Counties."[101] The atelier also kept track of the schools and libraries the TVA helped furnish in the region.[102] In 1947, two years after Fontana Dam had been completed, George Richardson sent her a photograph of the Manual Training Building at Fontana with the suggestion that it might be converted into a library.[103]

In 1940 Rothrock helped organize the Tennessee Valley Library Council to further implement her vision. The council worked for nine years and only ceased operations with the publication of the government-sponsored *Southeastern States Cooperative Library Survey* in the fall of 1949.[104] The TVA planners and architects joined this conversation as well. Menhinick, who attended the 1944 meeting, told the audience that he hoped the libraries would provide the residents of the region with scientific information, now that "science is the dominant factor in modern life."[105] Wank, for his part, prepared proposals for a series of rural libraries, distinguished by size and method of construction; he imagined both conventionally built and prefabricated buildings. Graves prepared landscape designs for each of the alternatives, suggesting specific plants while noting that the design would have to be adapted to each location.[106] Bianculli continued this design effort when he replaced Wank as head architect for the TVA, and he used the *Architectural Forum* once again to disseminate the ideas. The essay included plans for seven typical library buildings

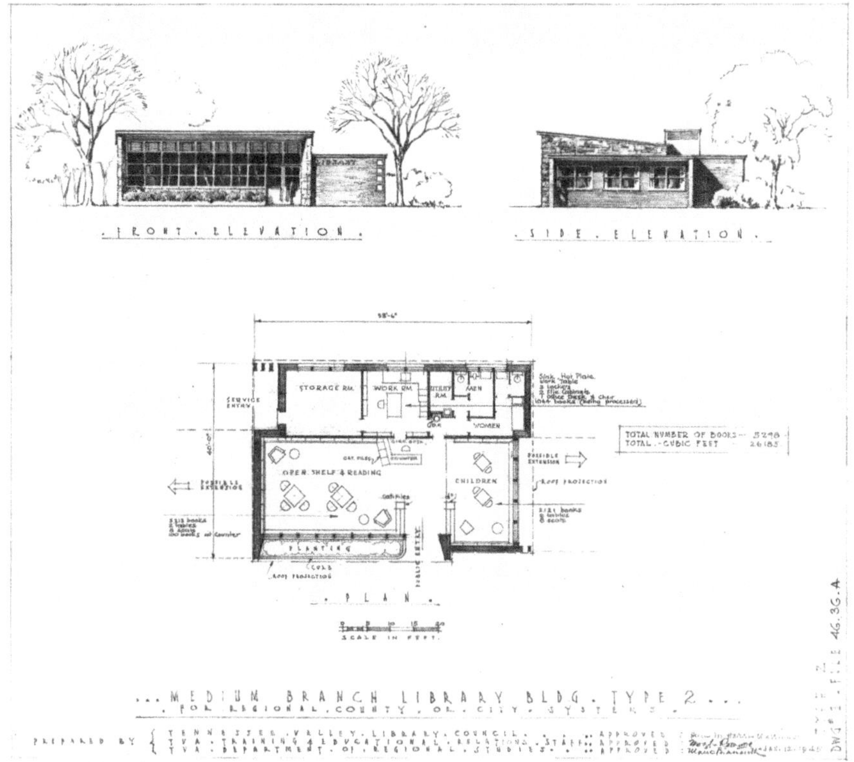


**Figure 66.** Design for a "Medium Branch Library Building" approved by Mario Bianculli on January 12, 1945. This drawing was part of a series of prototypes developed by the TVA architects for the Tennessee Valley Library Council. The Type 2 building was designed to provide a base for community action in a county or city.

of various sizes. While based on Wank's sketches, they were much developed by Bianculli (fig. 66). The council then used copies of this essay as part of their informational material. Requests for copies were received from librarians across North America, including Michigan, Connecticut, British Columbia, and Ontario.

Rothrock's efforts were recognized as a model for rural library services across the country.[107] They also had a real-world application. In Knoxville, Tennessee, a group of businessmen, a garden club, and several church groups sponsored the Burlington branch of the city library.[108] They requested that the architects, Bealer & Wilhoit, follow the TVA Type No. 2 closely (fig. 67). The modern design of the building was an abrupt departure from local design norms, but the *Architectural Forum* reported

**Figure 67.** The C.O.N.N.E.C.T Ministries at 3615 Martin Luther King Jr Ave., Knoxville, Tennessee. The building was originally built as the Burlington Branch Library, based on the design by the TVA shown in figure 66.

that both librarians and patrons appreciated the light-filled space and the radiant heat. This library thus combined the atelier's utopian ideals with professional knowledge they had developed in the course of their work. The book repository has moved to a larger facility; today the building is the home of a nonprofit organization committed to revitalizing the neighborhood. The dire need for this revitalization points to the limited development of a "planning region" in Knoxville and its surroundings, but it also indicates the power of community action the atelier had worked so hard to engender.[109]

# 5

# MODERN HOUSES

## Low-Cost Houses

Houses, specifically single-family homes, played an outsized symbolic role in the garden ideal. As progressive reformers, the Tennessee Valley Authority atelier members were convinced that a well-built, well-sited, and well-appointed house was the best environment for individuals to fulfill their dreams, engage in meaningful family life, and learn to participate in a democratic society.[1] The architects designed such houses at Norris, Tennessee, as part of Arthur E. Morgan's regional demonstration (see chapter 1). They disseminated detailed information about them, including plans and specifications, as part of the effort to lead by design. They also repeated the design and construction of such houses in the next two dams. At Wheeler Dam the houses vary in size from three to ten rooms; all have three-fixture bathrooms, screened porches, and laundries. These houses are still available as vacation cabins through the Alabama state park system (fig. 68). The "permanent" houses at Pickwick Landing (which were later moved to the Gilbertsville camp and village) were similar in layout but were finished with wood siding and not brick. Knoxville architect Charles I. Barber oversaw these designs during his brief spell on the TVA staff.

**Figure 68.** Cabin No. 9 at the Joe Wheeler State Park cabins in Alabama. Built by the TVA in the early 1930s, these houses were rented to engineers and their families and later to operators of the dam. They are among the only examples of permanent homes constructed by the TVA outside of Norris, Tennessee.

Harcourt A. Morgan and David El Lilienthal's insistence on grassroots action put a stop to any hope of populating the region with direct derivatives of the Norris houses. The atelier, however, continued to engage with this building type; they made them the center of their research efforts. This shift flowed naturally from Lilienthal's insistence that "the people" were the experts, but they would also benefit from professional knowledge. It also aligned the atelier members with their engineering and social science colleagues and opened a door to interdepartmental collaborations. Designs for single-family homes were eminently suited to research and inquiry. Knowledge developed through such efforts could have a wide impact; the questions surrounding good houses—plan, price, and performance, and systems of construction—were not limited to a specific region. In addition, they spanned the public and private divide; houses, unlike communities, were of interest not only to planners and public entities but also to individual builders and commercial companies. The shift to research also aligned the TVA staff with progressive peers who were developing similar programs. Douglas Haskell was especially vocal about the role architects should play in the house-building industry, arguing: "Unless housing can be made very much cheaper and better, the mass of the people can afford only the cheapest kind."[2] Looking back at the 1930s, James Marston Fitch recalled that "almost every component of today's modern building—prefabricated panels, air-conditioning, radiant heating, automatic controls, indirect lighting, fluorescent tubes, welded steel construction, special glasses—these were all known in 1939 to be perfectly practical: they were regarded as inevitable, 'just around the corner.'"[3]

The first houses built at Norris all have wood-frame structures, but the atelier investigated the durability and economy of different sheathing materials. As part of this investigation, each house in the town is finished with a unique pallet of materials, including brick, wood, stone, and even steel. This commitment required an investment of about 20 percent more than the cost of construction, but the TVA board approved this expenditure as part of its wider efforts to develop a base of scientific knowledge for the region. This initial investigation, however, did not reduce the price of the houses, which in some cases exceeded that of a custom-designed home. The atelier then began cutting construction costs, confident that good siting would compensate for structures that were less expensive. A second set of houses, built in 1934, was interspersed among the first group, enjoying the same careful siting of the original houses. The town was doubled in density without a significant loss in what the atelier prized as the pleasing aspects of its homes. The houses were small, consisting of a living room, kitchen, bath, and two bedrooms, as well as the requisite screened porch to "prevent any feeling of cramped quarters."[4] Thirty-two such houses were built at the cost of $2,400 each, less than half the cost of the electrified version. The most important innovation was the use of cinder blocks instead of the original wood frame (fig. 69).

The atelier later reused the cinder-block building system when it had to extend the town of Norris to accommodate the unskilled laborers in housing they could afford to rent. They built over eighty homes on two new roads, which were located nearer the construction camp and slightly removed from the main town. In these houses the cinder blocks remained exposed, and the roof was made of metal, minimizing the cost of maintenance. They were rented unfinished to save on paint but were renovated once the dam was complete to conform to higher standards.[5] These houses include both single-story and two-story types; most are still in use today (fig. 70).

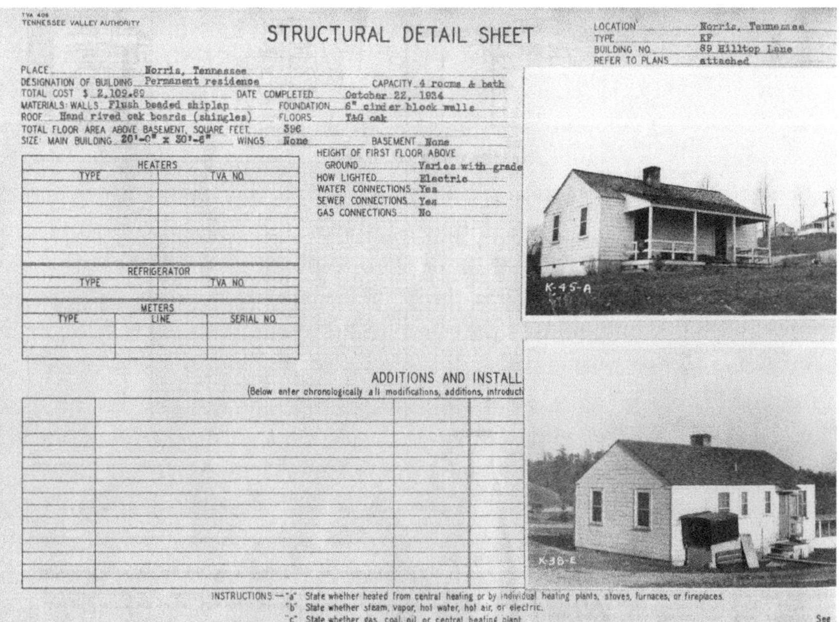
TVA 406
TENNESSEE VALLEY AUTHORITY

STRUCTURAL DETAIL SHEET

LOCATION Norris, Tennessee
TYPE KF
BUILDING NO. 89 Hilltop Lane
REFER TO PLANS attached

PLACE Norris, Tennessee
DESIGNATION OF BUILDING Permanent residence CAPACITY 4 rooms & bath
TOTAL COST $ 2,109.89 DATE COMPLETED October 22, 1934
MATERIALS: WALLS Flush beaded shiplap FOUNDATION 6" cinder block walls
ROOF Hand rived oak boards (shingles) FLOORS T&G oak
TOTAL FLOOR AREA ABOVE BASEMENT, SQUARE FEET 396
SIZE: MAIN BUILDING 20'-0" x 30'-6" WINGS None BASEMENT None
HEIGHT OF FIRST FLOOR ABOVE GROUND Varies with grade
HOW LIGHTED Electric
WATER CONNECTIONS Yes
SEWER CONNECTIONS Yes
GAS CONNECTIONS No

| HEATERS | |
|---|---|
| TYPE | TVA NO. |

| REFRIGERATOR | |
|---|---|
| TYPE | TVA NO. |

| METERS | | |
|---|---|---|
| TYPE | LINE | SERIAL NO. |

ADDITIONS AND INSTALL
(Below enter chronologically all modifications, additions, introducti

INSTRUCTIONS—"a" State whether heated from central heating or by individual heating plants, stoves, furnaces, or fireplaces.
"b" State whether steam, vapor, hot water, hot air, or electric.
"c" State whether gas, coal, oil, or central heating plant. See



**Figure 69.** "Structural Detail Sheet" prepared by the TVA architects for a permanent residence built of cinder blocks in Norris, Tennessee. These and similar houses were designed to blend in with the houses built the previous year but to cost significantly less.

The additional houses in Norris were a practical solution to an immediate problem, but they also played a rhetorical role. In September 1935 Earle S. Draper, director of the Land Planning & Housing Division (LP&H) introduced these houses to the readers of the *Architectural Forum:* "TVA's Yardstick for housing . . . is a cinder-block house costing from $2,325 for one story and four rooms to $3,150 for two stories and five rooms."[6] The term "yardstick" was taken, of course, from David E. Lilienthal power machine program, which had a dual goal; to augment the demand for electricity and to keep the price of electric appliances low. The yardstick was also intended to provide a "standard of performance for evaluating the efficiency of privately owned companies."[7] Thinking of houses as yardsticks expanded their institutional role. The costly houses in Norris were emblems of Arthur Morgan's top-down regional planning approach; the design and construction of cheaper models fit into the realm of grassroots action.

Studying and developing low-cost houses also served the TVA in a practical way;

**Figure 70.** Low-cost employee housing on Oak Road in Norris. This house type was developed for the families of unskilled laborers and built of cinder concrete blocks, with concrete floors and a metal roof. The building was rented unfinished at the lowest possible rent but was renovated after World War II.

as the river machine outlined in the 1936 "unified plan" took shape, it was clear that the need for such low-rent housing would persist and even expand.[8] The atelier set about creating a "reservoir of information" intended to produce "considerable saving in time and money on future house construction projects."[9] Louis Grandgent took the lead in this project, seeing it as a way to "keep in active touch with progressive developments in that field."[10] His research project included a study of the completed TVA houses, beginning with the low-cost models at Norris. In 1936 Grandgent prepared a report, "Houses at Norris, Tennessee: A Review of Costs."[11] He would have relied on work by his colleagues, including Ben A. Batson and C. J. Price's report, "Housing vs. Single-Family Housing in Low Cost Groups—Norris, Tennessee."[12] Though not all of them were widely circulated, these studies were intended for housing authorities and architects.[13]

Grandgent's interest in housing low-income workers proved prescient. In 1937, as part of the wider reorganization of the Authority, the board adopted a new housing policy to meet the TVA's responsibility to provide housing for its low-income workers. The rationale was influenced by the middle-class norms that shaped the TVA: "Laborers cannot afford to pay abnormal transportation costs. Neither can they afford rents much higher than they are accustomed to. If housing is not available at low rental, they will often be forced to double up in congested, unsanitary living quarters in the region, or to find shelter in substandard shacktown development outside the control of the Authority. Most of the workers have children who will be affected by adverse social conditions at a formative period of their lives."[14] The policy distinguished between permanent homes on the one hand—high-quality structures built to house the construction professionals and, afterward, the dam operators—and temporary houses on the other, "that provide wholesome living conditions on a minimum basis for the necessary length of time, but no more; that is, houses which are sanitary but of temporary construction, to be removed after the job is over."[15]

The 1937 housing policy was written after the villages at Norris, Wheeler, Pickwick Landing, and Guntersville had been constructed and when the Hiwassee village was nearly complete. In fact, the policy was in part a response to conditions that developed first at Pickwick and then near the Hiwassee Dam.[16] Due to the lack of adequate housing, workers had crowded into the available houses and had also constructed small shacks on the roads leading to the sites, which lacked even basic sanitary arrangements. Draper worried that any recurrence of these developments would be a "serious reflection upon the Authority."[17] He and his staff urged the board to act, first preparing a "carefully considered recommendation" and then working to make this policy a reality.[18] They developed several new types of houses that, they argued, met acceptable minimal standards for living and were low-cost. The relied in part on minimum requirements of space, light, privacy, and sanitation as outlined in a report by the Committee on the Hygiene of Housing of the American Public Health Association.[19] True to the Norris precedent, considerable study was given to the location of houses, so that the different types of houses would fit the topography and would relieve "monotony in the exterior appearance at very small cost."[20]

The new low-cost houses were first implemented at Hiwassee, where there was an acute demand for housing for low-income married employees. These houses were similar in layout to the low-cost houses at Norris but were finished with weather-resistant wallboard sheets made from paper pulp. Although the bid specifications did not specify the use of Homasote, the detailed requirements for the exterior walls made it virtually unavoidable.[21] These houses cost as little as $975 per unit (in direct cost of labor and materials), significantly less than the earlier house types.[22] The construction of these homes did not resolve all the housing problems at the camp, where many laborers continued to live in shacks, but it inaugurated the new housing policy and its underlying assumption that individual houses were superior to shared housing.[23] Grandgent argued that they embodied "several progressive ideas, such as modular layout and employment of sheet material in standard sizes for exterior and interior wall surfaces."[24] Indeed, these new houses were considered so satisfactory that dormitories and other buildings were patterned after them in other TVA construction sites.

The TVA architects constantly (and proudly) compared their work to that of other entities interested in low-cost houses. George L. Richardson kept plans drawn by other government agencies such as the Farm Security Administration.[25] In 1938 Draper reported that the TVA houses "were hailed as the first example of truly low-cost government houses meeting reasonable minimum standards," an accolade repeated in the annual report submitted to Congress by the TVA board.[26] Grandgent prepared a physical model of these houses in the same year (fig. 71).[27] The purpose of this model, he explained, was "to facilitate TVA study and checking of the design, and to serve the convenience of other interested agencies."[28] The model represented a slightly larger layout than the one used at Hiwassee; it was expected to cost about $1,250 and rent for $12.50 a month—still within reach of the TVA laborer. The proposal included heating by coal rather than electricity, and it highlighted the temporary nature of the house. (Grandgent estimated that a more permanent version would cost about $1,000 more.) This model was the basis for houses at the Watts Bar and the Gilbertsville villages.[29]

After completing the work on the low-cost model, Grandgent left the TVA to join the United States Housing Authority (USHA) and then joined the Atlanta office of the Public Housing Administration in 1942—continuing to develop low-cost housing for the rest of his career. His work as part of the atelier had given his career a new direction: housing was a far cry from designing a monumental window for a railroad terminal or a park pavilion for orchestral concerts, the projects for which he had won prizes as a student at MIT.[30] It was also a significant departure from his professional practice designing upper-middle-class homes in the 1920s.[31] At his retirement party Grandgent reflected: "While a person may lose something

**Figure 71.** Model of a low-cost house prepared by Louis Grandgent in 1938. The model was used as a "research" tool—a way to share the design with other agencies interested in low-cost housing.

of individuality in serving as part of a big organization . . . yet he enjoys the thrill of big doings, the miracle of organized accomplishments, and enterprises that are worth while in the public interest. This thrill is our recompense in public housing."[32] Grandgent's trajectory is typical of the way many progressive architects reinterpreted their roles in the 1930s and laid the groundwork for theoretical changes after World War II.

## Prefabricated Houses

The atelier's work housing the employees of the TVA river machine took them into the realm of prefabrication, which received widespread interest in the 1930s and

1940s, in what Gilbert Herbert calls *The Dream of the Factory-Made House.*[33] Douglas Haskell regularly expounded on this issue, connecting it clearly with regional planning. In 1934 he explained that "the ideal of mobile shelter gives us all a greater opportunity than before to occupy locations that are usefully planned."[34] He also collaborated with the John B. Pierce Foundation to produce a series of essays for the *Architectural Forum* on the history of prefabrication, which were later complied in a book, even as he recognized that "the factory promises no Utopias."[35] For Haskell, as for Carroll A. Towne and his staff at the TVA, the object was not to copy European examples but to develop an American type of prefabricated house that would allow families to remain in the locations where they had already forged a community. Such houses were truly a garden in the machine—a house that could "re-site" itself, so to speak, as needed.

The TVA architects designed and produced an impressive range of prefabricated houses. This in part indicates how the term functioned as "a catchword for an array of processes and products," but it is also a sign of the wide interest within the atelier itself.[36] Roland A. Wank had joined the TVA with an established interest in industrial house production, and he advocated that the process be brought under government control.[37] Alfred Clauss, the architect on staff in the Office of Information (also known as the Department of Information), contributed to the effort to develop industrial housing, though his proposal was not pursued.[38] Grandgent and Towne, together with George Richardson and Woodruff Purnell, eventually took the lead in this field within the TVA, recognizing and pursuing various opportunities to experiment with this idea.

The atelier embraced prefabrication as a design goal rather than a substitute for the conventionally built house. As early as 1934 Grandgent had detailed a model prefabricated house in a report to the TVA board of directors titled "Truckable Unit House."[39] Also referred to as the "Pioneer House," the house he proposed was very similar to the Norris houses, which Grandgent called "fit for general purposes in this region."[40] More specifically, he drew on Type K, the wood-framed, low-cost house designed for Norris, and he borrowed the breezeway and attic plans from Type D-2, another of the recurring types built in the town. Grandgent assumed that truckable houses would be heated by coal-burning furnaces, based on technical developments and tests undertaken by the TVA.[41] The experience at Norris—in particular, the dimensions of the trucks used for transportation in dam construction—also influenced the design of the house by providing rough measurements consistent with road transportation. Grandgent's Pioneer House in turn influenced the layout and exterior appearance of the low-cost houses the atelier developed.[42]

The Pioneer House was never constructed. Arthur Morgan and Draper approved the production of one or more trial houses—this was their support for architectural and site planning research—but the funds for this project were never released.[43] Still, the house set the direction of the TVA effort in the next decade by presenting a novel approach to the process of construction. Most prefabrication designs in the 1930s relied on the shop for only part of the construction, producing carefully designed panels that would be assembled into units on location. Grandgent considered this approach wasteful; he argued that whatever the basic unit, "construction in the field, by hand, costs more than production of commodities by mechanical process."[44] The Pioneer House offered an alternative; it was composed of five sections or slices of the house: "*whole* [*sic*] pieces of house, each comprising one fifth of the cubic volume of the house."[45] Grandgent later shared his proposal at the conference of the American Society of Mechanical Engineers and was delighted when a chief engineer at the Federal Housing Administration referred to his plan as "the only scheme for real *prefabrication* of a house that had yet been offered."[46] Even after Grandgent had transferred to the USHA, this emphasis on shop production and the sectional approach would characterize the TVA designs.

The TVA's institutional structure played a large role in preserving and expanding Grandgent's proposal. First, the atelier remained vigorous even after Grandgent's departure; Towne became "interested in this notion of his."[47] Second, the advent of defense spending and the war did not curtail the TVA's work but, on the contrary, opened new possibilities for exploration. Towne negotiated this situation and took advantage of it, securing funding for a truckable house demonstration. This effort began modestly, with the construction of six houses known as the Pickwick Cottages. These were intended to be used immediately as temporary housing during the emergency—as they were, first at Pickwick Landing Park and later in other locations, including Parson, Tennessee.[48] Towne and his colleagues also expected them to be converted to vacation cabins (discussed in the next chapter), but this did not happen.

The Pickwick Cottages were very simple designs, which allowed Towne and his

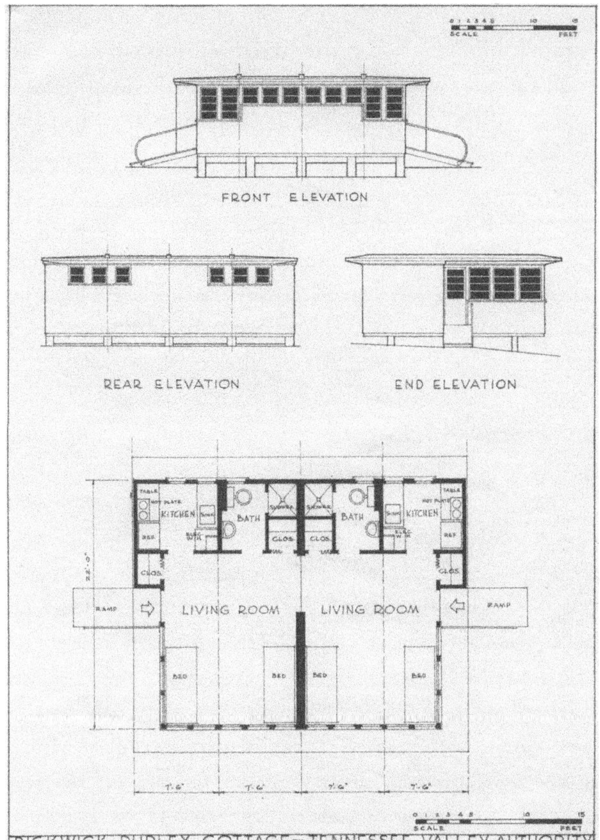


**Figure 72.** Presentation drawing of the "Pickwick Duplex Cottage." The TVA architects developed these cottages as a research project; their practical application was limited. The cottages did, however, play an important rhetorical role in publicity material (such as this drawing) prepared by the TVA's Department of Regional Studies.

group to experiment with Grandgent's sectional approach. The four single-family houses had three sections each, and the two duplex houses consisted of four (fig. 72). Richardson oversaw the organization of a fabrication shop in an empty building in Muscle Shoals, Alabama. Here the fabricators began by creating floor frames for each section and then belting them together, as a base for conventional (rather than prefabricated) construction. When the houses were ready, the sections were unbolted and each was hoisted and placed on a truck trailer.[49] The TVA engineers,

Towne recalled, scoffed at the effort, predicting that "as you pick one of these three-dimensional sections up and start to move it, the plumbing will come apart and the light fixtures will fall out and the glass will break in the windows."[50] The architects, however, were adamant that this direction was worth investigating. They also used this opportunity to introduce a modernist style into work, something that had not been attempted when Arthur Morgan was still in command.

The Pickwick Cottages were designed and built even as the atelier was experimenting with moving houses from one construction camp to another (see chapter 4). The use of such demountable houses was expanded in the following years, especially after the United States joined World War II and began building dams high in the mountains on tributaries of the Tennessee River. The atelier, working under Towne's supervision and with Wank's assistance, identified multiple uses for their demountable construction system, which they began to refer to as "prefabricated." In 1940 Gordon R. Clapp agreed to secure Grandgent as a consultant, to be loaned to the TVA from USHA.[51] (Several of their colleagues were at that time working on projects outside the Authority.) Towne and Purnell focused on the technical development of the prefabrication process.[52] Maurice Abramowitz used these ideas in the design and construction of the dormitories for TVA camps, and Seth Harrison Gurnee, who had produced bucolic perspectives of the Norris houses, now designed the homes themselves.

The emergency and wartime economies delivered to the atelier the task of "defense housing."[53] In 1941, when the TVA reopened the nitrate plant at Muscle Shoals, housing was needed for hundreds of defense workers in the vicinity, and the Authority was contracted by Federal Works Administration (FWA) to build 250 houses.[54] Clapp, then general manager of the TVA, saw this assignment as an example of decentralization and a move away from the surveillance of Washington. Clapp also credited the "loose, flexible, decentralized scheme of administration" of the TVA as giving the agency "the opportunity to do the best job that has ever been done in every field we tackle."[55] The atelier had an important advantage in this field—it could undertake both community planning and house construction—and it continued as agent for the FWA and then for its successor, the Federal Public Housing Authority.[56] The houses designed under these contracts had to adhere to mandated specifications as well as to "local preferences"; they are decidedly more

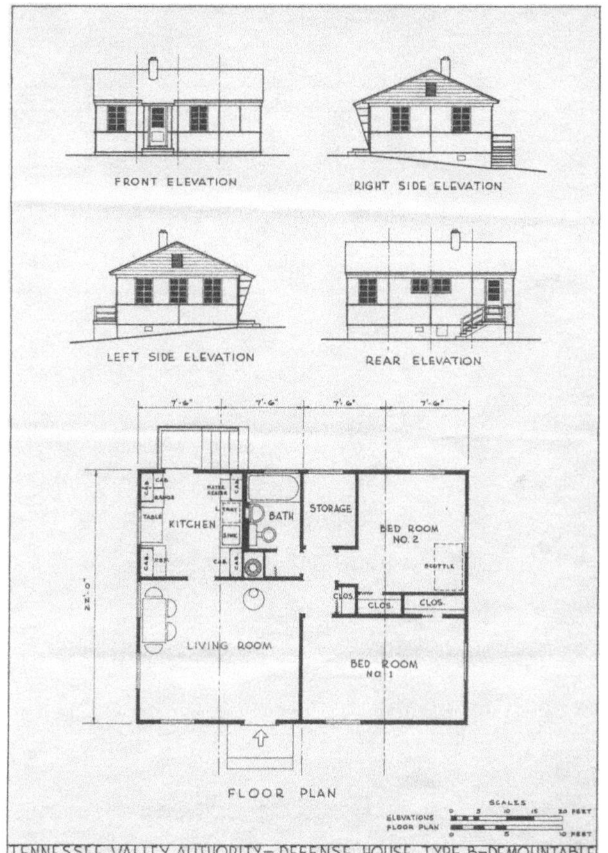


**Figure 73.** Presentation drawing of a Type B-demountable house designed by the TVA architects in their role as agents for the Federal Works Administration and then for its successor, the Federal Public Housing Authority. The architects abided by expectations for "local preferences" in the aesthetics of the houses but used the design process to further develop their sectional approach to prefabricated housing.

traditional than the Pickwick Cottages in their aesthetic, including a slanting roof (fig. 73).[57] Still, they gave the TVA architects an opportunity to refine their prefabrication system. Richardson explored configurations for plants in which to produce prefabricated houses, and in 1944 he prepared a "Study for Panel Storage Warehouse & Assembly Building."[58] Such a building would have staged the construction of house sections by house part: floor, wall, roof, and so on (fig. 74).

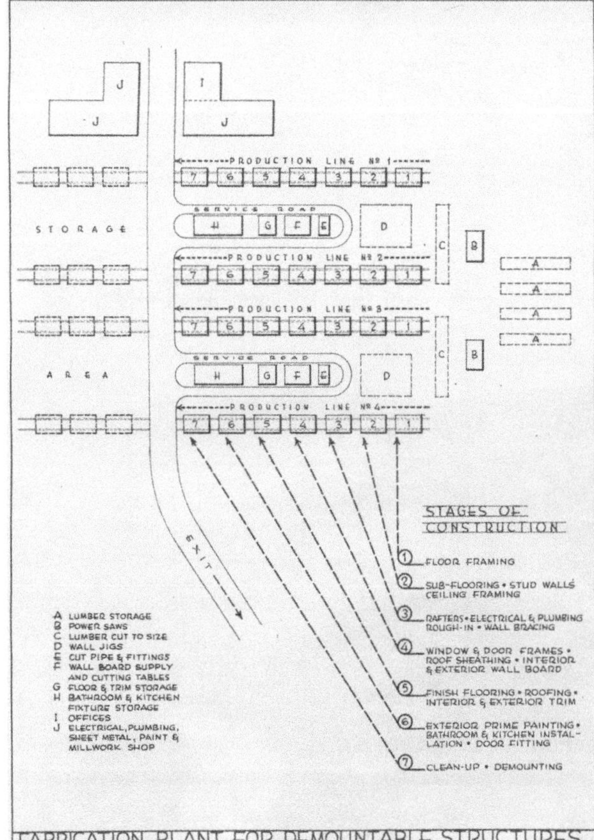


**Figure 74.** Schematic diagram of a fabrication plant for demountable structures. Carroll A. Towne and the staff of the Architecture Research Division were eager to share the values and the technical knowledge that underlay their prefabrication efforts with a wide audience. This drawing supplemented information on the houses themselves (seen in figs. 72 and 73).

The defense housing projects provided the atelier with opportunities to expand the reach of their ideas. The Lanham Act authorizing this work included the directive that all housing constructed for defense purposes would be taken off the market at the end of the war—a nod to pressure from National Association of Home Builders, who worried about the future of their own industry. The act also specified that the housing for the war effort was to be built by both public and private entities, incentivizing companies to join the experimental efforts. In grassroots manner,

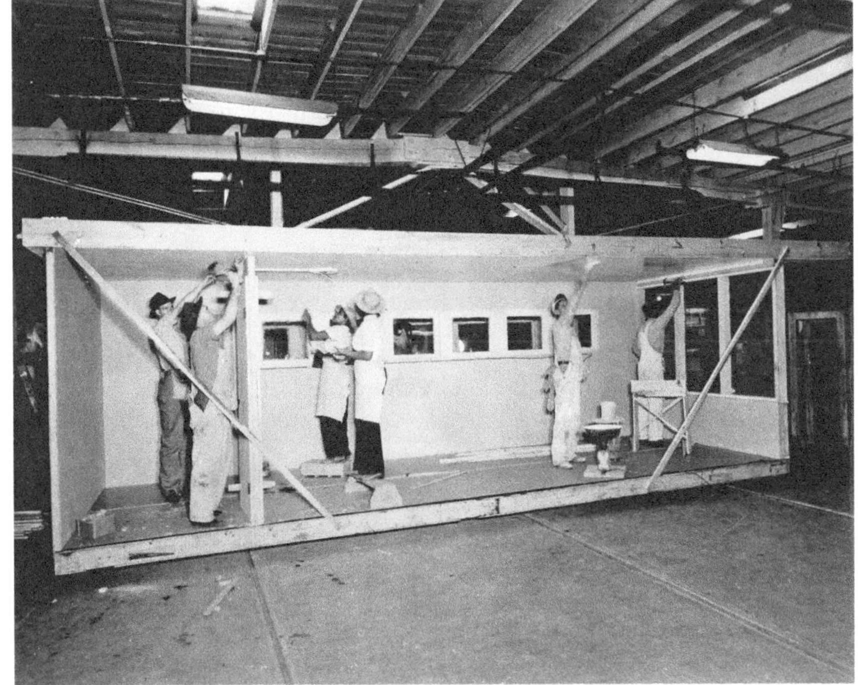

**Figure 75.** Photograph of the construction of a two-bedroom Type B-1 house. The TVA architects designed these houses for the Fontana village and worked with commercial companies to produce them. They considered this process an extension of the research they had already completed and as a way of disseminating knowledge about prefabrication.

the atelier collaborated with companies in western Tennessee that had also secured FWA contracts. Towne created a Defense Housing Section within the Division of Recreation and Public Grounds (DRPG), whose specific responsibilities included site acquisition, project design, award of contracts, coordination of construction, and cost control.[59] Its staff included Ben A. Batson, Albert S. Ware, and George Marsch. The TVA also produced prefabricated houses to plans by the firm Skidmore, Owens and Merrill for the town of Oak Ridge, Tennessee, which was built to support the development of the atomic bomb.[60] The models for Oak Ridge (E and F) were larger than the previous models and could be customized though using different sections or "cells."[61] The TVA housing systems, including the wartime prefabricated houses, made their way to the journal *L'Architecture D'aujourd'hui.*[62]

The atelier's collaborations with industry partners were based on shared objectives; as Timothy Mennel explains, corporate rhetoric about houses also cast them as a form of utopia, a means for perfecting society.[63] The collaborations were also an answer to a concern Grandgent raised in 1937, when he wondered whether "actual development of truckable unit housing belongs within the scope of the Authority's activities or whether it should be abandoned to private enterprise."[64] This question was on the atelier's mind when they were developing house types for the Fontana village (see chapter 4). A portion of these houses were based on developments in techniques for lightweight plywood engineering, which were already being used by commercial trailer companies. These methods meant the house slices were much lighter and could be towed by a small truck or even an ordinary car. The architects first designed a sample house (which Towne credited to Abraham W. Celler). Then, instead of involving the "already overtaxed TVA construction forces," they contracted four commercial trailer companies to produce a sample house under the supervision of a TVA representative.[65]

The Authority eventually ordered one hundred trailer homes from Schult Trailers, Inc., of Elkhart, Indiana, who adjusted their production system to create units with one open side (fig. 75).[66] These light houses could also be moved by crane (fig. 76). The TVA did not build foundations for these houses but did attend to their immediate surroundings and connected them to the village's system of paths and roads (fig. 77). The houses were inhabited immediately after they arrived, providing families with private space for work and relaxation (fig. 78). With these accommodations, Haskell's vision and Grandgent's sectional proposal reached its practical conclusion. The houses combined the atelier's insistence on good siting with the technical expertise they had developed. Towne saw them as "evidence that complete factory fabrication is not an idle dream[;] it has been done."[67] The TVA circulated data about their work and also employed visual rhetoric to make their case. In published images we see clusters of mechanically produced homes nestled within a lush forest, veritable machines in the garden (fig. 79). The reality of Fontana village was more complex; the highly designed trailer homes were interspersed with every other type of TVA housing, as well as community washhouses and purchased trailers (fig. 80). Even as they had become a topic for research, the houses did not lose their symbolic role as sophisticated designs.

**Figure 76.** Delivery of the Type B-1 house seen in fig. 75.

**Figure 77.** Photograph of Type B-1 houses in Fontana village during World War II, surrounded by the lush forest of the Appalachian Mountains. These houses were produced in a factory and shipped to the site in sections. They were used as vacation cabins after the dam was complete.

**Figure 78.** Photograph of an interior of a Type B-1 house in Fontana village. George. L Richardson and his associates documented the houses they had designed with an eye toward marketing their ideas.

**Figure 79.** A photograph of Fontana village during World War II. The TVA architects selected this and similar images to publicize their work. The framing highlights the contrast between the machines for living, which had been produced in factories, and the lush environment in which they were placed.

**Figure 80.** Another view of Fontana village during World War II. The image, shot by George L. Richardson (or an associate), captures a communal washhouse, commercial trailers, factory-built prefabricated houses, and traditional frame dwelling of different sizes and layouts. This photograph, and those like it, was not used in TVA promotional material, but it better captures the reality of living conditions in a community in times of war (compare with fig. 79).

## Electrified Houses

Research into low-cost and prefabricated houses was a product of the TVA's housing demands; a part of the effort to build the river machine. The atelier, however, was always conscious of its overall goals for the Tennessee Valley, and in this sphere the power machine and rural electrification played a larger role. As David E. Nye explains, the impact of electricity on the schedule of a farm was easy to measure in longer and more flexible working hours. Electric current also changed the buildings on farms, eliminating the need for structures such as smokehouses and outdoor privies.[68] Water heaters improved health and sanitation; refrigerators allowed families to preserve fresh food for longer periods. Electricity was especially important in powering pumps and providing humans and livestock with a steady supply of water. Longtime farmer Mary Heaton Vorse wrote: "When water was piped into the kitchen sink, women had their first great liberation."[69]

For the TVA, however, technological improvement was only the first step, as George W. Kable, chief of the Agricultural Engineering Section explained in 1937: "*The end for electric service is not lines, lights and radios. It is better homes, better health, and better profits*" (emphasis in original).[70] Lilienthal explained further: "When an electric range or refrigerator comes into a farm kitchen the effect is always much the same: the kitchen gets a coat of paint, is furbished up; not long after, the rest of house spruces up; new rooms are built on, pride begins to remake the place—pride supported by the added income that comes from 'smart' use of electricity for farm purposes. You can follow the trail of new electric lines in many sections by observing how many houses have been thus tidied up."[71] Well-tended farmhouses were thus yet another yardstick for the TVA, a sign that "progress was made on a democratic basis."[72] In 1946 the TVA board of directors provided data to support this claim, telling Congress that in Georgia, since 1935, at least 289 homes were painted, 299 screened, and 232 remodeled. They also recorded 181 water systems and 173 new sanitary toilets. They even counted new lawns, totaling 221. They estimated the costs of these improvements at $35,000,000.[73]

The TVA used images to reinforce the point. A set of photographs, commissioned from photographer Arthur Rothstein, document the lives of Julien H. Case and his wife on their farm in Lauderdale County, Alabama. Case is shown unloading TVA fertilizer, fixing an electric connection, and resting in the shade of one of the one-hundred-year-old white oaks on his farm; inside the home he is seen using an electric shaver and fluorescent light. One image shows the couple leaving their well-maintained house for a camping trip on the shores of one of the TVA lakes. The farmer's wife (who is not identified by name) is depicted preparing and serving dinner using an electric refrigerator, a stove, and other appliances.[74] As in all the TVA projects (and also in programs administrated by the Rural Electrification Administration) farmers were assumed to conform to established gender roles.[75]

Rural electrification, however, was a double-edged sword. For the TVA staff, including the atelier, it was but a first step on the way to the utopian garden and especially to a healthy balance between urban and rural life.[76] But the advent of electricity did not necessarily inspire homeowners to adopt the civic and social ideals that directed the reformers' zeal. Becoming a (layman) expert often meant becoming a consumer; Valley residents stocked the farmhouse with appliances rather than developing the individual and family responsibility the TVA aspired to create. Under these conditions the house lost its symbolic role and became a container for more and more technology. As Reyner Banham comments: the house became "an undifferentiated shell within which the gizmos can do their work, and its external form acquires a slightly improvised quality, an indecisive shape."[77] It might be a technologically modern house, but it did not symbolize a larger vision. This tendency undermined the atelier's utopian goals, but it also opened another avenue for research; the TVA would promulgate "objective" and "scientific" knowledge pertaining to heating and insulating houses that farmers (and others) could adopt to elevate their homes and lifestyles to a higher level.

The investment in this inquiry began, once again, at Norris, Tennessee, and by 1935 it was formalized as a research project.[78] Allen Twitchell was in contact with an organization in Wilkinsburg, Pennsylvania, named Consulting and Research Association about the design of an experimental electric panel for one of the Type 41 houses in the town.[79] The system was installed but was later abandoned when its operational time lag proved too long for the Tennessee winters.[80] Even at this early date the atelier members expected their knowledge to contribute to a moribund building industry and thus "to the country as a whole."[81] This research was reinvigorated in 1937 when six vacant houses in Norris, as well as several inhabited dwellings, were monitored to accurately record thermal conditions.[82] The atelier was especially interested in insulating materials: "Two houses electrically heated and occupied, one insulated and one not insulated, were carefully compared and the insulation in this case was found to effect a saving of 44.75 per cent at best. Reports of these tests, among the first of their kind, served as a valuable guide for future TVA work. The results of this work were presented to the insulation industry at a meeting sponsored by the National Mineral Wool Association and have been extensively used to further the work of the industry."[83]

In 1938, as atelier members used the American Public Health Association report to set standards for low-cost houses, they also collaborated with the Committee on the Hygiene of Housing to produce another document: "A Study on the Heating of Houses at Norris."[84] A five-page bulletin was then distributed to the occupants of the Norris electrified houses, explaining the practical applications recommended in that report. While recording data on electrified homes, the TVA teams not only developed new notation standards but also recorded the inhabitants' response to their electrified homes. Grandgent compiled this data in the report "Heating at Norris, Tennessee: A Study of Thermal Efficiency in Heating."[85]

Woodruff Purnell produced many of the drawings for the Norris houses and would have been aware of the research, and possibly participated in it; he took charge of the next phases in the research project. One house in the Gilbertsville village (renamed Kentucky Dam Village) was designed specifically to compare the performance of electric and oil heaters. It was constructed of weather-resistant fiberboard and had an interlocking, galvanized metal roof. This house was relatively large, an indication of the TVA's interest in a range of housing options. It included, in addition to the living and dining areas and two bedrooms, an attached garage, separated from the house by a screened porch (fig. 81). The resulting report (produced once again in conjunction with the APHA) was titled "Studies in the Heating of Small Houses."[86] With these studies, as Harry B. Tour later explained, the TVA "demonstrated to their own satisfaction, and were able to demonstrate to others after, that electric heating for houses was feasible."[87]

The TVA's changing policies as to permanent housing, together with the development of defense housing, heightened the atelier's focus on research. Menhinick, moreover, was more attuned to changing professional mores than was Draper, at least in the early stages of the TVA project. In 1942 he established the Architecture Research Division (ARD) within Towne's unit—Recreation and Public Grounds (DRPG)—under the umbrella of the Department of Regional Studies (DRS). Architectural research was thus formally put on par with architectural design and site planning. Purnell oversaw this unit, assisted by Max H. Wiese.[88] Carroll Towne was excited by this institutional change, explaining that the ARD would be a base from which the architects could collaborate with other departments in the TVA. As World War II came to an end, the ARD prepared a detailed plan for future research, part of a wider effort by the DRS to outline postwar plans. This proposal combined a recognition that at least 160,000 houses would be needed in the Tennessee Valley in coming years to meet an increasing population.[89] It was also an effort to expand the research work to rural housing and small farm buildings, to be undertaken in collaboration with universities, experiment stations, and similar organizations in the

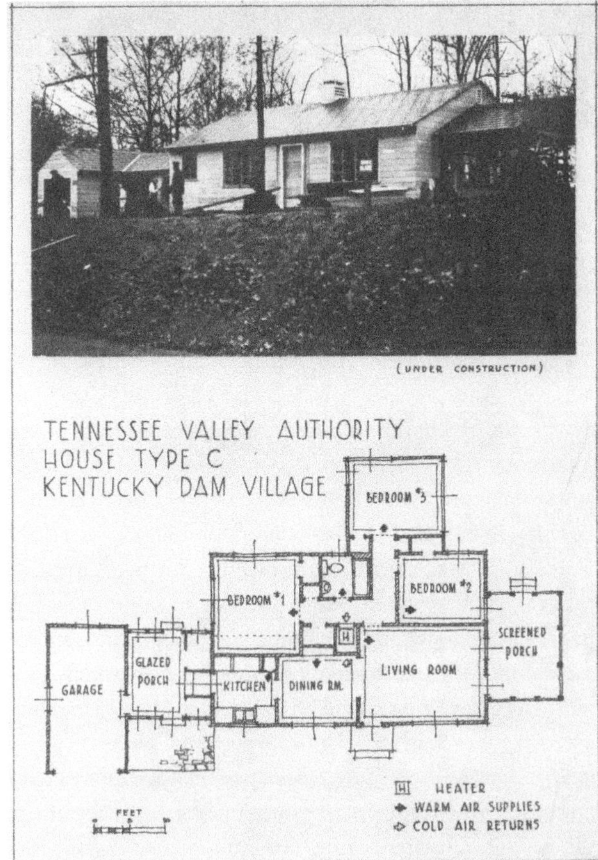


**Figure 81.** Presentation drawing and photograph of a Type C house at the Kentucky Dam (first called Gilbertsville) village. This house was built as a site for thermal research. Experiments in this house were the basis for a report titled "Studies in the Heating of Small Houses." It is now part of the Kentucky Dam Village State Park.

region. Taking a cue from their previous work on houses and other structures, it was to be called "small structures."[90]

The ARD staff was in contact with housing research centers outside the TVA. In April and May 1941 (even before the unit was formalized), Purnell corresponded with the John B. Pierce Foundation on technical matters. He explained that his goal was to develop simple applications and make them available to the architectural profession.[91] Three years later he shared detailed technical information with Vernon DeMars, at the time chief of the Housing Standards Section in the technical division of the National Housing Agency (NHA).[92] NHA staff also visited the Schult Trailer corporation and appraised the TVA prefabricated houses, noting their compliance with the agency's standards.[93] The correspondence with DeMars is also an indication of the central role Wank played, or at least was seen to play, in the housing project. When DeMars sent the TVA reports by the NHA, he addressed them to Wank, who then shared them with Towne and Purnell.[94] Other atelier members contributed as well; Augur wrote Towne about an article in the magazine *Nation's Business* devoted to new uses of cotton in house construction. He advocated studying this work carefully and checking if the new methods held any promise for the Tennessee Valley specifically.[95]

The ARD was especially proud of the development of the prefabrication systems. This project, more than any other, combined TVA requirements, the garden ideal, and cutting-edge professional interests. It also meshed with the other research interests; studies for the Fontana houses included an analysis of double glazing and curtains as methods of insulation. Towne continued to invest in the prefabrication efforts and insisted that the goal of the research was to produce good products and not just cheap alternatives. He hoped to "ignore all limitations and produce a TVA version of the 'House of the Future.'"[96] He also acted to publicize the work, fielding questions and writing extensively. In 1942 he issued an essay titled "Portable Housing: TVA Experience Leads to Trailer-Houses."[97] The essay included photographs of models of the sections system and was followed by a more personal account in 1944 (fig. 82).[98] The TVA recognized Towne for this work in 1944. The language of this decision makes clear that the atelier's insistence on combining theory and practice was institutionally recognized. Towne was commended for "outstanding success in the development of TVA demountable houses, which achievement has been inestimable assistance to TVA construction schedules and in addition has been accorded recognition by the War Department, the British Purchasing Commission, and the prefabrication housing industry."[99]

The TVA research was indeed well received. In 1951 Burnham Kelly, director of the Bemis Foundation, located at MIT in Cambridge, Massachusetts, recognized the TVA houses as "probably the most important government effort in prefabri-

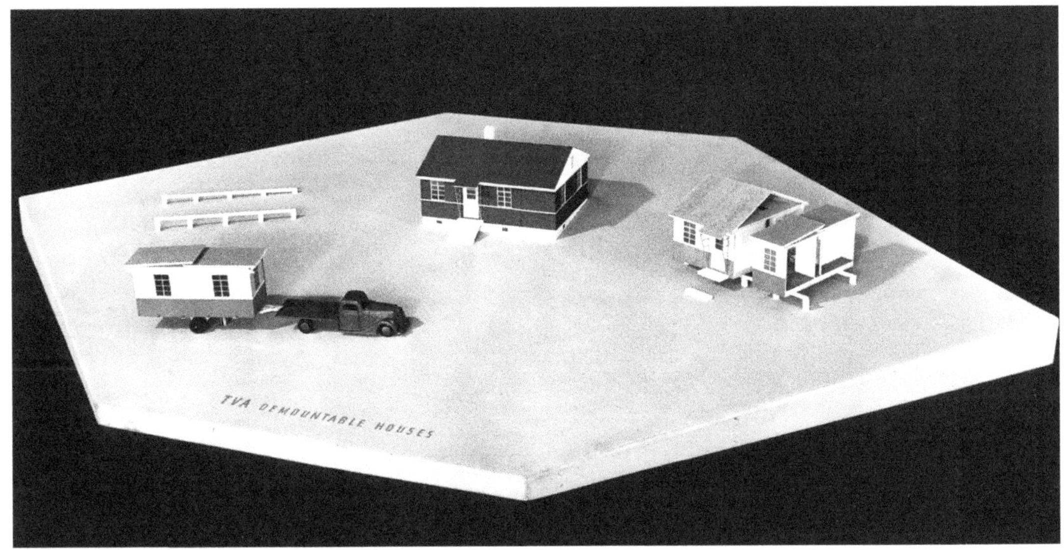


**Figure 82.** A model prepared by the TVA Architecture Research Division to explain the different systems for house construction they had developed. This and similar images were used to illustrate an essay Carroll A. Towne published in *Progressive Architecture* in 1942, titled "Portable Housing: TVA Experience Leads to Trailer-Houses."

cated building during this period, at least from a developmental standpoint."[100] Images of the houses, like the dams and powerhouses before them, were included in a 1942 exhibit at the Museum of Modern Art in New York, titled SCENE 6: Quantity Production of Houses.[101] They also featured in the *Architectural Record, The Technocrat,* and in a handbook for defense houses.[102] A 1943 "Portfolio of Low Cost Homes and Rental Housing Units," published by a commercial entity, includes an item on "Well Built Knoxville Homes."[103] The segment describes the work of an unnamed builder who was constructing a "smokeless community" on the southern edge of Knoxville. The item includes images from the builder's advertising material, which bear an uncanny resemblance to the TVA design—the plans are similar to the houses in Gilbertsville village, and the entrance to the house is articulated like the TVA houses. Importantly, the grassroots approach that underlaid the TVA research into modern houses offers yet another measure of success. The sectional approach the architects championed still underlies the production of manufactured houses in the region today. In particular, it is the basis for operations at Clayton Homes, one of the largest producers of such houses in the nation.[104] Towne and his colleagues would likely have considered this the most important impact of their work.

# 6

# REGIONAL DEVELOPMENT

## A New Industry

In 1921 Benton MacKaye published a proposal for the Appalachian Trail, a hiking path along the ridge of the mountains from Maine all the way to Georgia, in the *Journal of the American Institute of Architects.*[1] The plan had four layers: the trail itself, shelter camps, community camps, and food and farm camps; the latter two elements were versions of garden cities. MacKay posited that solving the "problem of labor" (i.e., increasing the efficiency of the working hours) was best approached by reversing the question. He asked: "Can we increase the efficiency of our spare time?"[2] The Appalachian Trail would make spare time more "efficient" by increasing opportunities for outdoor recreation; he compared the experience of being in a forest to that of being in a home, arguing that both were crucial for the development of a cultural identity and a meaningful life. MacKaye believed that recreation, especially hiking, was also key to wilderness preservation. People who were familiar with the scenery and enjoyed it, he reasoned, would be more likely to support its preservation, in turn benefitting their own culture. MacKaye's proposal echoed the ideas of Patrick Geddes, who had argued for firsthand "rustic experiences" as the antidote to "hooliganism."[3] Ideally, Geddes elaborated, youth will partake in the upkeep of parks and gardens, which will introduce them to forestry as well as the conservation of resources. Geddes saw the development of such experiences as a pillar of regional planning.[4]

The Appalachian Trail was intended, as Garrett D. Nelson comments, to "fuse leisure and industry, environment and labor, community development and wilderness preservation into an interrelated project."[5] Members of the Committee on Community Planning of the American Institute of Architects called this plan "the most far-seeing project in regional planning yet conceived in America."[6] The Regional Planning Association of America, which emerged from this committee, hoped it would be the seed of regional planning in the Appalachian Mountains, and the nation as whole. The trail itself was still under construction when the Tennessee Valley Authority began its operations, but the idea was well known among regional planners and wilderness enthusiasts. Managed forests and hiking trails were part of the model region Arthur E. Morgan directed the Land Planning & Housing Division (LP&H) to assemble around the first TVA dam at Norris, Tennessee. In 1935 the TVA designated the Norris Lake Forest (now known as the Norris Watershed) as an "integrated economic unit" in which resource conservation (a responsible timber industry) could be combined with regional planning (forest recreation). The TVA also designated several renovated farmhouses as lodging for the forestry workers.[7]

The AT never fulfilled its utopian goals. As Ronald Foresta discusses, the recreational features—the trail and the shelters—were given early attention, but eventually they were the only elements to be completed.[8] A similar fate awaited MacKaye's attempts to make his vision a blueprint for the TVA's regional planning. He called this vision "habitability," a term that captured his multilayered goals but that did not garner support in the institutional setting of the TVA. MacKaye left the Authority in 1936 without convincing Arthur Morgan to adopt his terminology. Still, the idea, or at least elements of it, was championed by staff in the LP&H and later at the Department of Regional Studies (DRS). Earle S. Draper, the first director of these units, agreed that at least some preservation of "primeval" landscapes was in the public interest.[9] Draper was even more interested in developing recreational opportunities and was, importantly, able to identify institutional mechanisms to support his goal. He knew to "translate" the ideas from utopian, vague language into actionable plans. He ultimately considered this project his biggest success at the TVA:

"As far as the recreation field goes, over many objections, we finally accomplished everything that we had hoped for in getting it accepted as part of the development of the resources."[10]

A central obstacle to comprehensive recreation opportunities and wilderness conservation was land ownership. MacKaye's vision was specifically tied to public land. The TVA did acquire land in the Tennessee Valley but restricted its purchases to what was needed to build dams and create reservoirs. These areas were then utterly transformed by the river machine. TVA directors Harcourt A. Morgan and David E. Lilienthal, moreover, insisted that the decisions about the land use be made by the Tennessee Valley residents, in what they called grassroots action. These residents preferred agriculture and industry; few saw an economic future in recreation. Still, the TVA land machine did include a mechanism—its forestry program—for changing people's minds. The conservation and renewal of the nation's forests had been a topic of widespread interest for several decades, having been brought to public attention by Theodore Roosevelt and Gifford Pinchot. It was a two-pronged attack. Conservatists lobbied public entities to buy land and transform it into forests; foresters, including MacKaye at the start of his career, developed scientific techniques to manage these lands.[11] Forestry combined the utilitarian and the aesthetic—a concern for timber supplies balanced by an appreciation for the beauty of these landscapes.[12] Federal interest in the forests of Appalachia also had a history; in 1901 a survey of the southern Appalachian region included a proposal to create an Appalachian forest reserve.[13] By the early 1930s counties in the mountainous parts of the region were petitioning the federal government for help in preserving forest and scenic amenities.[14]

Unlike "habitability," forestry was clearly outlined in the TVA Act; the sight of denuded and exploited forests had contributed, after all, to making the Tennessee Valley the first federal planning project in the United States. By the 1930s, moreover, the national timber companies had largely abandoned the region, leaving those who depended on them for their livelihood without work.[15] They had also left behind barren mountains and second- or third-growth forests, which were of inferior quality and could not support a renewed, regionally based timber industry. The need for proper management and scientific techniques to revive these landscapes seemed self-evident.[16] In addition, the TVA engineers had a practical interest in maintaining forest cover: they worried that widespread erosion, as had been previously experienced in the region, would clog the reservoirs they were building with silt, rendering them useless.

The TVA foresters eagerly undertook the project, encouraging regional government entities to purchase mountain tracts using federal funds under the Fulmer Act.[17] They also trained would-be foresters, offering them the chance to learn about preventing and controlling fires, constructing trails, and planting trees and shrubs.[18] The TVA maintained tree nurseries, one at Clinton, Tennessee, and one near Norris Dam, in which they cultivated regional trees (fig. 83).[19] They were especially interested in identifying trees that would help in erosion control and provide quick cash returns. After evaluating a range of species, including persimmons and locusts, the TVA foresters promoted the black walnut.[20] Knowledge gained from these experiments was also "made generally available," along with the TVA's information on farming techniques and house improvement.[21] The TVA also distributed seedlings without charge. Landowners who chose to participate in the program could enter into an agreement with the TVA; the Authority would provide trees and the farmer would maintain them for five years.[22]

President Franklin D. Roosevelt was especially interested in forestry. This focus was manifested, as Neil M. Maher shows, in his creation of the Civilian Conservation Corps (CCC), which set itself the goal of planting as many trees as possible across the nation.[23] The TVA forestry effort was supported by this organization; in the summer of 1933 twenty five camps moved to the Tennessee Valley from the high mountains of the West.[24] For eighteen months they divided their time between public and private land but then limited their work on farms to extreme cases only.[25] This was another example of a three-way cooperation that placed the TVA in the role of professional expert. The Authority supplied plans, technical supervision, and inspection; the Department of Agriculture, through the Forest Service, managed the work; and the young men enrolled in the CCC camps performed the physical labor.[26] In 1941, a year before the program was terminated, the CCC annual report described the corps' contribution to the Tennessee Valley: "During the past year over 13 million young trees were planted on 1,043 erosion projects on over 9,000 acres of severely eroded private lands."[27]

The key to making the development of recreation part of the forestry effort was to describe it as the basis for a new, promising tourist industry. This was a masterful move; it took an element of MacKaye's utopian idea of "habitability" and married it

**Figure 83.** The Norris Experimental Nursery planted by the TVA below Norris Dam in the 1930s. The trees are arranged by species and identified by signs. By the 1970s the TVA had developed the Songbird Trail, which connects the dam and the nursery along the Clinch River and is popular as a short hiking path.

with the language of resource conservation. This approach allowed the TVA to promote recreation as an economic development, even as it retained some of its social reform. Recreation implied the conservation of both natural and human resources, as Conrad L. Wirth, assistant director of the National Park Service (NPS) wrote in 1937: "We must realize that in park work we are dealing with conservation in its broadest meaning. Our job concerns not only conservation of natural resources, but conservation of human resources. The greatest resource of any nation is its human wealth, and in the conservation of the human wealth recreation plays a major part."[28]

Howard K. Menhinick, who replaced Draper as director of the DRS, subscribed to this point of view. Speaking with the Tennessee Valley Library Council in 1944, he explained that he had always assumed that "the building of a factory by a manufacturer added to the wealth of a community but the building of a hospital or a school or a playground by the local government impoverished the community."[29] Working for the TVA shifted his view; he came to appreciate that the service occupations were as productive as agriculture and industry and that "a growing forest, a swimming beach, a lake or even a beautiful view may be a greater economic asset than a cornfield."[30] This point of view recognized that a region based primarily on agriculture would not be viable; farmers could not make a living on marginal plots of land. Unless a use was found for these locations there would not be enough resources to support a robust population. This observation further enforced the idea that economic development was a path to social reform, or as Daniel Schaffer explains, that progressive resource conservation and economic development "were one and the same."[31]

In 1939 the TVA recognized recreation, together with agriculture, forestry, and industry, as an optimal (and therefore legal) use for land. This decision allowed the atelier members to allocate TVA-owned land on the shores of the rising reservoirs to this use. As we shall see, this allocation included land that remained in the Authority's domain, tracts that were transferred to other public entities, and even parcels sold to individual landowners. They also included areas set aside for quasi-public uses, such as for the 4-H Clubs, which enrolled school children and teenagers. The TVA statement recognizing recreation also stipulated that although the agency could not expend funds directly for this purpose, it could invest in demonstrations as authorized by the TVA Act.[32] In addition, this work had to be undertaken "with due regard to sound economy of operation."[33] The development of recreation was thus rooted—even more than community planning and house construction—in the grassroots approach. As such it was yet another opportunity for atelier members to engage in developing professional expertise, especially that directed toward securing "high standards of appearance, sanitation, and safety in all recreational developments actually carried out."[34]

Forestry and recreation were not unknown in the mountainous regions of the Tennessee Valley. The Appalachians were dotted with expensive and exclusive resorts that offered wealthy families a respite from the urban centers of the Northeast. By 1930 the Biltmore Estate had been opened as a tourist destination. Designed and constructed in the late nineteenth century, the estate was the pet project of George Vanderbilt, the grandson of steamboat and railroad magnate Cornelius Vanderbilt. Fabulously wealthy, Vanderbilt hired architect Richard Morris Hunt and premier landscape architect Fredric Law Olmsted to lay out a self-sufficient, scientifically managed unit complete with forestry programs, farms, and a dairy; Gifford Pinchot worked here in the early part of his career. The atelier drew on these precedents but recognized that to promote a larger preservation effort they would have to appeal to a much wider swath of society. The TVA would have to join the move to "federalize public recreation development," in Phoebe Cutler's phrase.[35] This work followed about two decades of rising popular interest in recreation, driven, in part, by a concern that efficient farming and industry would result in a sharp rise in leisure time. As Galen Cranz points out, the phrase "leisure time" (which first appeared in 1907) suggested a gap to be filled, as opposed to just "leisure," which denoted a stroll or a picnic. Reformers were worried about how people would fill this leisure time, and the design of environments to ensure against "wrong" interpretations (i.e., drinking and gambling) was part of progressive work from the early twentieth century.[36] The public's interest in recreation continued to grow during the Great Depression and became a serious enterprise, with more people "working at play."[37]

The atelier's first move was to anchor their recreation efforts in data and surveys; their goal was to develop methods for quantifying the value of recreation to fit it into the TVA engineering mindset.[38] They spoke of recreation as a renewable resource: unlike timber or minerals, recreation areas could be used over and over, especially if they were properly planned, designed, and managed. True to the managerial style of the TVA, the responsibility for "Recreation and Conservation" was assigned to a dedicated section in the LP&H.[39] Malcolm Dill helped establish this section, but Robert M. Howes, who joined it in June 1934, became its central force. Howes, a landscape architect from Massachusetts, was the right man for this intricate assignment. He appreciated the complexity of both the terrain and the institution, remarking: "I often think how much the agency reflects the river with which it works—the Tennessee. The controversial and consequential qualities of the agency reflect the same qualities in the river."[40] He was independent and self-driven, and he explored both the TVA technical library and the Knoxville Municipal Library to broaden his understanding of the Tennessee Valley. (This self-directed academic program also introduced him to his future wife.) Howes spent his entire career at the TVA and was devoted to it and its goals. As a stalwart member of MacKaye's Philosophers Club, he often joined him on hikes in the mountains. Howes's writing also displays a sensitivity to local customs and traditions. He later became a central advocate for creating a recreation park on the Norris Reservoir for Black citizens of the region, which would have been the first in the state.

In its self-assumed role as coordinator of federal, state, and local agencies, the atelier focused on forests, roads, and tourist safety. It participated, for example, in collaborative studies of forest resources in the Southeast. Much attention was given to planning roads for recreation throughout the region, including roads that could support vacation trailers.[41] This interest was later part of the development of the TVA prefabricated house system (see chapter 5). The atelier also supported legislation that would protect these new roadways from "dangerous roadside encroachments" such as billboards.[42] In grassroots style, this work was pursued in cooperation with many entities, including the National Resources Committee, the American Civic Association, the state highway commissions, the Bureau of Public Roads, and the CCC. The atelier also worked to ensure the health and safety of tourist accommodations and to develop a system to license such establishments.[43] Atelier members studied tourist camps, trailers, and trailer camps, creating a bibliography to share with state planning boards and similar agencies throughout the Valley.[44] In addition, they helped draft legislation that would form the basis for ongoing inspection of these sites. MacKaye and Howes, for their part, designed a layout for a series of leaflets on the Tennessee Valley, intended to guide the expected tourists during their visit and point them to the most attractive locations (fig. 84).[45]

In 1935 the atelier completed a study of "Non-Urban Recreation," a detailed classification of outdoor recreation, which MacKaye had advocated as an important step in promoting "habitability."[46] The report, written by Dill and Howes, was distributed widely.[47] In 1937 Draper reported on it in the *Architectural Record* as part of a discussion of "community recreation."[48] The report is basically a flow chart that allows readers to locate different recreation areas within a larger matrix of terms. The authors' goal was to provide a unified vocabulary for the different federal agencies engaged in recreational development. This project drew on the mapping capabilities the TVA had developed, and it resulted in a series of maps. One section of this report discusses travelways, which were a central preoccupation for the atelier and the LP&H. The proposal outlines a system of freeways like the Norris Freeway, which were to be a "separate and distinct phase of the regional highway problem."[49]

"Non-Urban Recreation" was the implicit focus—though not initially proposed as such—of the most important report TVA produced at this time. *The Scenic Resources of the Tennessee Valley,* a study developed over several years by Howes and his team, was completed in 1938 (fig. 85). In each stage of the project, the researchers studied a particular subregion of the Valley, beginning with the eastern moun-

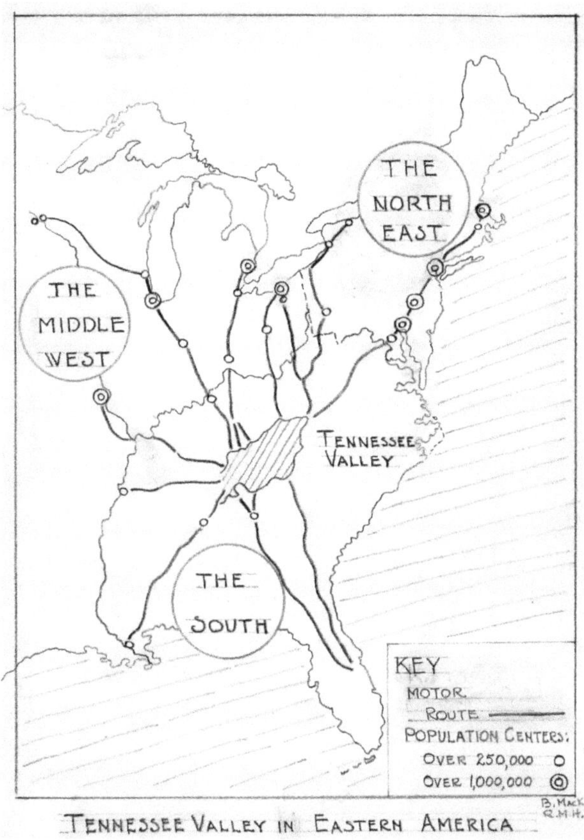


**Figure 84.** This diagram by Benton MacKaye and Robert L. Howes was included in a proposal for a series of pamphlets directing tourists to points of interest in the Tennessee Valley.

tains (which they considered best suited to recreation) and moving toward the west (where the "problems" were more "serious").[50] The title of the report illustrates how the atelier reframed their focus on recreation to fit within the TVA's broader resource conservation approach. MacKaye wanted to call this work a study of "habitability" rather than "recreation potential," the titled preferred by the Resort and Recreation Committee, which was chaired by Tracy B. Augur, Draper's deputy.[51] The agreed title, *Scenic Resources,* balanced between these two and also allowed the board to describe the report as a "byproduct of investigations into the resources of

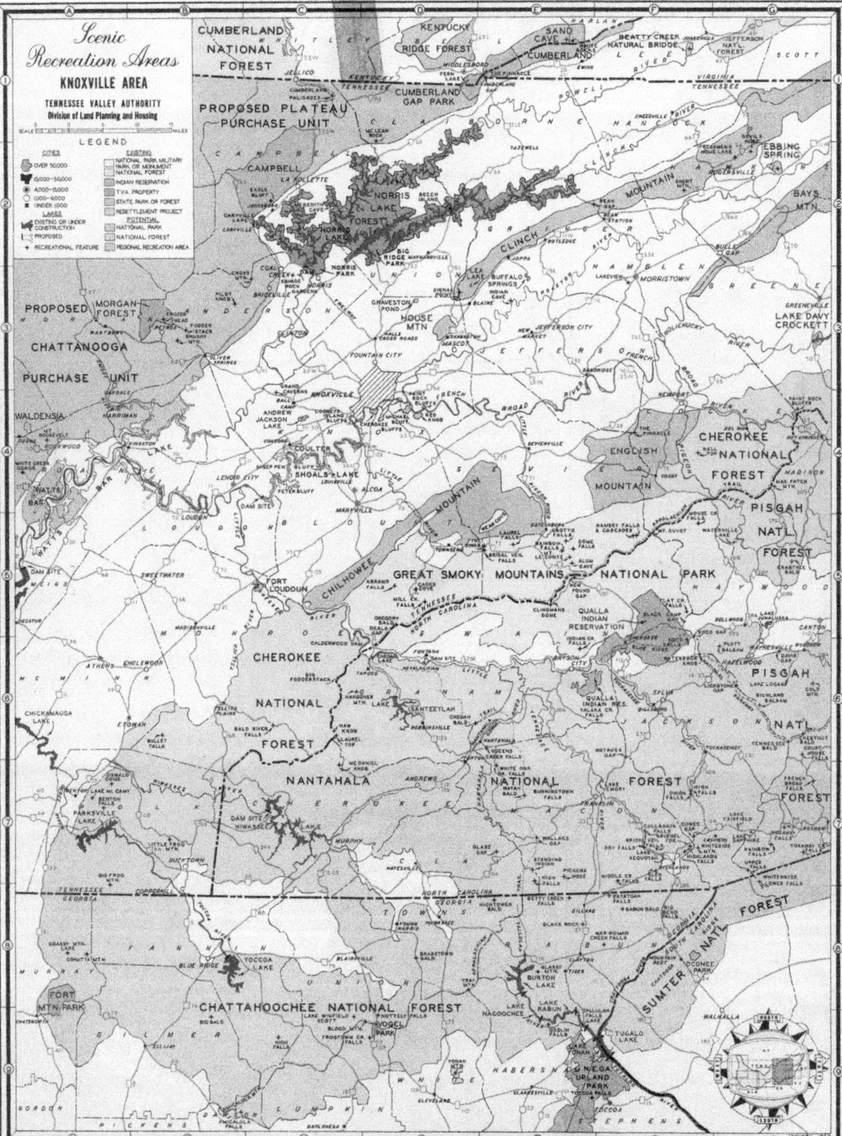


**Figure 85.** Map of the *Scenic Recreational Area Knoxville Area* prepared for the *Scenic Resources of the Tennessee Valley* report completed in 1938. Landscape architect Robert L. Howes developed this project, which took Benton MacKaye's insistence on habitability and translated it into the language of resource conservation. This map includes the Great Smoky Mountains National Park, the Norris "reservation," and a part of the "Proposed Chattanooga Purchase Unit" and the "Proposed Plateau Purchase Unit."

the area."[52] In preparing the survey, the team made use of the new mapping techniques developed in the TVA, such as infrared cameras.[53] They also cooperated with other departments in the Authority and examined a range of materials prepared by individuals, private organizations, and public agencies in the region.[54] The Regional Planning Council read and commented on an early draft of the report, an indication of its role in promoting the garden ideal.[55]

In a third report, *Recreational Development of the Southern Highlands Region: A Study of the Use and Control of Scenic and Recreational Resources,* the atelier made specific recommendations for resource conservation and the development of recreation in the Tennessee Valley. The report also nodded to the interest in grassroots institution building and included an analysis of existing statutes along with recommendations for new legislation that would support these goals. The *Southern Highlands* report includes practical suggestions, including identifying districts recommended for immediate development, while recognizing the limited financial resources of most counties in the region. Based on this study the TVA supported the creation of the Southern Highlands Recreation Committee, composed largely of representatives of federal, state, and local government agencies concerned with recreation. The purpose of this committee was to plan and guide the conservation and development of these natural—and through them human—resources.[56]

## A Rustic Experience

In 1938 the DRS compiled a report on the work undertaken by its predecessor, the LP&H, under the rubric of "regional planning."[57] The report included a map, *Lakefront Parks on TVA Reservoirs,* dated July 1938. This map points to another element in the atelier's development of recreation: the planning, design, construction, and management of public parks. Strictly speaking, these parks were the work of the NPS and the Tennessee Department of Conservation, and they were built by teams of young men in the CCC. The atelier, however, had envisioned their scope, developed the design drawings, and supervised the construction.[58] The parks were intended to provide the residents of the Tennessee Valley with "early training which will prepare them for successful and creative use of their leisure time."[59] The TVA earned accommodation fees from visitors staying in these parks, and by 1937 this income was sufficient to defray the costs of operating them. The seven parks included in the 1938 map—Norris, Big Ridge, Cove Creek, Harrison Bay, Wheeler, Muscle Shoals, and Pickwick (from east to west)—were only the largest projects. Pursuant to the TVA policy, the atelier had also been involved in smaller projects undertaken in Tennessee by other entities, such as the Shelby County Forest Park near Memphis and a children's area at Chilhowee Park in Knoxville.[60]

The TVA forestry and recreation efforts were undertaken in parallel with another major regional project, the creation of the Great Smoky Mountains National Park. Much of the land included in the park had been ravaged by timber companies, and it too had to be "salvaged" before becoming a national amenity. The Smokies were also transformed by the work of CCC camps, a project welcomed by residents of the surrounding areas, who recognized the potential for increased tourism and, thus, income.[61] The TVA work, however, is more profitably compared to the efforts of the state park system. State parks predated the Depression—a few appeared as early as the 1880s—but the concept was not fully developed until 1921, with the first National Conference of State Parks organized by Stephen Mather, the first director of the NPS. This conference did not agree on a single definition of state parks but did expect them to buffer between urban and wilderness regions and to offer recreation to large swaths of the population. In 1925 the Tennessee General Assembly officially recognized the importance of such parks and established the State Park and Forestry Commission, which was empowered to buy properties for public use. As part of their efforts at creating "a planning region," the TVA suggested that this commission be replaced by a nimbler organization. This reorganization was accomplished in 1937 when the Tennessee Department of Conservation was established, which included a State Parks Division and the Division of Forestry. Sam Brewster, who had worked for the TVA as a landscape architect in Muscle Shoals, Alabama, was the first commissioner, and two years later he became director of state parks.[62]

An important practice shared by the TVA and the state park movement was the attention to land with little obvious utility. Transforming "submarginal" land into locations for recreation gave these tracts new life, turning abandoned property into a public resource, the very goal of resource conservation. This approach is evident in the title of the 1938 map—*Lakefront Parks on TVA Reservoirs.* The new bodies of water swelling behind the TVA dams were reservoirs; they were subject to the machine logic of their engineering role. The level of the water, for example, depended on the changing needs of flood control and power production (see fig. 3 in chapter 1). The TVA nevertheless began referring to them as lakes—as resources to be developed. Draper explained to *Architectural Forum* readers in 1937: "The TVA realizes that this chain of lakes extending for hundreds of miles through the Valley will enhance the attractions of a region already rich in scenery and climate—the raw materials of the recreation industry."[63] A photograph issued by the TVA (taken by Arthur Rothstein) shows Kenneth C., Helen Louise, and Peggy Hall rowing a boat on the Tennessee River, clearly enjoying a moment of peace and quiet.[64] At the time the photograph was taken, the family was living in defense housing in Sheffield, Alabama, near Muscle Shoals. Kenneth Hall worked as a foreman in the hot rolling mill at the Reynolds Metals Company, an aluminum plant using TVA electricity. Here again the TVA, spurred by the atelier, was highlighting the garden aspects of the new landscape, even as it acknowledged, and even celebrated, its machine accomplishments.

In designing the "Lakefront Parks on TVA Reservoirs," the atelier followed Geddes's and MacKaye's insistence on rustic experiences quite literally. Park buildings were designed in what Cutler calls "Government Rustic," a style that emphasizes the connection between building and site and keeps decoration to a minimum.[65] Christine Macy and Sarah Bonnemaison discuss the evolution of this style in detail.[66] The TVA structures fit naturally in the 1938 edition of *Park and Recreation Structures,* prepared by Albert H. Good, architectural consultant for the NPS.[67] These designs also gave visual form to a fundamentally illusory notion inherent in the TVA garden ideal: the continuity of history and experience between the frontier landscape and the TVA project. By weaving recreational and conservation elements into the reshaped landscape, the atelier could present a less intrusive face of progress to the region. As Torben H. Larsen observes, this choice located the TVA ideology in the specificity of the region.[68] The pairing of the TVA landscape with emblems of frontier life was not limited to the parks. A mural in the visitors' center of Boone Dam, which was completed after the war, made this connection in a straightforward manner. Todd Smith describes the composition as one that "weaves over two hundred years of regional history into a diorama punctuated by abstracted panels of color and perspective."[69] At the center of the mural are three figures: folk hero Daniel Boone (for whom the dam was named), a TVA engineer, and a fisherman. Their tools—a gun, technical drawings, and a fishing pole—are also depicted, drawing a clear connection between "pioneer to professional to leisure enthusiast."[70]

**Figure 86.** Caleb's Barn at Clear Creek below Norris Dam with the Norris Freeway behind it crossing on a stylized bridge. The barn had been moved from Morristown, Hamblen County, to this location so that visitors to the Norris Dam State Park could appreciate the conditions of the "pioneer days." The barn houses an exhibit of agricultural tools and is open on weekends in the summer months.

One point along the Norris Freeway encapsulates this rustic character. Just below the Norris Dam—the product of twentieth-century industry and technology—the TVA placed two relics of previous centuries, buildings that belonged to the frontier life that the dam had just destroyed. These buildings, a gristmill and a threshing barn, were purchased by the TVA and moved and reconstructed at the section of Clear Creek where it meets the freeway (fig. 86).[71] The mill had been in continuous operation by members of the same family for 140 years, and all of its mechanism are handmade. It was made operational once again by constructing a water channel at the new site; even today, tourists can still purchase souvenir bags of stone-ground cornmeal.[72] Draper explained this display: "In each park, relatively small areas were set aside for intensive development; the remainder perpetuating as nearly as possible the natural conditions of the upper Tennessee Valley during pioneer days."[73]

The atelier continued this practice in the nearby Norris Park, now the Norris Dam State Park, which is reached through a ceremonial traffic circle designed by Roland A. Wank for the eastern end of the Norris Dam (see chapter 3). This was not submarginal land; it had belonged to W. H. Longmire of Anderson County, Tennessee, until it was acquired by the TVA. In the early stages of the TVA project, however, the drive toward a model region was not yet tempered by the ideology of resource conservation. Work began in 1934, in cooperation with the NPS and the CCC.[74] After the park was opened in 1936, the TVA continued to manage it under an agreement with the NPS, first by the Norris town manager and later by the Department of Reservoir Properties.[75] The central building in the park is a tearoom (initially referred to as a lodge), which contains facilities for dining and dancing as well as a lakeside terrace. Built of wood on a stone foundation, the building is connected to the electric grid but also includes a fireplace, which symbolizes community even when it is not used for social gatherings (fig. 87). Opposite the lodge is its outdoor equivalent: a small theater built into a natural bowl. Split logs serve as benches in this primitive structure, and the stage is paved with local flagstone. The theater was designed for informal theatricals, lectures, and meetings, and it is still in regular use.[76] The atelier also supervised the construction of picnic shelters of similar style and made of the same materials.

The Norris Dam State Park does not offer a beach, as the shore is too steep, but the designers did develop a floating boat dock, a design that they refined and used in subsequent parks.[77] These docks offered access to the lake, expanding the opportunities for recreation. The Architecture Research Division (ARD) included floating equipment in its research program, and the National Boat and Engine Manufacturer's Association included examples of these structures in their publications.[78] The park also included a stable where horses could be rented for use on eighteen miles of trails. These trails were also rustic in one sense—they commemorated the routes used by the farmers living in the area before the dam was built (fig. 88). A second set of buildings, just below the lodge, is also part of the original design. These are twenty vacation cabins, of which five are duplex models. Finished in lapped shiplap and wood shingles, they are small versions of the Norris houses and include fireplaces, screened porches, and miniature three-fixture kitchens (figs. 89, 90).[79] In 1942 the

**Figure 87.** A photograph of the interior of the lodge at Norris Park on June 1, 1938. Built by the TVA as a demonstration of "rustic recreation," the building is still used as the Tea Room in the Norris Dam State Park.

TVA also moved in the very basic cabins built for construction workers at the Norris camp so they could be used by tourists; these were later replaced by newer buildings. Demand was so high at first that even the unused dormitories in the construction camp were opened to visitors before being dismantled and removed.[80]

Big Ridge State Park is also located on the Norris Reservoir, built at the same time as Norris Park.[81] Carroll A. Towne was especially proud of having identified the perfect location for this park, along with Dill. When the two men visited the reservoir area, after it had been cleared of vegetation but before it was flooded, they came upon a small valley near Loyston, a town that would be inundated by the reservoir. They envisioned creating a lake in the valley that, unlike a reservoir, could be kept at a constant level by means of a small auxiliary dam. Back in Knoxville they proposed this park plan, but the engineers scoffed at their casual method of siting such a dras-

**Figure 88** Photograph of the horse stable in Norris Park on June 1, 1938. Riders could explore a system of trails based on the routes used by the farmers living in the area in the late nineteenth and early twentieth centuries.

tic transformation of the landscape. Doing their own assessment, the engineers traveled to the head of the valley, where they found an old mill complete with its wheel and sluiceway. Towne tells the story with some satisfaction: "[They] spent about an hour throwing chips in the sluiceway and measuring with a stop watch the speed at which the chips rolled down the sluice, scratched their heads a while and came back to Knoxville. And so a day or two later they called us back and said, 'Well, you boys have done the impossible. You have found the one location in Norris Lake where we think we can possibly build a dam that will hold water.'"[82] The dam, a concrete structure, was eventually built at the site, creating a forty-five-acre "lake" at the heart of Big Ridge State Park.[83] The landscaping artifice did not end with the dam. Ten miles

**Figure 89.** A historic cabin in Norris Dam State Park, design by the TVA architects and constructed with Civilian Conservation Corps labor. This cabin can still be rented for a rustic vacation.

of wire fencing, some supplied by the forestry department, were installed to protect the wildlife in the park area from predators outside it, creating a kind of wilderness-made-for-man.[84]

Similar to Norris Park, Big Ridge also boasts a public lodge and cabins as well as a rustic gateway structure. These structures were completed in 1936, but four years later the public lodge was renovated to provide restrooms accessible from the exte-

**Figure 90.** A July 1952 photograph of the interior of a vacation cabin at the Norris Dam State Park. The juxtaposition between the handcrafted interior and the mechanized kitchen is emblematic of the TVA architects' approach to design, especially in the early 1930s.

rior of the building (fig. 91). The mill discovered by the engineers is also part of the park, dominating one arm of the lake. Beyond it, the atelier developed an example of a quasi-public group campground, which was to serve organized groups such as the Boy Scouts, Campfire Girls, and the 4-H clubs. The campground accommodation and dining structures are very basic, but they are supported by water, sewage, and electricity. Located directly on the lake, Big Ridge has two communal elements that were not part of the Norris Park—a boathouse and a swimming beach, which used to include a diving tower. After its first season the beach was improved by concreting the wading pool and adding a sequence of stone walls and benches, which helped keep the water from getting muddy. In June 1939 the atelier was busy planning and supervising the installation of a chlorination and recirculation system.[85] The beach

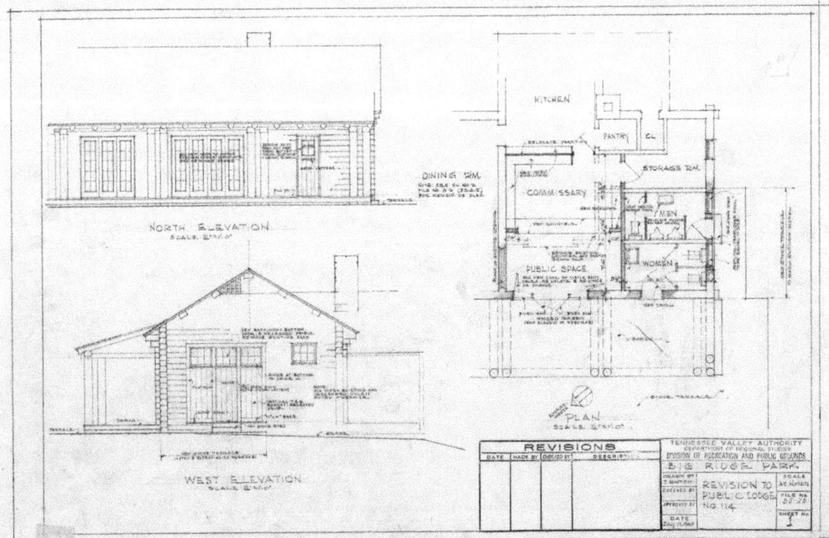


**Figure 91.** A drawing of renovations to the public lodge in Big Ridge Park by architect Troy Minton. The lodge had been completed in 1936, but the renovations added restrooms accessible from the exterior of the building.

is also serviced by a bathhouse, which was enlarged considerably when it proved inadequate for the crowds the park attracted.[86]

Before the official end of Jim Crown segregation, the Norris Reservoir did not include a park officially open to African Americans; citizens in both Knoxville and Chattanooga organized committees to demand such development. In 1937 discussions were held between the DRS (represented by Dill), the Tennessee State Planning Board, and the Tennessee State Department of Conservation. These conversations produced a clear recommendation to establish parks on both the Norris and the Chickamauga Reservoirs, the first on TVA land and the second to be operated by the state Department of Conservation. Draper toured the Norris Dam area with representatives from the Knoxville citizen committee and identified a suitable location west of the dam. The legal department, however, worried that such use would not prove "prudent" economically and demanded more assurances that the park could be self-maintaining; the budget office voiced similar concerns. The Knoxville citizens, represented by Dr. J. Max Bond, argued that any such costs must be borne by the white community, since they demanded the segregation. Moreover, if a park

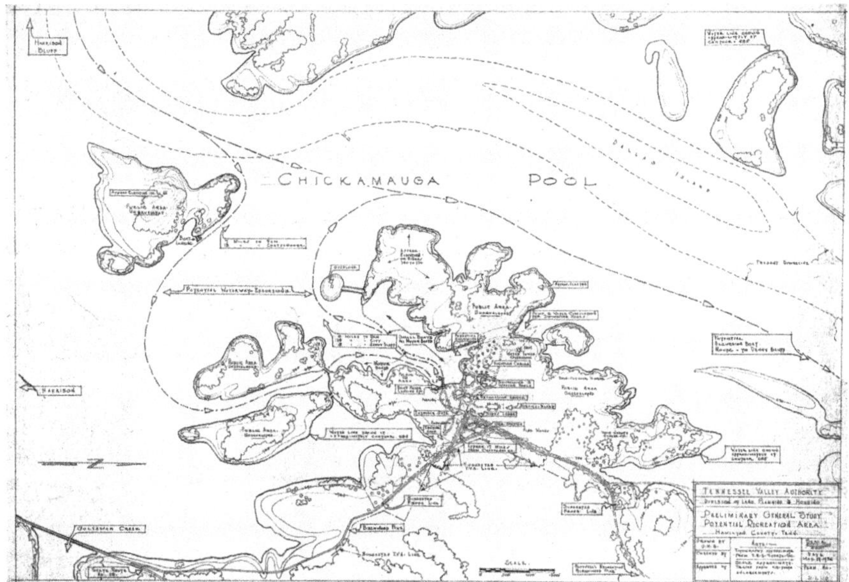


**Figure 92.** A "Preliminary General Study of Potential Recreation Area" in Hamilton County, Tennessee, drawn by Osborne H. Graves. Completed on May 29, 1936, for Land Planning and Housing, this plan is an early example of the TVA landscape architects' attention to recreation. Work on Chickamauga Dam, which would create this environment, had not yet begun.

was not built, they would continue to unofficially use the amenities offered at Norris Park, as they were already doing.[87]

The TVA decided to create a "Negro park" on Chickamauga Lake, closer to Chattanooga, a site they had been studying for several years (fig. 92). The decision was also based on a report that noted that the Black population near the more southern town was several times larger than that of Knoxville. The TVA thus prioritized the larger, underprivileged population over the wealthier but smaller group. The report also suggested allowing Black organizations to lease land on the Norris reservoir and develop it according to TVA guidelines.[88] The Booker T. Washington Park was developed on Chickamauga Reservoir, not far from the Harrison Bay Park, and both are now part of the state park system. Commenting on this park in later years, Towne betrayed a sentiment that was likely shared by at least some of his colleagues: "In the early days of the TVA the 'separate but equal' philosophy had not been discredited and, in fact, was regarded as a step ahead of the way in which the Negroes had been treated in that region before the TVA came. This was a very fine park. It had a beautiful view and its own boat basin and, as far as I know, it is still operating as a park."[89]

The atelier also developed parks in northern Alabama, the location of the existing Wilson Dam and two of the first TVA constructions, Wheeler and Pickwick Landing Dams. The shoreline of the Wilson Reservoir was almost all under private ownership. The TVA did have jurisdiction over a nearby area, however: the land surrounding the nitrate plants at nearby Muscle Shoals. Using CCC labor, and continuing to collaborate with the NPS, the atelier created three day-use parks. These parks were also segregated, with only one open to African Americans. In addition, the TVA supervised conservation of some 2,300 acres while it developed about 100 acres for camping, complete with Boy Scout cabins, a field museum, a lookout tower, a boathouse, and picnic area, all served by roads, trails, and a sewer system.[90] No project was too small to serve as a demonstration of the benefits of good planning and outdoor recreation (fig. 93). The picnic shelter in what is now called the CCC Park in Sheffield, Alabama, is similar to one constructed at nearby Wheeler Reservoir. The shelters include a stone floor, fireplaces, and a storage room for park main-

**Figure 93.** A picnic shelter in the CCC Park in Sheffield, Alabama. This shelter, designed by the TVA, shares a rustic design with similar structures on other TVA properties.

tenance equipment.[91] Like the Norris cabins, the shelters offer visitors an opportunity to create rustic outdoor experiences.

The importance of the rustic experience only grew after the United States engaged in defense and war projects in the name of democracy, as Harold l. Ickes, Secretary of the Interior, explained in his introduction to the *Yearbook Park and Recreation Progress* published in 1941:

> The real first line of defense lies in the soul of a people, and is anchored deeply in the land. In times of stress men and women draw peace, understanding and strength from the hills, the forests, the waterways—places where quiet abounds. If there are any among us today, particularly among our young people, who have become so confused by tragic world events that they are beginning to doubt the democratic way, let them go into our parks. . . . Surely then doubt, bewilderment and cynicism will give way to a deeper understanding and devotion to America and our democratic processes.[92]

## A Chain of Lakes

The atelier concluded its design and construction of demonstration parks with the Booker T. Washington Park. After the war the atelier turned its attention to supporting recreation in the Tennessee Valley through grassroots action. This powerful myth propelled the TVA's work, but for the designers it had a serious flaw. The atelier could not be sure that, in the hands of local and regional entities, recreational development would conform to their standards of good planning and design. To address this issue, Howes and his team engaged in institution building and provided technical advice, similar to the work of Raymond F. Leonard and Aelred Gray with communities in the region (see chapter 2). The recreation team had an advantage that the Assistance to Communities section (later renamed the Urban Community Relations section) did not: the TVA owned the shoreline along the reservoirs. After Arthur Morgan was dismissed from his position as director, the TVA ceased to purchase entire shorelines (as it had at Norris), but the river machine still required the transition of private lands into the public domain, and the TVA board of directors did authorize the acquisition of land to ensure public access to the reservoirs.[93] Harold Frincke recalled that the "recreation planning experts" would coordinate the allocation of land on TVA reservoirs, producing both a comprehensive plan and specific plans for each reservoir.[94]

The most elaborate plan was conceived for Chickamauga Reservoir, in part because of its location near Chattanooga—the largest city in the Tennessee Valley—and the fact that it would be accessible from both sides via highways and county roads.[95] The scenic resources report emphasized the importance of that location as the confluence of three distinct geographical areas: the Blue Ridge Province, most of which was public land in Cherokee and Chattahoochee National Forests; the river valley; and the Appalachian Plateaus.[96] The TVA did not buy land in this region, but it was able to work with Hamilton County, where most of the reservoir is located. TVA planners assisted in compiling countywide zoning regulations and agitated for the establishment of a county park commission.[97] The TVA directly contributed proposals for the shoreline in Dayton and Soddy, Tennessee, which they had prepared as part of their community planning efforts.[98] The atelier also developed the Chickamauga Boat Harbor on TVA-owned land, including a concession building with rest rooms and a tea terrace overlooking the lake and dam (fig. 94). The buildings were designed by Wank, along with Seth Harrison Gurnee and Mario Bianculli, and were constructed under the supervision of Towne and George Richardson. Their style represented a departure from the rustic style adopted in the demonstration parks at Norris. These overtly modern structures were made of weatherproof plywood and finished in natural colors that contrasted with a red concrete base. Photos and drawings of these buildings, together with architectural details, were published in *Pencil Points* in July 1941.[99]

In a 1953 staff report, Howes commented: "The two principal features of TVA's activities in recreation may be said to be their stimulative character and their flexibility."[100] This new advisory role was not always easy for the atelier members. Towne later recalled: "To those of us who were involved in the direct development, this came as a shock, and we found that we had to learn how to act as advisors to local agencies rather than having the fun of doing the designing and development ourselves."[101] The atelier persisted in this mission, however, and Menhinick reaffirmed Draper's dedication of a section to this task. In 1940 the unit consisted of Howes (classified as an associate regional planner) assisted by his junior colleagues Harry H. Wilkerson and S. F. Brandt. Two years later Howes was appointed recreation technician, with George Barker assisting him as an associate. Their responsibilities

**Figure 94.** The tea terrace of the concession building at the Chickamauga Boat Harbor on July 20, 1941. The TVA developed such sites as demonstrations for regional commercial entities.

included services to state planning commissions and conservation departments; the preparation of land purchase and land-use plans; and the recommendation of TVA lands to be allocated to recreational use, in cooperation with state and local planning agencies. In addition, they performed services "in connection with reservoir construction projects," particularly with the TVA Department of Reservoir Property Management (DRPM). In line with their self-appointed role as an atelier, they also took the knowledge they amassed to conferences arranged by the other organizations.[102]

Design—in the sense of imagining and drawing possible landscapes, buildings, and equipment—did not disappear entirely, but it was focused toward the development of professional expertise rather than built examples. Frincke recalled drawing plans and layouts for recreation parks and lake access as a way of inspiring local organizations to undertake their construction. He also worked on developing floating boat docks and other equipment based on the model first used at Norris.[103] These drawings were used by the River Transportation Division in the Commerce Department, in discussions with organizations outside the TVA.[104] Another project consisted of written standards and cost analyses of construction and operation for docks, cottages, and village services.[105] In early 1940 Howes suggested the atelier prepare standard plans for recreation structures, which Richardson listed four years later.[106] They included buildings developed for the demonstration parks, such as lodge buildings, bathhouses, boathouses, and cabins. Richardson also listed structures that the atelier developed in its work on the river machine: overlook buildings (both temporary and permanent), comfort stations, wash houses, and concession buildings. With typical thoroughness he also included practical elements such as curbs and guardrails, lockers, manholes, and even a gasoline- and oil-dispensing barge. These drawings were still in use in 1955 when Harry B. Tour borrowed the "master list."[107]

The atelier was especially interested in the development of vacation cabins and took on the hybrid role of coordinator, supervisor, and designer that was typical of their other work on small structures (see chapter 5). They made a list of reference material for weekend and summer houses, including both commercial material and articles in trade magazines such as *House & Garden.*[108] Their goal was to provide house builders with a clear standards.[109] The atelier also included information about the TVA demountable and prefabricated houses, adjusted for vacation purposes (fig. 95).[110] In 1945, for example, Harry H. Wilkerson transmitted a set of construction drawings for such houses to the manager of the properties in the Chattanooga area.[111] These were based on material calculations made specifically for this dissemination of knowledge.[112]

Designing and developing the shoreline of TVA reservoirs into lakes for recreation also highlighted the complexity of the land machine. Leasing land to governments—cities, counties, and state systems—was acceptable across the TVA. The forestry department, however, considered giving control to private companies and individuals "indefensible and intolerable."[113] For others, however, this was the logical conclusion of the grassroots approach, as well as a necessary policy for dealing with the many miles of new shoreline created by the dams. The atelier began experimenting with leasing land around the Norris Reservoir in August 1939. The following year

**Figure 95.** Drawing of a prefabricated house used as a vacation cabin. The TVA architects developed their prefabrication system in a time of crisis but were constantly anticipating the recreational opportunities of the postwar period.

plans were made for further sites there, as well as locations on the Pickwick Landing Reservoir.[114] These leases were awarded to commercial enterprises such as boat docks and to private citizens as well. Individual lessees were required to build a vacation house (confusingly also referred to as a cabin) on the land within two years. In 1939 the first such contracts were prepared, and over sixty lots were put up for public bid. The new tenants had to commit to comply with all TVA technical and engineering restrictions, including keeping the lower part of each lot, which may be flooded when the TVA raises the water level in the reservoirs, free of permanent structures. The atelier, for its part, brought the garden ideals it had first implemented in Norris, Tennessee, especially the careful attention to siting houses:

> We wanted to avoid that kind of speculation on land and exploitation of people. Our program started out with having sufficient size lots so that the

> house sites would be a reasonable distance from each other. It was not based on acreage per lot, but rather on house sites themselves as applied to the topography. So, we had many cases of very large lots because the hinterland was not developable, but it could be used for other kinds of private recreation, the shoreline being the most valuable, and we tried to get as many attractive house sites along a shoreline as possible. Another criterion was the quality and character of the roads themselves. We wanted good standards of roads that would not be just adequate to sell the lot, but that those who lived there in the future would have decent access to their home site.[115]

The Community Planning Division in the Department of Regional Planning Studies (DRPS, as it was still called in 1939) thus stepped into the field of subdivisions, in addition to their other work (fig. 96). Frincke notes that some of the standards they developed were later adopted by local planning commissions.[116] The architects, too, extended the scope of their work. Building on the knowledge developed in designing houses for Norris and Hiwassee, they created standards for houses on steep slopes—pertinent to most of the lakeside plots. Richardson insisted that at least some of these houses be given a "distinctive modern treatment," and proposed adding some examples of such modern designs to the collection used by the DRPM (fig. 97).[117] The architects also worked with individual lessees. One of them, George Tomlinson, submitted a rough sketch for a two-story cabin planned for Hurricane Hollow in Norris Reservoir area. Members of the atelier provided feedback, prompting him to revise his design to create—in Richardson's estimation—a "more desirable and compact layout which is, however, *modern* in treatment with simple lean-to roofs and quite contrary to the general architectural treatment of our present summer cabin designs."[118] Richardson's preference for modern design highlights the didactic aspect of the "rustic" parks the TVA had produced.

The leasing of lands at Norris was based on a 1935 amendment to the TVA Act that required the Authority to dispose of any real estate that was surplus to its needs and included recreation in the approved uses for the land.[119] Following the success at Norris and the other early reservoirs, the TVA sought to expand this legal basis. In January 1940 the TVA board submitted a report on its recreational activities to President Roosevelt. The report specifically asked that the law be amended to allow the TVA to "cooperate more fully with local governments and private indi-

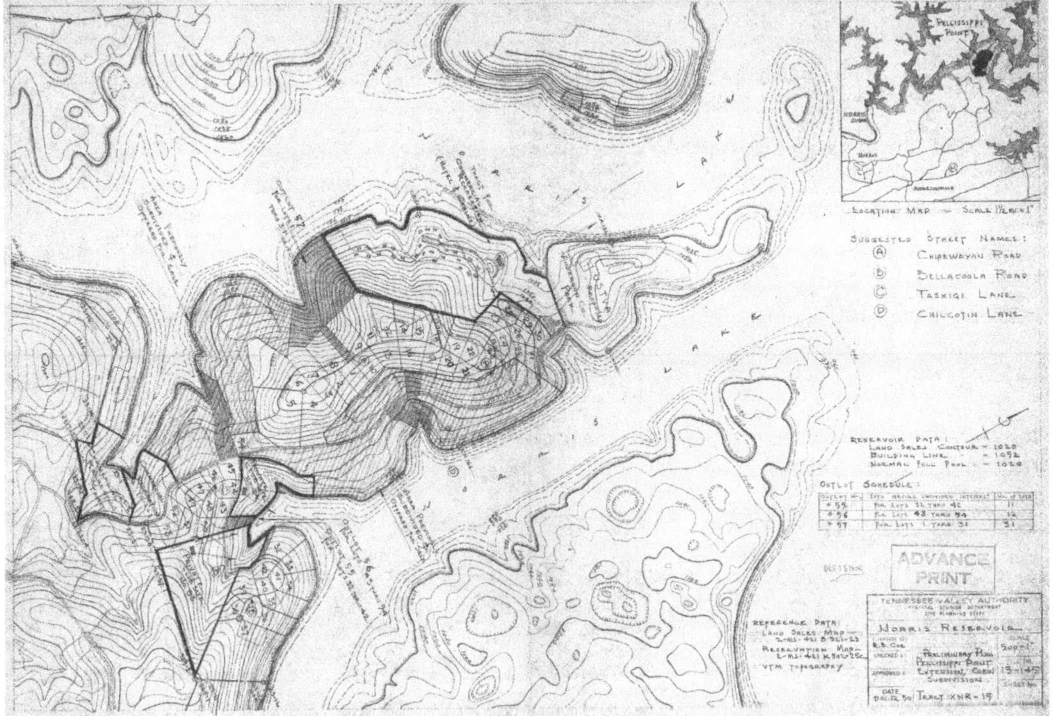


**Figure 96.** A preliminary plan for the "Pellissippi Point Extension Cabin Subdivision," dated December 12, 1950. The TVA was required by Congress to sell land that was surplus to the operation of the dams, and the Department of Regional Studies expanded its practice to include the design of subdivisions. Lots in these sites were sold to the general public—on condition that no permanent structure be built below the maximum water level.

viduals in furthering the recreational development of its reservoir properties."[120] It also requested permission to sell rather than lease land for recreational purposes. Roosevelt's transfer of the report to Congress was accompanied by a reminder that the TVA was created to promote regional planning and not only resource conservation.[121] When Congress approved another amendment to the TVA Act, which allowed such sales, Howes commented that this change "clearly established recreation along with hospitals and schools as a legitimate area of public policy."[122] This legislation was followed by other federal acts—such as the Recreation and Public

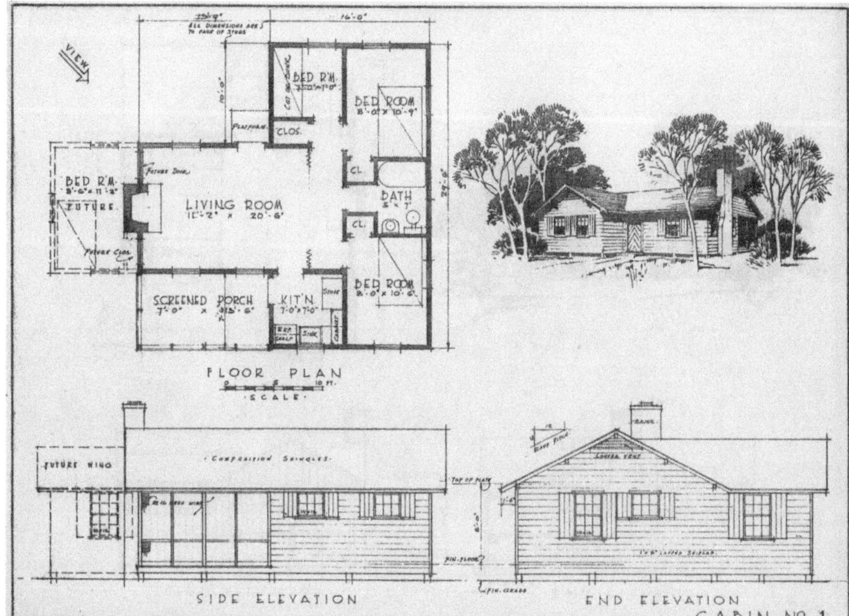


**Figure 97.** Drawing of a cabin—a vacation home—in a subdivision on a TVA reservoir. The TVA architects prepared this and similar drawings for the Department of Reservoir Property Management as example of "proper" development.

Purposes Act of 1954, the Fish and Wild-life Act of 1956, and the Federal Boating Act of 1958—that formally "recognized recreation as an official policy objective."[123]

In 1942 the National Resources Planning Board (NRPB) included recreation among its recommendations for immediate planning in the South, specifically calling for the creation of state systems of nonurban parks as well as the development of travelways and freeways for the "touring public."[124] These plans survived, though the board did not. The NRPB was abolished a year later, as the region and the nation began to move away from "governmental planning" and toward an "economic development" model, a move toward privatization that was typical of the fate of Roosevelt's New Deal policies more generally. [125] Lilienthal, however, was undaunted. He saw this public interest in recreation planning as a vindication of the grassroots approach he espoused, arguing in *TVA: Democracy on the March* that it was a "further illustration of how public interest in a natural resource—the use of

**Figure 98.** A boat dock on Watts Bar Lake.

these beautiful man-made lakes for recreation—and the private interest of businessmen in developing profitable enterprise can be harmonized."[126]

The atelier used the war years to continue to develop agreements with those state authorities that had the largest share in the TVA lakefront property: Alabama, Kentucky, North Carolina, and Tennessee. Howes explained that these memoranda, creating a level of state oversight, ensured that "at the end of World War II, TVA could sell reservoir lands with little fear that shantytowns and honkytonks would undermine their recreation advantages."[127] And it did. As tourists began pouring into the Tennessee Valley following the war, the Authority prepared surveys of surplus land for all of its reservoirs and slowly transferred ownership to government, commercial, and individual hands.[128] By 1950 it had also divested itself of the demonstration parks on the early reservoirs, transferring them to state or local governments. By this time, more than seven million private boats could be found on the chain of lakes yearly.[129] Today it is not always possible to distinguish who is responsible for the many sites that line the lakeshores (fig. 98). In 1965 researchers calculated that "the lakes attracted an estimated 50 million recreation-oriented visits with an associated value of 321 million dollars of ancillary facilities serving these visitors."[130] The TVA lakes, Ian Draves argues, became some of the most popular outdoor recreation sites in the United States. From a crazy idea supported by a small atelier, "recreation became a defining aspect of the relationship between people and nature in the Tennessee River Valley."[131]

# CONCLUSION

World War II changed the pace and focus of the Tennessee Valley Authority project without altering its basic organization, but the decade following the war brought profound change. In 1945 the TVA finished work on Kentucky Dam, the largest of the river dams, and by 1953 it had completed the entire river machine, as proposed in the 1936 "unified plan."[1] Erosion control, a central mission of the land machine, was largely achieved by 1941; in 1943 the TVA introduced a new type of fertilizer based on nitrogen rather than phosphates.[2] The Authority also transferred responsibility for forestry efforts to commissions that were established in each one of the Tennessee Valley states. The power machine, despite its halting start, was also in motion, and by late 1940 the TVA board was happy with its progress in the Valley's rural areas. Public perception of the Authority had also changed dramatically. The American public celebrated its contributions to the war effort and accepted it as an established institution.[3] In 1945 it was one of the largest agencies of the federal government, surpassed only by the US Postal Service, the Treasury Department, and the Department of Agriculture.[4] Lilienthal, who as chairman of the board during the war years had actively shaped TVA policies, left the Authority in September 1946 to head a new federal agency, the Atomic Energy Commission (AEC). About a decade later he established the Development and Resources Corporation, which worked to spread the TVA goals and model across the world.[5]

The TVA would now build steam plants together with its hydroelectric dams, in a dramatic shift of focus. The first such plant, after all, had been constructed during the war near the Watts Bar Dam, specifically to provide the energy needs of the Manhattan project in Oak Ridge; it was authorized by Congress only because of the war emergency. The TVA's requests for further appropriations for similar projects after the war encountered vigorous debate in Washington, though they too were eventually approved.[6] Steam plants were not mentioned in the TVA Act; the production of energy had superseded the original goals and ideals of the Authority—including maintaining a balance between environment and industry. This shift was registered within the organization as well: the new emphasis on producing cheap power gave that division of the Authority extra weight, disrupting the collaborative relationship that had been the basis for regional action. Harcourt A. Morgan appears to have resisted these trends, but he was unable to stem the flow of change.[7] As the TVA changed, it became a machine unmoored from the garden ideal. At its worst, the machine destroyed the garden through the proliferation of coal mines. The opportunities dwindled to pursue the admittedly utopian goal of renewing the garden. As William C. Harvard comments: "TVA now has a history where it once simply had a vision."[8]

Facing a new future, the TVA was determined to remain an independent agency focused on the Tennessee Valley. Franklin D. Roosevelt was gone. President Harry S. Truman was ambivalent toward the TVA, and Dwight D. Eisenhower's administration tried to curtail its role. The TVA also had a new chairman of the board, Gordon R. Clapp, who had risen through the ranks. Clapp had worked closely with Lilienthal and would later join him in directing the Development and Resources Corporation. A graduate of Lawrence College in Wisconsin, Clapp had pursued, but not completed, a master's degree in educational administration at the University of Chicago. He had joined the TVA in 1933 as assistant director of personnel, becoming director in 1936 and general manager of the entire agency in 1939. He became chairman of the board in 1947 and served until 1954, when he failed to gain reappointment. Clapp understood the TVA organizational structure well—no one understood it better—and he saw it as the key to TVA's survival, which was his chief mission. Clapp did not distinguish between regional planning and regional economic development more generally, and under his direction the TVA transformed into a de facto power company. By the late 1940s, moreover, all nonpower programs were subject to an annual review by Congress.[9]

The TVA reduced its staff as it completed its projects.[10] The board emphasized the transfer of responsibility to state and local agencies, whose technical staff the TVA staff had been assisting—ultimately at the expense of their own jobs.[11] The atelier also confronted an unprecedented problem in recruiting personnel because of "an almost total lack of suitable applicants."[12] Carroll A. Towne left in 1946 (with Lilienthal) to work at the AEC and later to serve as a community planner for NASA and retired in 1963. Tracy B. Augur left in 1948 to move to Washington, DC, where he championed decentralization in the spatial sense of dispersal, arguing that "Dispersal Is Good Business."[13] His efforts were outstanding, as David Krugler comments: "Among postwar dispersal advocates, few were as important as Tracy Augur."[14] By this time, Menhinick described the work of the division (no longer a department) he still directed in strictly advisory terms, explaining that it produced studies and recommendations and offered advice, but he did not mention planning and design.[15] In 1946 he too became a roving intellectual and was leading the team studying possible sites for the UN building in New York.[16] After leaving the TVA, Menhinick returned to teaching, at the Georgia Institute of Technology, where he also directed the graduate program in city planning.

Roland A. Wank's and Mario Bianculli's separation from their TVA assignments was gradual. Before leaving, Wank designed a new building for the Division of Chemical Engineering in Muscle Shoals, Alabama. The design included a reception lobby reminiscent of the visitor facilities in other TVA installations. The TVA mostly followed this design when it completed the structure between 1947–50, with some adaptations to new requirements outlined by the chemical engineers.[17] Still, when the building was featured in *Progressive Architecture,* it was billed as a joint project by the TVA and Fellheimer & Wagner, Wank's New York firm. Such credits emphasized the fluid nature of architecture work in the Authority.[18] Still at Fellheimer & Wagner, Wank also worked on designs for the New Jersey Turnpike, including everything from signs and maintenance facilities to rest areas and restaurants. He later formed a successor firm, Wank, Adams, Slavin and Associates, where he worked until his death from cancer in 1970.[19] Wank continued to publish on architecture, demonstrating his continued interest in designs for public spaces within machines. One essay discussed the design of visitor facilities, including a reception room, in small manufacturing plants. These facilities, he explains, welcome visitors who come to inspect the "attractive working conditions, efficient production and painstaking devotion to the excellence of the product."[20]

Bianculli replaced Wank briefly as head architect, but he, too, left for private practice, where he continued to design buildings for power boards and civic centers (see chapter 4). Based in Chattanooga, Tennessee, Bianculli is credited with bringing modernist architecture to the city.[21] His work, however, extended beyond the Tennessee Valley region, and he advised on power projects around the world. He commented in 1970: "Since my retirement I guess I've added another 15 or so [projects], which whether I like it or not, makes me an 'expert' in power house architecture."[22] Bianculli also continued to promote the values he shared with the atelier members. In a 1950 essay, published in the *Tennessee Planner* and titled "Planning and the Architect," he extolled the progress in the region and affirmed the importance of professional guidance in community planning.[23] Seth Harrison Gurnee, Wank's and Bianculli's close colleague, was still working on plans for libraries in 1944, but he disappeared from the roster a year later.[24] Alfred Clauss moved to Philadelphia where he engaged in a varied practice, collaborating with other architects and with his wife, Jane West Clauss.[25] Francis Stuart Chapin Jr., who had contributed to "Communities for Living," worked briefly as a city planner before joining the Department of City and Regional Planning at the University of North Carolina at Chapel Hill, where he was a faculty member from 1949 until 1978. He, too, would continue to promote community planning and professional expertise, contributing, for example, to a report titled, "Planning the Neighborhood: Standards for Healthful Housing."[26]

The skeletal atelier that remained in the TVA continued the projects that were already underway, but its structure now resembled the larger TVA organization. Rather than a group of dedicated individuals collaborating closely, it was dispersed into small groups, each responsible for a portion of what had once been conceived as a unified, idealistic project. Landscape architect Osborne H. Graves supervised the section in charge of Recreation and Public Grounds, working with George L. Richardson, Otto J. Priebe, Harold Frincke, Bernard Krauter, and Raphael Saraceni. This unit provided site planning for the housing the laborers required for the dams completed in the late 1940s and early 1950s. As the river machine was completed, their work turned increasingly to maintenance, a change documented in the commercial publication of Herbert S. Conover's *Grounds Maintenance Handbook* in 1958.[27] Robert M. Howes and Aelred J. Gray also remained with the Authority, continuing to work on recreation and community planning, respectively.[28]

The role of head architect, or what Bianculli called the design team, was now merged with the engineering division of design under Harry B. Tour. After Bianculli left, the TVA appointed a series of three head architects: Rudolph J. Mock, Frederick G. Roth, and Joseph R. Passonneau (who would become an influential dean at Washington University in St. Louis). Tour remembered them as "very high caliber," but he did his best to hire local architects as well.[29] In the late 1940s and 1950s Tour's office absorbed more and more of the architectural work. Many of his staff (including Hiram H. Ostrander, Richard Henry Owens, Laurence V. Gibney, Troy B. Minton, Ralph G. Bowman, and Robert T. Case) remained with the Authority into the 1960s.[30] The Department of Regional Studies, on the other hand, was slowly dismantled. First it was made a division of the Office of Reservoir and Community Relations, under the general manager. In 1951, when that office ceased to exist, the small division lost even more standing. Gray and David A. Johnson pinpoint the end as 1968, when the remnants of the regional planning staff joined with the navigation staff to form not a department but the Division of Navigation and Regional Studies. They explain that "in the process the regional studies group was divided into separate staffs: regional and city planning, economic research, and governmental relations. The result was that there was no longer an independent voice to represent before the Board a totality of area planning interests. The result was a further weakening of the already small influence this staff was able to exert on policy options."[31]

The architects and landscape architects continued—despite this organizational demotion—to explore opportunities to design and build beautiful architecture and landscapes. Mock, Roth, and Passonneau oversaw the design not only of the steam plants but also the power houses and visitor buildings in the last dams.[32] Their quality demonstrates how central Tour had been to the project all along.[33] These centers, however, were still ensnared in the system of racial segregation that marred the TVA's earlier designs—a defect that, paradoxically, may have arisen from its grassroots ethos. In these later designs the stand-alone overlook buildings were given special artistic attention. At Douglas, Fort Patrick Henry, South Holston, and Watauga Dams, the small structures (successfully) compete with the larger dam for attention

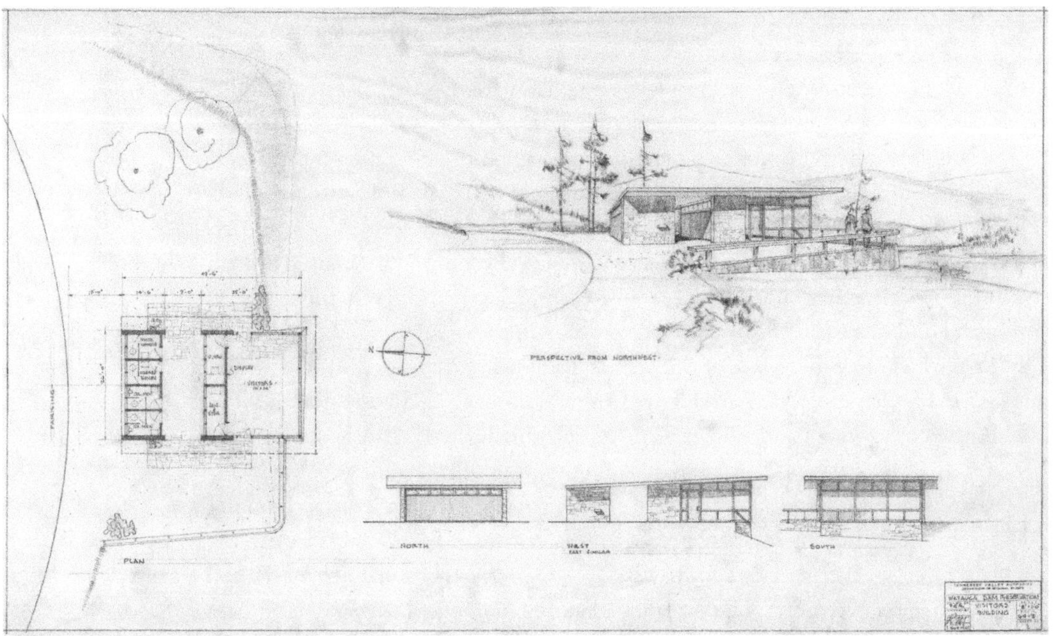


**Figure 99.** A drawing for the visitor center at Watauga Dam approved by Rudolph Mock on October 1, 1947. As head architect, Mock continued the design tradition begun by Roland A. Wank, but he preferred standalone visitor centers. The restrooms in this proposal are still segregated.

(figs. 99, 100). Still, they perform the same functions: to invite residents to make use of the surrounding landscape, to take a break from everyday life through sightseeing, walking, picnicking, boating, and fishing. As such they function at what Leo Marx calls a sentimental level.[34] But they also fulfill Marx's call for meaning: these installations anchor a public park—a garden—as much as they are part of the framework of the dam—a machine.

Utopian ideals are never fully reached, and the garden described here is no exception. The Tennessee Valley has seen many changes, but they are similar to those achieved by government agencies in other parts of the nation.[35] These changes, moreover, are rarely conceived of as elements of a comprehensive regional plan but rather as a series of smaller effects.[36] Neither did the region develop as a planning

**Figure 100.** The visitors' center at Fort Patrick Henry Dam on the South Fork Holston River near Kingsport, Tennessee. Completed in the early 1950s, this is one of the final dams in the TVA's "unified plan" proposed in 1936.

region: planning commissions do exist, and many adopted ordinances and codes the atelier developed while housing the TVA workers as they constructed the river machine.[37] Their power, however, tends to be limited to mitigating problems rather than instigating change. The landscape they preside over is traversed by many beautiful roads, but they are almost always lined with the kinds of shacks and road signs the atelier hoped to eliminate. These roads lead to large swaths of wilderness, but still only a fraction of what Benton MacKaye would have considered necessary to engender a robust culture. Residents and visitors are more likely to enjoy the developed sites: privately owned resorts, marinas and boat docks, state parks, and of course, the TVA maintained gardens.

The severe soil erosion of the 1930s has been stemmed, but the Tennessee Valley was not transformed through the TVA's actions into an agrarian paradise. The rurban setting many residents experience daily has many amenities, but it is a far cry from the vision of self-sufficient thriving communities. The houses in this landscape are connected to the electric grid, and they are better built than the log cabins and many of the pre-TVA farmhouses, but their siting—dependent on land ownership—is often haphazard and insensitive to the topography. The owners and renters of these houses, moreover, are more likely to work in one of the region's industries—especially the hospitality trades—than to engage in farming as a profession. Even more importantly, the Tennessee Valley has seen an influx of technologically skilled outsiders who are able to take advantage of the changes the TVA wrought. But, as Michael J. McDonald and John Muldowny comment, "Those who lived in it as it was have either left it or have been unable, in many respects, to secure the advantages which TVA was created to provide."[38]

This outcome is due, in part, to the nature of utopian ideals: they are mental and not physical constructs. More than that, they are often employed to mask deep contradictions that have no resolution. As James Dahir comments: "The geologists' maxim, 'Most faults are normal,' is ignored by the seeker after perfection."[39] The garden-in-the-machine ideal was shaped by opposing ideas, not least the logic of nature, the power of the machine, individual freedom, and the importance of community. Most glaring, however, was the deep tension between centralized planning and regional conceptions of democracy. Planners, architects, and landscape architects still tend to bemoan a public that refuses to understand their mission rather than recognize how radical their position is (at least in the American spectrum). Those who sought to plan in the Tennessee Valley had to contend with an entrenched system of public action that was already highly stratified. The TVA projects engendered opportunities across the region, but there was nothing inherent in their well-planned communities or dramatic dams that would assure their fair distribution. If anything, the TVA (and the New Deal more generally) "planned their own uplift and that of their broad constituencies, disregarding the less numerous or more powerless groups."[40] The entrenched system also allowed the atelier members to ignore the profound role that segregation and disenfranchisement played (and still play) in producing not only the economic but also the environmental conditions in the region.

Lilienthal's organizational myth of grassroots democracy did offer some resolution to the tension between planning and politics, but it also revealed further faults. For the planners, architects, and landscape architects the most urgent were the blurring between professional and homegrown expertise and between social reform and economic development. Their resolution of these tensions was registered in their work, resulting in competing measures of success. Which was more important: the number of garden cities or the number of planning commissions? Was the design for a house to be evaluated by the comfort it offered or by the number of times it was reproduced across the region? Is the number of tourists a good indication of a park's success, or does the fact that many come from outside of the region make it an irrelevant benchmark? Is knowledge useful if it sits in boxes in the special collections section of a university library? And, of practical importance, if the TVA atelier members develop a building material that is used by commercial companies for the next two decades (until replaced by newer developments), whose success is this—the TVA's or the commercial companies'?

The atelier members' biases in defining the nature of expertise were of special importance, because even as they were imagining a new Tennessee Valley, they were also actively shaping their professions. Regional planning was a new field in the United States in the 1930s, framed only by a utopian ideal and a progressive political position. As one of the largest and most stable New Deal agencies, and the only one with jurisdiction over a geographical region, the TVA was the foremost institution in which to translate these ideas into practice. When confronted by the realities of the institution in which they practiced, the planners and their collaborators responded in two ways. First was a focus on the first stages of the planning process—surveys and the preparation of master plans—rather than the political implementation of these proposals, which was left to other experts. This focus allowed the planners to develop the comprehensive visions they prized but distanced them from the process as a whole. The second approach was to rename some of the planning and design practices as "research." Though this work was not fundamentally different from other design work, the rhetoric carved out a space for professional expertise distinct from the homegrown variety.[41] These shifts from the ideal to the practical had the cumulative effect of moving the planning practice away from direct political engagement toward the more nebulous "public interest." From the messiness of democracy—in the sense of political action—toward managerial organization and technical knowledge. We can only speculate to what extent the atelier members made this shift consciously, but the outcome is that ultimately the garden ideal was replaced with a professional ideal that was more in line with the machine aspects of the TVA's work.

The TVA planners, landscape architects, and architects worked to make their ideas, and the professional standards they had developed, widely accepted. In the early 1940s the leaders of the TVA's Department of Regional Studies simultaneously filled leadership roles in the American Institute of Planners. In 1942 Draper was its president, Menhinick was secretary-treasurer, Augur was completing a term on the board of governors, and Wank was a member of its Committee on the War Effort.[42] Here they broadened the conception of planning from a focus on city planning to a wider engagement with regions. As Augur commented in 1940: "It was wholly characteristic of the planners' professional society to forsake the snug name City Planning Institute, and adopt the vague cognomen of Institute of Planners just when public understanding had advanced to the point where city planner was more apt to be listed under 'city' than under 'plumber' in the classified directory."[43] Their efforts were successful, and after World War II planning discourse in the United States was characterized by the technical bent developed in the TVA (and elsewhere). Indeed, the 1960s challenges to this hegemony (especially Ian McHarg's *Design with Nature*) were, in part, a resurgence of the garden ideal, including an emphasis on regions.[44]

The TVA legacy also impacted the more established professions of landscape architecture and architecture. In landscape design, the garden ideal and the TVA designs created a quandary: Was picturesque design, and the creation of rustic and pastoral-looking landscapes, a *radical* or a *reactionary* practice? The history of the profession of landscape architecture in the second half of the twentieth century still needs to be told, but one important element of the story must be the repeated calls for a radical landscape practice, mirroring the modernist tradition in architecture. For the architects, however, the situation is reversed. The TVA effort helped popularize architectural modernism, a development that was amplified after the war, when it swept both the profession and public attention. For architects, then, the challenge was to remain connected to the larger garden ideal or to develop architecture as an integral element in "environmental design."[45]

The move from the garden ideal to the machine emphasis was a gradual. Even as the TVA planners, architects, and landscape architects were standardizing their practices, they also insisted on collaboration. The term "atelier" is my own; I use it to suggest how effectively they were able to work within the institutional structure and to practice in this creative manner. It may also convey the success they had in integrating their professional and personal lives. They found "opportunity and interest, and not despair," much as Arthur Morgan had hoped.[46] They also attended to what Harcourt Morgan called "a need for 'a reason for being'—a purpose in life beyond that of immediate personal gain and satisfaction—a common mooring to help him understand his importance and his responsibilities in the eternal plan of life."[47] They were able to entertain both utopian ideas and forthright practices at once.[48] Perhaps collaboration—which kept these ideas together—was, ultimately, the garden most successfully cultivated by the atelier.

# NOTES

### Introduction

1. Samuel P. Hays, *Conservation and the Gospel of Efficiency: The Progressive Conservation Movement, 1890–1920* (Pittsburgh, PA: University of Pittsburgh Press, 2015), 11.

2. Leo Marx, "The Idea of Nature in America," *Daedalus* 137, no. 2, On Nature (Spring 2008): 8–21.

3. Frederick Jackson Turner, *The Significance of the Frontier in American History* (Madison: State Historical Society of Wisconsin, 1894).

4. Clayton R. Koppes, "Efficiency/Equity/Esthetics: Towards a Reinterpretation of American Conservation," *Environmental Review: ER* 11, no. 2 (Summer 1987): 130.

5. Neil M. Maher, *Nature's New Deal: The Civilian Conservation Corps and the Roots of the American Environmental Movement* (Oxford: Oxford University Press, 2008), 25.

6. Koppes, "Efficiency/Equity/Esthetics."

7. For a visceral description of these experiences, listen to Johnny Cash's song "Five Feet High and Rising." Cash is describing a flood on the Mississippi in 1937, which was equally devastating to the lowlands of the Tennessee Valley. Wikipedia, s.v. "Five Feet High and Rising," accessed June 13, 2022.

8. Paul K. Conkin, "Intellectural and Political Roots," in *TVA: Fifty Years of Grass-Roots Bureaucracy,* eds. Erwin C. Hargrove and Paul K. Conkin (Urbana: University of Illinois Press, 1983), 3–34.

9. Daniel Schaffer, "Environment and TVA: Toward a Regional Plan for the Tennessee Valley, 1930s," *Tennessee Historical Quarterly* 43, no. 4 (1984): 333–54.

10. Aaron Wildavsky, "TVA and Power Politics," *American Political Science Review* 55, no. 3 (1961): 576.

11. TVA, *Annual Report for the Fiscal Year Ended June 30, 1945,* 35.

12. Thomas K. McCraw, *TVA and the Power Fight, 1933–1939* (Philadelphia: Lippincott, 1971).

13. Benton MacKaye, "Tennessee—Seed of a National Plan," *Graphic Survey* May (1933): 252. Emphasis in original.

14. Walter L. Creese, "TVA as an Allegory," in *Built for the People of the United States: Fifty Years of TVA Architecture,* eds. Marian Moffett and Lawrence Wodehouse (Knoxville: Art and Architecture Gallery, University of Tennessee, 1983), 59.

15. Conkin, "Intellectural and Political Roots," 28.

16. David Ekbladh, "Meeting the Challenge from Totalitarianism: The Tennessee Valley Authority as a Global Model for Liberal Development, 1933–1945," *International History Review* 32, no. 1 (2010).

17. TVA, *Annual Report for the Fiscal Year Ended June 30, 1935,* 35.

18. Maher, *Nature's New Deal,* 87–88.

19. Leo Marx, *The Machine in the Garden: Technology and the Pastoral Ideal in America* (Oxford: Oxford University Press, 1964).

20. Benton MacKaye, "An Appalachian Trail: A Project in Regional Planning," *Journal of the American Institute of Architects* 9, no. 9 (September 1921): 325.

21. Jeffrey L. Meikle, "Leo Marx's the Machine in the Garden," *Technology and Culture* 44, no. 1 (2003): 152.

22. David E. Nye, *Electrifying America: Social Meanings of a New Technology, 1880–1940* (Cambridge, MA: MIT Press, 1990), 289.

23. Patrick Geddes, *Cities in Evolution: An Introduction to the Town Planning Movement and to the Study of Civics* (London: Williams & Norgate, 1915), 128.

24. Ibid., 96. Emphasis added.

25. Bruce Thomas, "Nature and the City in 1920s America: Sunnyside Gardens, Queens, New York," in *Rural and Urban: Architecture between Two Cultures,* ed. Andrew Ballantyne (London: Taylor & Francis, 2009), 137.

26. Ebenezer Howard, *Garden Cities of To-Morrow (Being the Second Edition of "To-Morrow: A Peaceful Path to Real Reform")* (London: S. Sonnenschein & Co., 1902).

27. For a discussion of this idea and the connection between Howard and Geddes, see Robert H. Kargon and Arthur P. Molella, *Invented Edens: Techno-Cities of the Twentieth Century* (Cambridge, MA: MIT Press, 2008).

28. Phillip D'Anieri, "A 'Fruitful Hypothesis'? The Regional Planning Association of America's Hopes for Technology," *Journal of Planning History* 1, no. 4 (2002): 279–89.

29. Derek H. Alderman and Robert N. Brown, "When a New Deal Is Actually an Old Deal: The Role of TVA in Engineering a Jim Crow Racialized Landscape," in *Engineering Earth: The Impacts of Megaengineering Projects,* ed. S. D. Brunn (Dordrecht: Springer Science+Business Media B.V, 2011).

30. Schaffer, "Environment and TVA."

31. Henry D. Shapiro, *Appalachia on Our Mind: The Southern Mountaineers in the American Consciousness, 1870–1920* (Chapel Hill: University of North Carolina Press, 1978).

32. Erwin C. Hargrove, *Prisoners of Myth: The Leadership of the Tennessee Valley Authority, 1933–1990* (Princeton, NJ: Princeton University Press, 1994); Philip Selznick, *TVA and the Grass Roots: A Study in the Sociology of Formal Organization* (Berkeley: University of California Press, 1949).

33. Arthur E. Morgan, "Tennessee Valley Becomes Laboratory for the Nation," *New York Times,* March 24, 1934.

34. The dismissal of Arthur Morgan created enough consternation to produce a Congressional investigation in 1939. The official record was published as *Investigation of the Tennessee Valley Authority, Hearings before the Joint Committee on the Investigation of the Tennessee Valley Authority, Congress of the United States. Seventy-Fifth Congress, Third Session, Pursuant to Public Res. No. 83, Creating a Special Joint Congressional Committee to Make an Investigation of the Tennessee Valley Authority* (Washington. DC: Government Printing Office, 1939).

35. Walter L. Creese, *TVA's Public Planning: The Vision, the Reality* (Knoxville: University of Tennessee Press, 1990).

36. Creese, "TVA as an Allegory," 60.

37. James Marston Fitch, "The Rise of Technology: 1929–1939," *Journal of the Society of Architectural Historians* 24, no. 1 (1965): 75.

38. Marx, *Machine in the Garden.*

39. Ibid.

40. Ibid.

41. Torben Huus Larsen, *Enduring Pastoral: Recycling the Middle Landscape Idea in the Tennessee Valley* (Amsterdam: Rodopi, 2006).

42. Christine Macy and Sarah Bonnemaison, *Architecture and Nature: Creating the American Landscape* (London: Routledge, 2003).

43. David E. Lilienthal, *TVA: Democracy on the March* (New York: Harper, 1944).

44. Tim Culvahouse, ed., *The Tennessee Valley Authority: Design and Persuasion* (New York: Princeton Architectural Press, 2007).

45. David E. Nye, *American Technological Sublime* (Cambridge, MA: MIT Press, 1994), xiii.

46. Todd Smith, "Almost Fully Modern: The TVA's Visual Art Campaign," in *The Tennessee Valley Authority: Design and Persuasion,* ed. Tim Culvahouse (New York: Princeton Architectural Press, 2007).

47. Timothy Mennel, "'Miracle House Hoop-La': Corporate Rhetoric and the Construction of the Postwar American House," *Journal of the Society of Architectural Historians* 63, no. 3 (2008): 340–61.

48. Roland A. Wank, "Time to Choose Our Destiny: Planning or Disintergration?," *Pencil Points* 26. no. 6 (June 1942): 47.

**1. Regional Planning**

1. MacKaye, "Tennessee—Seed of a National Plan," 251.

2. Edward K. Spann, *Designing Modern America: The Regional Planning Association of America and Its Members* (Columbus: Ohio State University Press, 1996); D'Anieri, "A 'Fruitful Hypothesis'?"

3. Avigail Sachs, *Environmental Design: Architecture, Politics, and Science in Postwar America* (Charlottesville: University of Virginia Press, 2018).

4. "Report on the Appalachian Project," *Journal of the American Institute of Architects* 11, no. 7 (July 1923): 292–93.

5. "The Regional Planning Association of America," *Journal of the American Institute of Architects* 11, no. 7 (July 1923): 292.

6. Ben A. Minteer, *The Landscape of Reform: Civic Pragmatism and Environmental Thought in America* (Cambridge, MA: MIT Press, 2006).

7. Ibid.

8. For a discussion of Geddes's theories, see Volker M. Welter, *Biopolis: Patrick Geddes and the City of Life* (Cambridge, MA: MIT Press, 2002).

9. Patrick Geddes, "The Twofold Aspect of the Industrial Age: Paleotechnic and Neotechnic," *Town Planning Review* 3, no. 3 (October 1912): 176–87.

10. Geddes, *Cities in Evolution,* 63.

11. Ibid., 96. Emphasis added.

12. Howard, *Garden Cities of To-Morrow.*

13. For a discussion of this idea and the connection between Howard and Geddes, see Kargon and Molella, *Invented Edens.*

14. Dugald Macfadyen, "Sociological Effects of Garden Cities," *Social Forces* 14, no. 2 (December 1935): 250–56.

15. Peter Hall, "The Neotechnic Vision," *Built Environment (1978–)* 8, no. 4, Classics Revisited (1982): 217–18.

16. Kermit C. Parsons, "Collaborative Genius: The Regional Planning Association of America," *Journal of the American Planning Association* 60, no. 4 (1994): 462–82.

17. Lewis Mumford, *The Culture of Cities* (New York: Harcourt, Brace, 1938).

18. Ibid.; Catherine Bauer, *Modern Housing* (Boston: Houghton Mifflin, 1934).

19. "Regional Planning Association of America."

20. MacKaye, "An Appalachian Trail."

21. G. Donald Hudson, "Geography and Regional Planning," *Journal of Geography* 34 (October 1935): 270–71.

22. Ibid., 269.

23. MacKaye, "Tennessee—Seed of a National Plan," 252.

24. Larry Anderson, *Benton MacKaye: Conservationist, Planner, and Creator of the Appalachian Trail* (Baltimore, MD: Johns Hopkins University Press, 2002), 250.

25. See Aelred J. Gray and David A. Johnson, *The TVA Regional Planning and Development Program: The Transformation of an Institution and Its Mission* (Aldershot, UK: Ashgate, 2005).

26. Anderson, *Benton MacKaye,* 250.

27. Martin Weil, "Frederick Gutheim Dies," *Washington Post,* October 4, 1993.

28. Origin of the Regional Planning and Development Concept in TVA Legislation (Memo from Howard K. Menhinick to L. L. Durisch and Tracy B. Augur, February 6, 1943), in Gray and Johnson, *TVA Regional Planning and Development Program* (Aldershot, UK: Ashgate, 2005).

29. Conkin, "Intellectual and Political Roots," 24.

30. TVA, *Annual Report for the Fiscal Year Ended June 30, 1935,* 35.

31. Hargrove, *Prisoners of Myth,* 24.

32. Robert E. Barde, "Arthur E. Morgan, First Chairman of TVA," *Tennessee Historical Quarterly* 30, no. 3 (1971): 299–314.

33. Gray and Johnson, *TVA Regional Planning and Development Program,* 9.

34. Arthur E. Morgan, "Tennessee Valley Becomes Laboratory for the Nation," *New York Times,* March 25, 1934.

35. Arthur E. Morgan, "Vitality and Formalism in Government," *Social Forces* 13, no. 1 (October 1934): 4.

36. "Social and Economic Implications of TVA," *Civil Engineering* 5, no. 12 ( December 1935): 757.

37. Margaret Crawford, "Earle S. Draper and the Company Town in the American South," in *The Company Town: Architecture and Society in the Early Industrial Age,* ed. John S. Garner (New York: Oxford University Press, 1992), 139–71.

38. Crawford, "Earle S. Draper and the Company Town," 161.

39. Oral History of the Tennessee Valley Authority, Interview with Dr. Earle S. Draper, December 30, 1969, 4, Mississippi Valley Archives, John Willard Brister Library, Memphis State University (collection hereafter cited as Oral History of the TVA, MVA).

40. TVA, *Annual Report for the Fiscal Year Ended June 30, 1935.*

41. Tracy B. Augur, "Industrial Growth in America and the Garden City" (MLA thesis, Harvard University, Cambridge, MA, 1921).

42. Tracy B. Augur, "The Size and Spacing of Urban Communities," *Journal of the American Institute of Planners* 15, no. 3 (1949): 42.

43. Oral History of the TVA, Draper Interview, MVA.

44. "Location of Urban Offices, August 1942," Reservoir Properties Papers, Box 33, National Archives at Atlanta (hereafter cited NAA).

45. Macy, "Architect's Office of the Tennessee Valley Authority," in Culvahouse, *Tennessee Valley Authority* (New York: Princeton Architectural Press, 2007), 26.

46. Anderson, *Benton MacKaye.*

47. Gray and Johnson, *TVA Regional Planning and Development Program,* 23.

48. Daniel Schaffer, "Benton MacKaye: The TVA Years," *Planning Perspectives* 5, no. 1 (1990): 5–21.

49. Benton MacKaye, "Regional Planning and Ecology," *Ecological Monographs* 10, no. 3 (July 1940): 349–53.

50. Anderson, *Benton MacKaye,* 254.

51. Schaffer, "Benton MacKaye: TVA Years."

52. Sonja Dümpelmann, "Three Men in Search of a Modern Arcadia: Landscape Architecture, Planning, and Conservation between Tradition and Modernism (Review Essay)," *Journal of Planning History* 6, no. 2 (May 2007): 166–86; Anderson, *Benton MacKaye,* 265.

53. Ronald Reed Boyce, "Geographers and the Tennessee Valley Authority," *Geographical Review* 94, no. 1 (January 2004): 23–42.

54. W. H. Droze, "TVA and the Ordinary Farmer," *Agricultural History* 53, no. 1, Southern Agriculture since the Civil War: A Symposium (January 1979): 188–202.

55. MacKaye, "Tennessee—Seed of a National Plan," 252.

56. Gray and Johnson, *TVA Regional Planning and Development Program,* 13.

57. "Annual Report of the Land Planning and Housing Division for Fiscal Year Ended June, 1934," Regional Studies Papers, Box 9, Folder 4G1, NAA.

58. TVA Commemorative Ceramic Plate, Artifact 2017.003, McClung Historical Collection, Knox County Public Library, Knoxville, TN.

59. Landscape architect Harold C. Fruncke, who was part of the team, attributed the name to

Tracy Augur. See Oral History of the TVA, Interview with Harold C. Frincke, December 30, 1970, MVA.

60. Earle S. Draper, "The TVA Freeway," *The American City* 49, no. 2 (February 1934): 47–48.

61. Ibid.

62. Department of Regional Planning Studies, TVA, *Recreational Development of the Southern Highlands Region: A Study of the Use and Control of Scenic and Recreational Resources* (Knoxville: Tennessee Valley Authority, 1938), 37.

63. Earle S. Draper, "Demonstration Parks in the Tennessee Valley," *Architectural Record* (June 1937): 126.

64. TVA, *Annual Report for the Fiscal Year Ended June 30, 1935.*

65. TVA, *The Scenic Resources of the Tennessee Valley: A Descriptive and Pictorial Inventory* (Washington, DC: Government Printing Office, 1938), 118–19.

66. TVA, *The Norris Project, a Comprehensive Report on the Planning, Design, Construction, and Initial Operations of the Tennessee Valley Authority's First Water Control Project, Technical Report No. 1* (Washington, DC: Government Printing Office, 1940), 174.

67. Oral History of the TVA, Draper Interview, 13, MVA.

68. Tracy B. Augur, "The Planning of the Town of Norris," *American Architect* 148 (1936): 24–25.

69. Oral History of the TVA, Interviews with Carroll A. Towne, December 31, 1969, second interview, 2–3, MVA.

70. Oral History of the TVA, Interview with Osborne H. Graves, June 11, 1971, 6, MVA.

71. Oral History of the TVA, Frinke Interview, part 2, p. 24, MVA.

72. Oral History of the TVA, Graves Interview, 9, MVA.

73. "Landscape Architectural Exhibition at the Pennsylvania State College," *Pencil Points* (December 1929): 872.

74. Oral History of the TVA, Towne Interviews, MVA.

75. "Norris Buildings Report," Construction Project Reports, Box 3, NAA.

76. Geddes, *Cities in Evolution.*

77. Oral History of the TVA, Draper Interview, 11, MVA.

78. Marian Moffett, "Looking to the Future: The Architecture of Roland Wank," *ARRIS Journal of the Southeast Chapter of the Society of Architectural Historians,* no. 1 (1989).

79. Mardges Bacon, "The Federation of Architects, Engineers, Chemists and Technicians (FAECT): The Politics and Social Practice of Labor," *Journal of the Society of Architectural Historians* 76, no. 4 (December 2017).

80. "Graduates of the Class of 1911," *Technology Architectural Record, Published Quarterly by the MIT Architectural Society* 4, no. 3 (June 1911).

81. "Design Awards for First Term, 1909–1910," *Technology Architectural Record, Published Quarterly by the MIT Architectural Society* 3, no. 2 (March 1910).

82. 1,946,970 Door and Operating Means Therefor (Patented February 13, 1934).

83. TVA, *Annual Report for the Fiscal Year Ended June 30, 1934.*

84. Brent Cebul, "Creative Competition: Georgia Power, the Tennessee Valley Authority, and the Creation of a Rural Consumer Economy, 1934–1955," *Journal of American History* 105, no. 1 (June 2018): 45–70.

85. Oxford Art Online, s.v. "Wank, Roland," by Marian Moffett, 2003, accessed July 20, 2022; Fredrerick A. Gutheim, "Roland Wank, 1898–1970," *Architectural Forum* 133, no. 2 (September 1970): 58–59; Moffett, "Looking to the Future."

86. Marx, *Machine in the Garden.*

87. Earle S. Draper, "The TVA's Forgotten Town: Norris, Tennessee," *Landscape Architecture,* 78, no. 2 (March 1988): 96–100. See also Creese, *TVA's Public Planning.*

88. Stephen Wallace Taylor, "Building the Back of Beyond: Government Authority, Community Life, and Economic Development in the Upper Little Tennessee Valley, 1880–1992" (PhD diss., University of Tennessee, Knoxville, 1996).

89. "No Monotony in TVA Houses" (Press Release by Earle S. Draper, Director of LP&H, TVA, for Release at Will, April 12, 1934), Regional Studies Papers, Box 46, Folder 156 N 132 Norris Housing 2 of 2, NAA.

90. Phoebe Cutler, *The Public Landscape of the New Deal* (New Haven, CT: Yale University Press, 1985).

91. Geddes, *Cities in Evolution,* 96. Emphasis added.

92. "Tennessee Valley Authority," *Architectural Forum* 71, no. 2 (August, 1939). The Library of Congress has similar photographs; see, for example, accessed June 23, 2022, www.loc.gov/item/2017871884/.

93. TVA, *Annual Report for the Fiscal Year Ended June 30, 1934,* 48.

94. "Annual Report of the Division of Land Planning & Housing, for Fiscal Year July 1, 1935 to June 30, 1936," Regional Studies Papers, Box 9, Folder 4G1, 29, NAA.

95. TVA, *Annual Report for the Fiscal Year Ended June 30, 1950.*

96. RG 142, Records of the Tennessee Valley Authority, 1918–2000, Lewis Hine Photographs for the Tennessee Valley Authority (TVA), 1933–1933 [*sic*], National Archives at College Park.

97. See National Archives Catalog online, accessed July 20, 2022, https://catalog.archives.gov/id/532731.

98. Thomas C. Hubka and Judith T. Kenny, "Examining the American Dream: Housing Standards and the Emergence of a National Housing Culture, 1900–1930," *Perspectives in Vernacular Architecture* 13, no. 1 (2006): 52.

99. See, for example, National Archives Catalog online, accessed June 23, 2022, https://catalog.archives.gov/id/532791, and other images of Mrs. Jacob Stooksbury's home in Loyston, Tennessee.

100. Hubka and Kenny, "Examining the American Dream," 59.

101. Thomas C. Hubka, *How the Working-Class Home Became Modern, 1900–1940* (Minneapolis: University of Minnesota Press, 2020).

102. Max H. Falkner, *Planning the Rural Home,* Circular 38, November 1937 (Knoxville: Agricultural Extension Service, University of Tennessee), 1.

103. TVA, *Annual Report for the Fiscal Year Ended June 30, 1935,* 35.

104. Paul K. Conkin, *A Revolution Down on the Farm: Transformation of American Agriculture since 1929* (Lexington: University Press of Kentucky, 2008).

105. Ibid.

106. Michael J. McDonald and John Muldowny, *TVA and the Dispossessed: The Resettlement of Population in the Norris Dam Area* (Knoxville: University of Tennessee Press, 1982).

107. Ibid., 266–67.

108. Matthew L. Downs, *Transforming the South: Federal Development in the Tennessee Valley, 1915–1960* (Baton Rouge: Louisiana State University Press, 2014), 83.

109. Carlton R. Ball, *A Study of the Work of the Land-Grant Colleges in the Tennessee Valley Area in Cooperation with the Tennessee Valley Authority* ([Place unknown]: Tennessee Valley Agricultural Correlating Committee, 1939), 27.

110. "Annual Report of the Division of Land Planning & Housing, for Fiscal Year July 1, 1935 to June 30, 1936," 29, Regional Studies Papers, Box 9, Folder 4G1, NAA.

111. Melissa Walker, "African Americans and TVA Reservoir Property Removal: Race in a New Deal Program," *Agricultural History* 72, no. 2, African Americans in Southern Agriculture:1877–1945 (1998): 417–28.

112. Ball, *Study of the Work of the Land-Grant Colleges,* 27–28.

113. Stuart Chase, "TVA: The New Deal's Greatest Asset, II. Broadening the Exchange Base," *The Nation,* June 10, 1936.

114. "Organizational Chart for the TVA," Board of Directors Papers, Box 157 Folder 321 (2) Duties and Activities, Power and Functions, General Policy, Etc., NAA.

### 2. A Planning Region

1. Paul Conkin describes him as an "early version of Buckminster Fuller—full of enthusiasm, innovative, almost utopian in his dreams, yet always a bit superficial." Conkin, "Intellectural and Political Roots," 24.

2. Harcourt A. Morgan and William M. Landless, "The Common Mooring—a Working Philosophy," *High School Journal* 30, no. 3, Health Educators at Work (May 1947): 117.

3. Chase, "TVA: II. Broadening the Exchange Base."

4. Elizabeth Cromley, "Domestic Space Transformed, 1850–2000," in *Architectures: Modernism and After,* ed. Andrew Ballantyne (Oxford: Blackwell, 2003).

5. Schaffer, "Environment and TVA."

6. Maher, *Nature's New Deal,* 61.

7. Conkin, "Intellectural and Political Roots."

8. Conkin, *Revolution Down on the Farm,* 72.

9. Koppes, "Efficiency/Equity/Esthetics," 131.

10. James Rorty, "TVA's H. A. Morgan, Made the TVA Safe for the Tennessee Valley," *The Commonweal,* June 18, 1948, 226–30.

11. Proposed Statement of Policy in the Planning Activities of the Tennessee Valley Authority (Memo from H. A. Morgan to A. E. Morgan and David E. Lilienthal, October 3, 1933), Board of Directors Papers, Box 134, Folder 221.31, NAA.

12. TVA, *Annual Report for the Fiscal Year Ended June 30, 1938,* 1.

13. TVA, *Annual Report of for the Fiscal Year Ended June 30, 1937.*

14. For an image of one such farmer, Julien Case, see photograph by Arthur Rothstein, Library of Congress, accessed June 16, 2022, www.loc.gov/item/2017832451/.

15. Harry B. Williams, "The County Agent Teaches Resource Use," *High School Journal* 29, no. 3 (May 1946): 167–71.

16. Droze, "TVA and the Ordinary Farmer," 194.

17. Willis M. Baker and William M. Landess, "Education for Sustained Regional Productivity," *Journal of Educational Sociology* 15, no. 3, The TVA Program—The Regional Approach to General Welfare (November 1941): 160–74.

18. David A. Lilienthal, "The TVA: An Experiment in the 'Grass Roots' Administration of Federal Functions," Address before the Southern Political Science Association, Knoxville, TN, November 10, 1939, 15.

19. Oral History of the TVA, Interview with Harold V. Miller, April 29, 1971, part 2, pp. 2–3, MVA.

20. Conkin, *Revolution Down on the Farm.*

21. Larsen, *Enduring Pastoral.*

22. Hargrove, *Prisoners of Myth.*

23. Selznick, *TVA and the Grass Roots.*

24. Nancy L. Grant, *TVA and Black Americans: Planning for the Status Quo* (Philadelphia: Temple University Press, 1990).

25. Rorty, "TVA's H. A. Morgan."

26. Hargrove, *Prisoners of Myth.*

27. Oral History of the TVA, Draper Interview, MVA.

28. Relation of Geographers and Foresters to Land Planning (Memo by C. M. Richards to Multiple Reciepients, August 20, 1936), Board of Directors Papers, Box 220, Folder 913.1, City, Community, Town Planning, and Zoning, NAA.

29. Responsibilities and Activities of the Division of Land Planning & Housing—TVA (Memo by Earle S. Draper, N.D.), Board of Directors Papers, Box 162, Folder 321-75-4 (2), Regional Studies Division: Duties, Activities, Policy and Procedure, Etc., NAA.

30. I*nvestigation of the Tennessee Valley Authority,* 3704.

31. Schaffer, "Benton MacKaye: The TVA Years."

32. Oral History of the TVA, Interview with Mario Bianculli, March 25, 1970, p. 13, MVA.

33. Responsibilities and Activities of the Division of Land Planning & Housing—TVA (Memo by Earle S. Draper, n.d.), Board of Directors Papers, NAA.

34. "Concise Defintion of Regional Planning," by E. S. Draper, November 14, 1934, Board of Directors Papers, Box 220, Folder 913.1, City, Community, Town Planning and Zoning, NAA.

35. Howard K. Menhinick and Lawrence Logan Durisch, "Tennessee Valley Authority: Planning in Operation," *Town Planning Review* 24, no. 2 (1953): 144–45.

36. "1940 Institute Roster," *Journal of the American Institute of Planners* 6, no. 1 (1940): 25–28.

37. "The Land Planning Program, Fiscal Year 1935–1936," Board of Directors Papers, Box 162, Folder 321-75-4 (2), 7, NAA.

38. "Annual Report of the Land Planning and Housing Division for the Fiscal Year Ended June 30, 1937, Earle S. Draper, Director," Regional Studies Papers, Box 9, Folder 4G1, NAA (hereafter cited as "Annual Report LP&H, 1937").

39. Boyce, "Geographers and the Tennessee Valley Authority."

40. Ibid.

41. T. Levron Howard, "The Social Scientist in the Tennessee Valley Authority Program," *Social Forces* 15, no. 1 (October 1936): 29–34.

42. "History and Indigenous Culture of Southern Highlands Region," LP&H, TVA, August, 1936, Regional Studies Papers, Box 45, Folder 123, L Southern Highlands, Vol. 4, NAA.

43. "Report on Relocation of 1,834 Families from Norris Purchase Area," by Charles M. Stephenson, Research Section, Social and Economic Division, August 19, 1935, Regional Studies Papers, Box 45, Folder 150 E 24, Relocation of 1,834 Families from Norris, NAA.

44. Letter from Charles H. Judd to Harcourt A. Morgan, April 22, 1938, Board of Directors Papers, Box 91, Folder 031.6-3, National Resources Planning Board, NAA.

45. Minutes of Meeting, 10:00 a.m. to 12:50 p.m., February 10, 1939, Board of Directors Papers, Box 162, Folder 321-75-4 (2), NAA.

46. "Regional Planning in the Tennessee Valley, Knoxville, Tennessee, August 8, 1938," Board of Directors Papers, Box 288, Folder 221.31, NAA.

47. "Purchase Boundary Suggestions for the Chatuge and Nottely Reservoirs: A Summary of Departmental Reports, August 15, 1941," Engineering Project Histories Papers, Box 336, NAA.

48. "Annual Report of the Division of Land Planning & Housing, for Fiscal Year July 1, 1935 to June 30, 1936," 5–6, Regional Studies Papers, Box 9, Folder 4G1, NAA.

49. Clarence Lewis Hodge, *The Tennessee Valley Authority: A National Experiment in Regionalism* (Washington, DC: American University Press, 1938).

50. Oral History of the TVA, Draper Interview, MVA.

51. Resolution Creating Department of Regional Planning Studies and Stating Policies Relating Thereto (Memo from E. S. Draper to John B. Blandford, July 7, 1937), Board of Directors Papers, Box 162, Folder 321-75-4 (1), Regional Studies Division: Creation, Organization, Etc., NAA.

52. Administrative Bulletin No. 8, July 13, 1937, Board of Directors Papers, Box 138, Folder 3320-5-1-1, Administrative Bulletins 1–52, NAA.

53. Future Work and Policy (Memo from Louis Grandgent to Carroll A. Towne, August 25, 1937), George Richardson Files, Box 14, Folder Prefabrication—Truckable Unit House, 2, NAA.

54. Lilienthal, "TVA: Experiment in 'Grass Roots' Administration."

55. *Investigation of the Tennessee Valley Authority*, 3723.

56. "Annual Report of the Department of Regional Planning Studies, for the Fiscal Ended June 30, 1938," Regional Studies Papers, Box 9, Folder 4G1, NAA.

57. "Annual Report of the Division of Land Planning & Housing, for Fiscal Year July 1, 1935 to June 30, 1936," 33, Regional Studies Papers, Box 9, Folder 4G1, NAA.

58. Administrative Bulletin No. 49-1, April 17, 1939, Organization of the Regional Planning Council Description and Membership, Board of Directors Papers, Box 138, Folder 320-5-1-1 Administrative Bulletins 1–52, NAA.

59. *Investigation of the Tennessee Valley Authority*, 3706.

60. "Report of Meeting of the Regional Planning Council in the Office of the General Manager, January 26, 1938 at 10 a.m.," Board of Directors Papers, Box 162, Folder 321-75-4 (2), NAA.

61. For further discussion, see Reinhold Martin, "Abolish Oil," *Places Journal*, accessed August 1, 2020, https://placesjournal.org/article/abolish-oil/.

62. Brian Black, "Organic Planning: Ecology and Design in the Landscape of the Tennessee

Valley Authority, 1933–1945," in *Environmentalism in Landscape Architecture,* ed. Michel Conan (Washington, DC: Dumbarton Oaks Research Library and Collection, 2000), 79.

63. Oral History of the TVA, Interview with Charles Krutch, November 10, 1969, 35, MVA.

64. Casey P. Cater, *Regenerating Dixie: Electric Energy and the Modern South* (Pittburgh: University of Pittburgh Press, 2019), 6.

65. Downs, *Transforming the South,* 101.

66. Robert Rook, "Race, Water, and Foreign Policy: The Tennessee Valley Authority's Global Agenda Meets 'Jim Crow,'" *Diplomatic History* 1 (January 2004): 55–81.

67. Schaffer, "Environment and TVA," 352.

68. David Cushman Coyle, ed., *Electric Power on the Farm: The Story of Electricity, Its Usefulness on Farms, and the Movement to Electrify Rural America* (Washington, DC: Government Printing Office, 1936).

69. M. M. Samuels, "Electricity Puts Its Hand to the Plow," *Pencil Points* 23, no. 12 (December 1942): 60.

70. Thomas K. McCraw, "Triumph and Irony—the TVA," *Proceedings of the IEEE* 54, no. 9 (September 1976): 1372–80.

71. Nye, *Electrifying America,* 302.

72. For a detailed discussion of this process, see McCraw, *TVA and the Power Fight.*

73. Richard Lowitt, "The TVA, 1933–1945," in *TVA: Fifty Years of Grass-Roots Bureaucracy,* ed. Erwin C. Hargrove and Paul K. Conkin (Urbana: University of Illinois Press, 1983), 40.

74. Downs, *Transforming the South.*

75. "Annual Report of the Department of Regional Planning Studies Fiscal Year 1939," Regional Studies Papers, Box 9, Folder 4G1, NAA.

76. David E. Lilienthal, *TVA: Democracy on the March* (10th anniversary ed.) (New York: Harper & Row, 1953), 8.

77. Lilienthal, "The TVA: Experiment in 'Grass Roots' Administration."

78. Nye, *Electrifying America.*

79. Cater, *Regenerating Dixie,* 114.

80. Lilienthal, *TVA: Democracy on the March* (10th anniversary ed.), 20.

81. Hargrove, *Prisoners of Myth.*

82. Droze, "TVA and the Ordinary Farmer," 194.

83. Samuels, "Electricity Puts Its Hand to the Plow," 60.

84. "Proposals for Electric Demonstration Farms" (Attached to Letter from George W. Kable to F. W. Hunter, September 26, 1936), Board of Directors Papers, Box 223, Folder 926.9–36, Rural Electrification, NAA.

85. Ibid.

86. Michelle Mock, "The Electric Home and Farm Authority: 'Model T Appliances' and the Modernization of the Home Kitchen in the South," *Journal of Southern History* 80, no. 1 ( February 2014): 73–108.

87. Barry M. Katz, "Ideology and Engineering in the Tennessee Valley," in *The Tennessee Valley Authority: Design and Persuasion,* ed. Tim Culvahouse (New York: Princeton Architectural Press, 2007), 80–95.

88. TVA, *How Cheap Electricity Pays Its Way—TVA* (Washington, DC: Government Printing Office, 1938); Proposed Program of Electrical Education outside the TVA Service Area (Memo from W. I. Nichols to Llewellyn Evans, June 19, 1935), Board of Directors Papers, Box 223, Folder 926.9–36, Rural Electrification, NAA.

89. G. E. Henderson and Jane A. Roberts, *Wiring and Lighting the Farmstead: A Combined Text and Laboratory Manual* (Knoxville: Department of Agricultural Industries, Tennessee Valley Authority, 1939).

90. Mock, "Electric Home and Farm Authority,."

91. George D. Munger, Carroll A. Towne, and Philip W. Voltz, "Education in the Adaptation of the Valley People to New Factors in the Environment," *Journal of Educational Sociology* 15, no. 3, The TVA Program—The Regional Approach to General Welfare (November 1941): 174–84.

92. Cebul, "Creative Competition."

93. Mock, "Electric Home and Farm Authority."

94. Gregory B. Field, "'Electricity for All': The Electric Home and Farm Authority and the Politics of Mass Consumption, 1932–1935," *Business History Review* 64, no. 1, Government and Business (Spring 1990): 58.

95. Hargrove, *Prisoners of Myth.*

96. Ibid.

97. Lilienthal, "The TVA: Experiment in 'Grass Roots' Administration."

98. Field, "Electricity for All."

99. Hargrove, *Prisoners of Myth.*

100. Benjamin Higgins, "The American Frontier and the TVA," *Society* 32, no. 3 (1995): 34–42.

101. William Wade Drumright, "A River for War, a Watershed to Change: The Tennessee Valley Authority during World War II" (PhD diss., University of Tennessee, Knoxville, 2005).

102. Hargrove, *Prisoners of Myth.*

103. Downs, *Transforming the South,* 119.

104. Ekbladh, "Meeting the Challenge from Totalitarianism."

105. Creese, "TVA as an Allegory," 61.

106. Lilienthal, "The TVA: Experiment in 'Grass Roots' Administration," 29.

107. Lilienthal, *TVA: Democracy on the March.*

108. Memo from T. B. Augur to C. A. Towne, February 4, 43, Reservoir Properties Papers, Box 33, NAA.

109. Lilienthal, *TVA: Democracy on the March* (10th anniversary ed.), 186–87.

110. Julian Huxley, *TVA: Adventure in Planning* (Surry: Architectural Press, 1943).

111. Ekbladh, "Mr. TVA."

112. Wank, "Time to Choose Our Destiny," 45.

113. "Planned Communities: A Speculative Survey of Their Future," *Architectural Record* 93, no. 2 (February 1943): 48.

114. Downs, *Transforming the South,* 97.

115. Conkin, "Intellectural and Political Roots."

116. Downs, *Transforming the South,* 94.

117. TVA, *Navigation and Economic Growth, Tennessee River Experience: A Report Prepared Pursuant to Section 22 of the TVA Act and Executive Order No. 6161 (June 8, 1933)* (Knoxville: Tennessee Valley Authority, 1966).

118. Downs, *Transforming the South.*

119. Hodge, *Tennessee Valley Authority: A National Experiment.*

120. Gray and Johnson, *TVA Regional Planning and Development Program,* 50.

121. "The Land Planning Program, Fiscal Year 1935–1936," 20–21, Board of Directors Papers, Box 162, Folder 321-75-4 (2).

122. Oral History of the TVA, Bianculli Interview, 7, MVA.

123. "Annual Report of the Division of Land Planning & Housing, for Fiscal Year July 1, 1935 to June 30, 1936," Engineering Project Histories Papers, NAA.

124. "Basic Reports of Land Planning & Housing Division, Tennessee Valley Authority, May 1, 1936," Engineering Project Histories Papers, Box 40, NAA.

125. "Annual Report of the Division of Land Planning & Housing, for Fiscal Year July 1, 1935 to June 30, 1936," 22, Engineering Project Histories Papers, NAA.

126. Paul E. Ryan and Raymond F. Leonard, "Industrial Studies in Physical Regional Planning," *Planners' Journal* 2, no. 2 (1936): 29–34.

127. "Annual Report of the Department of Regional Planning Studies Fiscal Year 1939," Regional Studies Papers, Box 9, Folder 4G1, NAA.

128. "Summary of Studies of the Research Section in the Social and Economic Division Relating to Norris Commercial Facilities," Regional Studies Papers, Box 46, Folder 156 T 345, Summary of Studies 1935, NAA.

129. Editor Howard K. Menhinick and Consulting Editor Henry V. Hubbard, "Editorial," *1,* no. 1 (1935).

130. Theodora Kimball Hubbard and Henry Vincent Hubbard, *Our Cities Today and Tomorrow: A Survey of Planning and Zoning Progress in the United States* (Cambridge, MA: Harvard University Press, 1929), vi.

131. Ibid.

132. Ibid., 360.

133. Downs, *Transforming the South,* 95.

134. Oral History of the TVA, Interview with Howard K. Menhinick, June 24, 1970, 34–39, MVA.

135. Hargrove, *Prisoners of Myth.*

136. "Annual Report of the Division of Land Planning & Housing, for Fiscal Year July 1, 1935 to June 30, 1936," 13, Engineering Project Histories Papers, NAA.

137. Oral History of the TVA, Menhinick Interview, 34–39, MVA.

138. Downs, *Transforming the South,* 147.

139. James Dahir, *Region Building—Community Development Lessons from the Tennessee Valley* (New York: Harper & Brothers, 1955), 87.

140. Aelred J. Gray and Victor Roterus, *The Tennessee River Valley: A Case Study* (Washington, DC: [Housing Division, International Cooperation Administration], 1960).

141. Downs, *Transforming the South.*

142. "Basic Reports of Land Planning & Housing Division, Tennessee Valley Authority, May 1, 1936," Engineering Project Histories Papers, Box 40, NAA.

143. Gordon R. Clapp and Howard K. Menhinick, "The Approach of the TVA to the Solution of Regional Problems," *Journal of Educational Sociology* 15, no. 3, The TVA Program—The Regional Approach to General Welfare (1941): 136–49.

144. "Annual Report of the Department of Regional Planning Studies Fiscal Year 1939," Regional Studies Papers, Box 9, Folder 4G1, NAA.

145. Albert Lepawsky, "Government Planning in the South," *Journal of Politics* 10, no. 3 (1948): 536–67.

146. Oral History of the TVA, Menhinick Interview, 32–34, MVA.

147. Ian Draves, "'It's Easier to Pick a Tourist Than It Is a Bale of Cotton': The Rise of Recreation on the Great Lakes of the South," *Southern Cultures* 20, no. 3, Southern Waters (2014): 87–104.

148. Lilienthal, *TVA: Democracy on the March* (10th anniversary ed.), 67.

149. Downs, *Transforming the South,* 133.

150. Earle S. Draper, "Urban Development in the Southeast: What of the Future?," *Social Forces* 19, no. 1 (October 1940): 19.

### 3. Public Architecture

1. Oral History of the TVA, Interview with Harry Tour, March 11 1970, MVA.

2. Thank you to Tracy Moir-McLean for pointing out this beautiful balance to me.

3. Oral History of the TVA, Tour Interview, 9, MVA; Marian Moffett and Lawrence Wodehouse, "Noble Structures Set in Handsome Parks: Public Architecture of the TVA," *Modulus* 17 (1984): 75–83; "Tennessee Valley Authority," *Architectural Forum* 71, no. 2 (August 1939): 73–113.

4. Christine Macy, *Dams* (New York: Norton & Co., 2009).

5. Oral History of the TVA, Bianculli Interview, 6, MVA.

6. TVA, *Annual Report for the Fiscal Year Ended June 30, 1938.*

7. Linda Nash, "The Changing Experience of Nature: Historical Encounters with a Northwest River," *Journal of American History* 86, no. 4 (2000): 1600–1629.

8. Nye, *American Technological Sublime,* xiii.

9. "Power & Beauty," *Knoxville News-Sentinel* magazine, November 28, 1937.

10. John T. Moutoux, "Architects and Engineers Unite Talents on TVA Dams," *Knoxville News-Sentinel* magazine, November 28, 1937.

11. "Moon, Mist Afford Unusual View of Dam," *Knoxville News-Sentinel,* September 10, 1937.

12. See Library of Congress, accessed June 16, 2022, www.loc.gov/item/2017877241/.

13. Smith, "Almost Fully Modern."

14. Culvahouse, *Tennessee Valley Authority: Design and Persuasion.*

15. "Huge Crowds Visit Norris Dam Project," *Knoxville News-Sentinel,* May 18, 1934.

16. "Norris Leads Boulder Dam," *Knoxville Journal,* September 18, 1934.

17. "Norris Dam Draws 230,000 Visitors from Out State," *Knoxville News-Sentinel,* September 3, 1937.

18. Gwendolyn Wright, *USA,* Modern Architectures in History Series, ed. Vivian Constantinopouolos (London: Reaktion Books, 2008), 119–20; Macy and Bonnemaison, *Architecture and Nature.*

19. Board Agenda Item #651, Board of Directors Papers, Box 203, Folder 800.1303, Architectural Studies, NAA.

20. Oral History of the TVA, Menhinick Interview, 23–24, MVA.

21. Oral History of the TVA, Draper Interview, 41, MVA.

22. "Tennessee Valley Authority Architecture," *Pencil Points* 20, no. 11 (November 1939).

23. Employees Recommended for Maximum Salary Rates in Positions at Grades of $4600 Entrance and above (Memo from C. L. Richy to A. S. Jandrey, December 20, 1940), Board of Directors Papers, Box 134, Folder 221.31, NAA.

24. Oral History of the TVA, Tour Interview, 39, MVA.

25. "TVA Architect and First Mayor of Pioneer New Town, Norris: Winner of Many Honors" (Obituary for Harry B. Tour), *AIA Journal* 56, no. 5 (November 1971): 62.

26. Gavin Townsend, "Mario Bianculli, Chattanooga's First Modernist," *ARRIS, Journal of the Southeast Chapter of the Society of Architectural Historians* 21 (2010): 4–19.

27. Oral History of the TVA, Bianculli Interview, MVA.

28. Letter from George Slover to Nathan Straus, December 7, 1938, Board of Directors Papers, Box 107, Folder 050-113.6, US Housing Authority, NAA.

29. Moffett, "Looking to the Future."

30. *Report to the Congress on the Unified Development of the Tennessee River System, Submitted by the Board of Directors of the Tennessee Valley Authority, March 1936* (Knoxville: Tennessee Valley Authority, 1936).

31. Ibid.

32. "Tennessee Valley Authority," *Architectural Forum* 71, no. 2 (August 1939): 91.

33. Oral History of the TVA, Tour Interview, 51–52, MVA.

34. Oral History of the TVA, Menhinick Interview, 23–24, MVA.

35. Architectural Budget Estimate—Fiscal Year 1938 (Memo from Harry B. Tour to B. M. Jones, March 26, 1937), Engineering Project Histories Papers, Box 35, NAA.

36. Harry B. Tour, "Engineers and Architects Cooperate on TVA Projects" (Letter to the Editor), *Civil Engineering* 11, no. 5 (1941).

37. Employees Recommended for Maximum Salary Rates in Positions at Grades of $4600 Entrance and above, Board of Directors Papers, Box 134, Folder 221.31, NAA.

38. Macy, "Architect's Office of the Tennessee Valley Authority."

39. Oral History of the TVA, Graves Interview, Part 2, p. 3, MVA.

40. Oral History of the TVA, Bianculli Interview, 35–36, MVA.

41. Mardges Bacon, "Le Corbusier and Postwar America: The TVA and *Beton Brut*," *Journal of the Society of Architectural Historians* 74, no. 1 (2015): 13–40.

42. Oral History of the TVA, Bianculli Interview, 19, MVA.

43. TVA, *Annual Report for the Fiscal Year Ended June 30, 1934*, 56.

44. The Library of Congress Prints and Photographs Division has an image of this mural: accessed June 16, 2022, www.loc.gov/item/2017877224/.

45. MacKaye, "Tennessee—Seed of a National Plan," 252.

46. "Annual Report LP&H, 1937," Regional Studies Papers, Box 9, Folder 4G1, NAA.

47. "Tennessee Valley Authority," *Architectural Forum* 71, no. 2 (August 1939): 73–113.

48. Talbot F. Hamlin, "Architecture of the TVA," *Pencil Points* 20, no. 11 (1939): 728.

49. "Final Report on the Chickamauga Project, Design of Permanent Structures, Part IV—

Section B, Architecture and Landscaping, by A. N. Krieger," Engineering Project Histories Papers, Box 399, Folder 7–200-IV-B, Architecture and Landscaping, NAA.

50. John H. Kyle, *The Building of TVA: An Illustrated History* (Baton Rouge: Louisiana State University Press, 1958).

51. "TVA Steam Plant," *Progressive Architecture* 35, no. 11 (November, 1954): 81.

52. Sarah K. Rovang, "Modernization and Architecture under the Rural Electrification Administration, 1935–1945" (PhD diss., Brown University, Providence, RI, 2016).

53. Letter from John M. Carmody to H. A. Morgan, November 14, 1938, Board of Directors Papers, Box 102, Folder 047.2–30, Rural Electrification thru 1941, NAA.

54. Employees Recommended for Maximum Salary Rates in Positions at Grades of $4600 Entrance and above, Board of Directors Papers, Box 134, Folder 221.31, NAA.

55. Rovang, "Modernization and Architecture."

56. "REA Headquarters Buildings for a Program of Rural Electrification," *Architectural Forum* February (1943).

57. Rovang, "Modernization and Architecture."

58. "REA Headquarters Buildings for a Program of Rural Electrification."

59. Roland A. Wank, "Co-Op Buildings Typify Progressive Democracy: REA Headquarters Buildings Are Community Centers," *Rural Electrification News* 6, no. 10 (1941): 6.

60. "REA Headquarters Buildings for a Program of Rural Electrification."

61. Ibid.

62. "Tennessee System Headquarters Has Many New Features," *Rural Electrification News* 5, no. 10 June (1940).

63. Howard K. Menhinick, "The Tennessee Valley and Its Development," *Journal of the American Institute of Architects* 6, no. 4 (1946).

64. Lilienthal, *TVA: Democracy on the March* (10th anniversary ed.), 197.

65. "TVA Creates a New Form of Display, Designed by Alfred Clauss," *Architectural Record* 82, no. 2 (July 1937): 86–88.

66. Carole Gabler, "Philadelphians at Home: The Clausses Drew a Blueprint for a Happy, Working Marriage," *Sunday Bulletin,* October 30, 1960, 8.

67. The Library of Congress Prints and Photographs Division has an image of this shed, accessed June 16, 2022, www.loc.gov/item/2017871863/.

68. The Library of Congress Prints and Photographs Division has images of these displays: see, for example, accessed July 20, 2022, www.loc.gov/item/2017877248/.

69. Oral History of the TVA, Menhinick Interview, 25–26, MVA.

70. Oral History of the TVA, Tour Interview, MVA.

71. McCraw, "Triumph and Irony—the TVA."

72. Culvahouse, *Tennessee Valley Authority: Design and Persuasion.*

73. See Talbot F. Hamlin, "Architecture of the TVA," *Pencil Points* 20, no. 11 (1939): 721–31; Kenneth Reid, "Design in TVA Structures," *Pencil Points* 20, no. 11 (1939): 691–720; "TVA Details," *Pencil Points* 20, no. 11 (1939): 732–38; "Tennessee Valley Authority," *Architectural Forum* 71, no. 2 (August 1939): 73–113; Roland A. Wank, "TVA Details," *Pencil Points* 22, no. 7 (1941): 475–82.

74. "One Hundred Years of Significant Building," *Architectural Record* 121, no. 4 (1957).

75. Frederick Albert Gutheim, *One Hundred Years of Architecture in America, 1857–1957: Celebrating the Centennial of the American Institute of Architects* (New York: Reinhold Publising, 1957).

76. "T.V.A. Architecture and Design," *Bulletin of the Museum of Modern Art* 8, no. 4 (April–May, 1941).

77. Ibid.

78. Douglas Haskell, "Architecture of the TVA," *The Nation,* May 17, 1941, 592. Emphasis in original.

79. Lewis Mumford, "The Architecture of Power," *New Yorker,* June 7, 1941, 58.

80. Moffett and Wodehouse, "Noble Structures."

81. Oral History of the TVA, Graves Interview, 12, MVA.

82. Osborne H. Graves, "TVA Land Planning, Landscape Architecture in a Resource Development Agency," *Landscape Architecture* 53 (July 1953): 154.

83. "Report on Status of Landscaping at Norris Dam, January 1937," Regional Studies Papers, Box 45, Folder 152 P, Report on Status of Norris Dam Landscape Work, NAA.

84. Swimming Instruction—Norris Quarry (Memo from O. H. Graves to Robert M. Howes, March 24, 1948), Board of Directors Papers, Box 44 Folder C40, Norris Dam Reservation, 1947–48, NAA.

85. Black, "Organic Planning," 76.

86. "Annual Report LP&H, 1937," Regional Studies Papers, Box 9, Folder 4G1, NAA.

87. Oral History of the TVA, Frincke Interview, 23, MVA.

88. "Annual Report LP&H, 1937," Regional Studies Papers, Box 9, Folder 4G1, NAA.

89. *Investigation of the Tennessee Valley Authority,* 3709.

90. Moffett and Wodehouse, "Noble Structures."

91. F. Stuart Chapin, *Communities for Living: Prepared for the Advisory Panel on Regional Materials of Instruction for the Tennessee Valley* (Athens: University of Georgia Press, 1941), 15.

92. Rough Draft OJP 1/9/43 (Outline of Status of Site Development at Various Dam Sites), Reservoir Properties Papers, Box 34, NAA.

93. Statement of General Landscape Planting Policy Recommended for TVA Dam Reserva-

tions (Memo from O. H. Graves and O. J. Priebe to Carroll A. Towne, Chief, Recreation and Public Grounds Division, March 4, 1944), Reservoir Properties Papers, Box 34, Folder B30b, Misc. Landscape 1944–46, NAA.

94. H. S. Conover, *Public Grounds Maintenance Handbook* (Knoxville: Tennessee Valley Authority, Division of Reservoir Properties, 1953); Herbert S. Conover, "Improvement and Maintenance Techniques at Certain TVA Dams, Areas 'Built for the People of the United States,'" *Landscape Architecture* 39, no. 2 (January 1949): 53–59; Conover, *Grounds Maintenance Handbook* (New York: F. W. Dodge Corp., 1958).

95. Oral History of the TVA, Towne Interviews, second interview, 10–11, MVA.

96. TVA, *Annual Report for the Fiscal Year Ended June 30, 1942,* 5.

97. Oral History of the TVA, Menhinick Interview, 25, MVA.

98. Oral History of the TVA, Tour Interview, 58, MVA.

99. Taylor, "Building the Back of Beyond."

100. Oral History of the TVA, Frincke Interview, 24–25, MVA.

### 4. Community Planning

1. Roland A. Wank, "Architecture in Rural Areas: A Report on TVA Experience," *Pencil Points* 23, no. 12 (December 1942): 47–53.

2. Lilienthal, *TVA: Democracy on the March* (10th anniversary ed.), 121.

3. "The Closed Shop on Public Works," by Arthur E. Morgan, Chairman of the Board, Tennessee Valley Authority, before Local #24, United Federal Workers of America, Knoxville, Tennessee, at 8 p.m. on November 17, 1937, Tennessee Valley Authorty Information Office, Engineering Project Histories Papers, Box 25, NAA.

4. *Downs, Transforming the South.*

5. "Construction Camp Standards" (Report by the Community Planning Division, January 27, 1938), George Richardson Files, Box 16, Folder Construction Camp Standards, H&S Dept. Sanitation Standards, NAA.

6. Eric L. Rousey, "The Worker's Life at Kentucky Dam, 1938–1945," *Filson Club History Quarterly* 71, no. 3 (July 1997): 347–66.

7. Oral History of the TVA, Menhinick Interview, 7–8, MVA.

8. Future Work and Policy (Memo from Louis Grandgent to Carroll A. Towne, August 25, 1937), 2, George Richardson Files, Box 14, Folder Prefabrication—Truckable Unit House, NAA.

9. Oral History of the TVA, Towne Interviews, second interview, 2–3, MVA.

10. "TVA Camp Presents Model Night Life," *Knoxville News-Sentinel,* July 8, 1934.

11. "Annual Report LP&H 1937," Regional Studies Papers, Box 9, Folder 4G1, NAA.

12. The Library of Congress Prints and Photographs Division has an image of this building: accessed June 16, 2022, www.loc.gov/item/2017877215/.

13. "The Land Planning Program, Fiscal Year 1935–1936," 6, Board of Directors Papers, Box 162, Folder 321-75-4 (2).

14. "Construction Camp Standards" (Report by the Community Planning Division, January 27, 1938), 9, George Richardson Files, Box 16, Folder Construction Camp Standards, H&S Dept. Sanitation Standards, NAA.

15. Ibid., 7.

16. Oral History of the TVA, Menhinick Interview, MVA.

17. "Construction Camp Standards" (January 27, 1938), 24, George Richardson Files, Box 16, Folder Construction Camp Standards, H&S Dept. Sanitation Standards, NAA.

18. Ibid., 2.

19. "Basic Principles of Healthful Housing: Preliminary Report of the Committee on Hygiene of Housing, American Public Health Association," *American Journal of Public Health and the Nation's Health* 28, no. 3 (March 1938): 351–72.

20. "Construction Camp Standards" (January 27, 1938), 12, George Richardson Files, Box 16, Folder Construction Camp Standards, H&S Dept. Sanitation Standards, NAA.

21. These cabins were later moved to the Norris Park to be used by tourists and were eventually replaced with larger models.

22. Downs, *Transforming the South.*

23. Taylor, "Building the Back of Beyond."

24. Rook, "Race, Water, and Foreign Policy."

25. Larsen, *Enduring Pastoral.*

26. Clayton Cranston, "The TVA and the Race Problem," *Opportunity, Journal of Negro Life* 12, no. 4 (April 1934): 111.

27. Downs, *Transforming the South,* 93.

28. Alderman and Brown, "When a New Deal Is Actually an Old Deal," 1913.

29. Negro Program (Undated Memo), Mary Rothrock Papers, Box 13, Folder 346, McClung Historical Collection.

30. He then took his work abroad, to Haiti, Liberia, Afghanistan, Tunisia, Sierra Leone, and Malawi. His son, J. Max Bond Jr., became an architect and taught at Columbia University. "J. Max Bond Sr., 89, an American Who Headed Liberian University," *New York Times,* Dec. 18, 1991.

31. Alderman and Brown, "When a New Deal Is Actually an Old Deal."

32. Downs, *Transforming the South,* 85.

33. J. Max Bond [Sr.], "The Educational Program for Negroes in the TVA," *Journal of Negro Education* 6, no. 2 (April 1937): 144–51.

34. "Construction Camp Standards" (January 27, 1938), George Richardson Files, Box 16, Folder Construction Camp Standards, H&S Dept. Sanitation Standards, NAA.

35. Lowitt, "The TVA, 1933–1945," 58–59.

36. Rousey, "Worker's Life at Kentucky Dam."

37. Lowitt, "The TVA, 1933–1945," 58–59.

38. Sachs, *Environmental Design.*

39. TVA, *The Kentucky Project: A Comprehensive Report on the Planning, Design, Construction, and Initial Operations of the Kentucky Project, Technical Report No. 13* (Washington, DC: Government Printing Office, 1951).

40. Rousey, "Worker's Life at Kentucky Dam."

41. "Construction Camp Standards" (January 27, 1938), 4, George Richardson Files, Box 16, Folder Construction Camp Standards, H&S Dept. Sanitation Standards, NAA.

42. TVA, *Annual Report for the Fiscal Year Ended June 30,* 1946, 2.

43. Hargrove, *Prisoners of Myth.*

44. Oral History of the TVA, Bianculli Interview, 16, MVA.

45. Oral History of the TVA, Graves Interview, 11, MVA.

46. Departmental Responsibilities for Program Planning and Design (Memo from Menhinick to Members of the DRS, August 22, 1941), 2, Regional Studies Papers, Box 9, Folder 4 E, Departmental Administrative Releases (Bulletins, Memoranda), NAA.

47. Disposition of TVA Housing (Memo from Howard K. Menhinick and Louis N. Allen to Gordon R. Clapp, General Manager, December 18, 1940), Chairman and the Members of the Board Papers, Box 96, Folder 622.1, Houses for TVA Employees, NAA.

48. Cross Index Sheet Dated 8-11-43, Board of Directors Papers, Box 189, Folder 621.1–17 (Douglas), NAA.

49. Carroll A. Towne, "Portable Housing: TVA Experience Leads to Trailer-Houses," *New Pencil Points* 23, no. 1 (1942): 50.

50. Gilbertsville Dam—Utilization of Pickwick Houses (Letter from T. B. Parker to J. B. Blandford, April 22, 1939), Board of Directors Papers, Box 189, Folder 622.1–9 (Gilbertsville), NAA.

51. "News," *Architectural Forum* 80, no. 4 (April 1944): 69.

52. Disposition of Vacant Guntersville Houses (Memo from Howard K. Menhinick to Gorson R. Clapp, July 16, 1943), George Richardson Files, Box 7, Folder Guntersville House Moving, NAA.

53. "Guntersville Housing—Cost Analysis," George Richardson Files, Box 7, Folder Guntersville House Moving, NAA.

54. Estimate on Removing House from Guntersville Dam to Guntersville Town (Memo from M. L. Beeler to W. H. Purnell, July 24, 1943), George Richardson Files, Box 7, Folder Guntersville House Moving, NAA.

55. "Removal of a Guntersville House to Occee No. 2" (Set of Photographs by George L. Richardson), George Richardson Files, Box 1, NAA.

56. "Demountable Housing for Defense Workers," *American Builder and Building Age (1930–1948)* 64, no. 3 (March 1942): 76.

57. Postwar Reconversion of TVA Prefabricated Houses (Memo from Howard K. Menhinick to Paul Ager, December 18, 1943), General Manager's Office Papers, Box 586, Folder 622.101, Low Cost Houses in General, NAA.

58. "Low Cost Houses," *Architectural Forum* 84 (April 1946); Roland A. Wank, "Demountable Houses: Smith Creek Village, Apalachia Dam, TVA," *Pencil Points* 25, no. 3 (March 1944): 77–79.

59. "Smith Creek Village, Community Center," *Pencil Points* 25, no. 2 (February 1944): 44–46.

60. Taylor, "Building the Back of Beyond."

61. Oral History of the TVA, Menhinick Interview, 13, MVA. See also Drumright, "A River for War."

62. Letter from Gordon R. Clapp to C. F. Palmer, October 15, 1941, Board of Directors Papers, Box 200, Folder 681.3–5 (Hiwassee), NAA.

63. Loan of Services of Carroll A. Towne to Federal Public Housing Authority (Letter from George Slover to George F. Gant, May 18, 1942), Board of Directors Papers, Box 107, Folder 050.128.3, Federal Public Housing Authority, NAA.

64. "Discussion of Community Facilities for Isolated Communities" (Transcript by the National Housing Agency, Federal Public Housing Authority, May 20, 1942), Reservoir Properties Papers, Box 33, Folder B30a, Misc. General Jan.–June 1942, NAA.

65. Taylor, "Building the Back of Beyond."

66. Alternate Camp Sites for Fontana Dam (Memo from Carroll A. Towne to E. S. Draper, April 29, 1936), Engineering Project Histories Papers, Box 48, NAA.

67. Oral History of the TVA, Graves Interview, 11, MVA.

68. Recreation (Undated Memo), Mary Rothrock Papers, Box 13, Folder 346, McClung Historical Collection.

69. "News from Fontana Dam, North Carolina," Mary Rothrock Papers, Box 12, Folder 336, McClung Historical Collection.

70. "Fontana Sketchbook," Mary Rothrock Papers, Box 12, Folder 336, McClung Historical Collection.

71. Ibid.

72. Future Status of Fontana Camp and Village (Memo from J. Ed Campbell and Howard K. Menhinick to Gordon R. Clapp, October 3, 1944), Board of Directors Papers, Box 200, Folder 681.3–8, Fontana, NAA.

73. Loren C. Hastings, "Fontana . . . Top Find in Low Cost Vacations," *Better Homes and Gardens,* April 1947.

74. TVA, *The Kentucky Project,* 285–86.

75. Extention of Loan Assignment of Tracy B. Augur to Federal Public Housing Authority (Letter from George Slover to George F. Gant, June 17, 1942), Board of Directors Papers, Box 107, Folder 050.128.3, Federal Public Housing Authority, NAA.

76. Loan of Services of Tracy B. Augur to Federal Public Housing Authority (Letter from George Slover to George F. Grant, March 19, 1942), Board of Directors Papers, Box 107, Folder 050.128.3, Federal Public Housing Authority.

77. Tracy B. Augur, "Planing Principles Applied in Wartime, Planning the Postwar Community . . . What It Promises to Be and How It Can Be Made That Way," *Architectural Record* 93 (January 1943): 72–73.

78. "Proposed Outline for Fontana Site Plan" (Syllabus for Architecture 2b and Landscape Architecture 2b, 2c, 4c, Fontana Site Plan—TVA, Due February, 20, 1951), Special Collections, Loeb Library, Harvard University, Cambridge, MA.

79. Downs, *Transforming the South.*

80. Conkin, *Revolution Down on the Farm,* 84.

81. Ibid., 90.

82. Leo Marx, "The American Ideology of Space," in *Denatured Visions: Landscape and Culture in the Twentieth Century,* ed. Stuart Wrede and William Howard Adams (New York: Museum of Modern Art, 1994), 76.

83. Dewey W. Grantham, "TVA and the Ambiguity of American Reform," in *TVA: Fifty Years of Grass-Roots Bureaucracy,* ed. Erwin C. Hargrove and Paul K. Conkin (Urbana: University of Illinois Press, 1983).

84. Chapin, *Communities for Living,* viii.

85. Ibid.

86. Andrew M. Shanken, *194X: Architecture, Planning, and Consumer Culture on the American Home Front* (Minneapolis: University of Minnesota Press, 2009); "The Visual Culture of Planning," *Journal of Planning History* 17, no. 4 (2018): 300–319.

87. Chapin, *Communities for Living,* 10.

88. Ibid., 43.

89. It is interesting to compare this schematic design to the short-lived, but very influential, drive-in market, which flourished in southern California in the second half of the 1920s. See Richard W. Longstreth, *The Drive-in, the Supermarket, and the Transformation of Commercial Space in Los Angeles, 1914–1941* (Cambridge, MA: MIT Press, 1999).

90. "Rural Activities Center, Tenn. Valley," *Architectural Forum* 80, no. 4 (April 1944): 89–93.

91. Ibid., 93.

92. Expressing the collaborative nature of the TVA, the authors thank a Mr. P. W. Voltz for advice on the "agricultural aspects of the project." Ibid., 89.

93. Ibid., 93.

94. "Power Board and Municipal Building," *Architectural Forum* 84, no. 3 (March 1946): 139.

95. "Community Buildings, Architectural Record's Building Types Study Number 113," *Architectural Record* 99, no. 5 (May 1946): 97.

96. Erin McCullough, "City Hall Added to National Register of Historic Places," (Tullahoma, TN) *Times,* August 17, 2018.

97. American Library Association, *Books for the South* (Chicago: American Library Association, 1933).

98. Mary U. Rothrock, "Tomorrow's Rural Libraries," *Bulletin of the American Library Association* 31, no. 13 (December 1937): 962.

99. Mary U. Rothrock and Helen M. Harris, "A Regional Library in the Tennessee Valley," *ALA Bulletin* 35, no. 12 (1941): 658–64.

100. TVA, *Annual Report for the Fiscal Year Ended June 30, 1950.*

101. Library Service Map (Memo from J. Harry Scott to Mary V. Rothrock, October 21, 1942), Mary Rothrock Papers, Box 16, Folder 421, McClung Historical Collection.

102. School and Library Facilities Furnished by the TVA (Memo from J. Ed Campbell to Malcolm G. Littel, March 12, 1943), Mary Rothrock Papers, Box 25, Folder 578, McClung Historical Collection.

103. Memo from George Richardson to Mary U. Rothrock, April 15, 1947, Mary Rothrock Papers, Box 13, Folder 346, McClung Historical Collection.

104. Mary Edna Anders, *The Tennessee Valley Library Council, 1940–1949: A Regional Approach to Library Planning* (Atlanta: Southeastern Library Association, 1960).

105. Discussion at Tennessee Valley Library Council Meeting, Gatlinburg, Tennessee, October 25, 1944 (Memo from Howard K. Menhinick to Mary U. Rothrock, November 6, 1944), 6, Mary Rothrock Papers, Box 31, Folder 726, McClung Historical Collection.

106. Typical Planting Plan for Medium Branch Library Building, Type 2 (Memo from O. H.

Graves to Mary U. Rothrock, July 18, 1946), Mary Rothrock Papers, FL 9–12, Q 3, McClung Historical Collection.

107. US Department of Agriculture, *Rural Library Service: Farmers' Bulletin No. 1847* (Washington, DC: Government Printing Office, 1949).

108. Ernest I. Miller, *Buildings for Small Public Libraries: Remodeled and Adapted, Including New Designs for Branches* (Chicago: American Library Association, Committee on Library Architecture and Building Planning, 1950).

109. Thank you to Allie Ward Chamberlain for introducing me to this nonprofit and its important work.

### 5. Modern Houses

1. Mennel, "Miracle House Hoop-La."

2. Douglas Haskell, "The House of the Future," *New Republic,* May 13, 1931, 344.

3. Fitch, "Rise of Technology," 76.

4. Earle S. Draper, "TVA's Yardstick for Housing," *Architectural Forum* 63, no. 3 (September 1935): 1623–70.

5. "Tennessee Valley Authority," *Architectural Forum* 71, no. 2 (August 1939): 73–113.

6. Draper, "TVA's Yardstick for Housing."

7. McCraw, "Triumph and Irony—the TVA."

8. TVA, *Report to the Congress on the Unified Development of the Tennessee River System.*

9. "Land Planning Program, 1935–1936," 20–21, Board of Directors Papers, Box 162, Folder 321-75-4 (2), NAA.

10. Future Work and Policy (Grandgent to Towne, August 25, 1937), 4, George Richardson Files, Box 14, Folder Prefabrication—Truckable Unit House, NAA.

11. "Houses at Norris, Tennessee, a Review of Costs by Louis Grandgent, March 14, 1936," Regional Studies Papers, Box 45, Folder 156 N 132, NAA.

12. Basic Reports of Land Planning & Housing Division, May 1, 1936, Engineering Project Histories Papers, Box 40, NAA.

13. "Land Planning Program, 1935–1936," 19, Board of Directors Papers, Box 162, Folder 321-75-4 (2), NAA.

14. "Construction Camp Standards" (January 27, 1938), 38, George Richardson Files, Box 16, Folder Construction Camp Standards, H&S Dept. Sanitation Standards, NAA.

15. Ibid., 39.

16. "Employee Housing on the Hiwassee Project, Summary" (Report by the Social and

Economic Research Division, December 14, 1938), Board of Directors Papers, Box 189, Folder 622.1–5 (Hiwassee), NAA.

17. Ibid.

18. "Annual Report LP&H, 1937," Regional Studies Papers, Box 9, Folder 4G1, NAA.

19. "Basic Principles of Healthful Housing."

20. "The Low Cost Houses at Hiwassee Dam" (TVA Information Office, May 16, 1938), George Richardson Files, Box 10, NAA.

21. "Employee Housing on the Hiwassee Project" (December 14, 1938), Board of Directors Papers, Box 189, Folder 622.1–5 (Hiwassee), NAA.

22. *Investigation of the Tennessee Valley Authority,* 3710.

23. "Employee Housing on the Hiwassee Project" (December 14, 1938), Board of Directors Papers, Box 189, Folder 622.1–5 (Hiwassee), NAA.

24. Future Work and Policy (Grandgent to Towne, August 25, 1937), 4, George Richardson Files, Box 14, Folder Prefabrication—Truckable Unit House, NAA.

25. "Plan of Farm Labor Home, Type 'K' by the Farm Security Administration," George Richardson Files, Box 9 (1944).

26. "Annual Report of the Department of Regional Planning Studies, for the Fiscal Ended June 30, 1938," Regional Studies Papers, Box 9, Folder 4G1, NAA.

27. Ibid.

28. Explanation of House Model (Memo by Louis Grandgent, July 15, 1938), Regional Studies Papers, Box 46, Folder 156 N 132, Norris Housing 2 of 2, NAA.

29. TVA, *The Watts Bar Project: A Comprehensive Report on the Planning, Design, Construction, and Initial Operations of the Watts Bar Project, Technical Report No. 9* (Washington, DC: Government Printing Office, 1949); TVA, *The Kentucky Project.*

30. "The Technology Architectural Record, Devoted to the Study of Architecture and to the Welfare of the Department of Architecture of the Massachusetts Institute of Technology."

31. "Residence of Dr. R. B. Taft, Belmont, Mass. Grandgent & Elwell, Architects," *Architectural Record* 47, no. 2 (February 1920): 178–80.

32. "Louis Grandgent," *Journal of Housing* 16, no. 10 (1959): 350.

33. Gilbert Herbert, *The Dream of the Factory-Made House: Walter Gropius and Konrad Wachsmann* (Cambridge, MA: MIT Press, 1984).

34. Douglas Haskell, "Bringing Shelter Up to Date: II Unchaining the House from Land," *The Nation,* May 23, 1934.

35. Alfred Bruce and Harold Sandbank, *A History of Prefabrication* (New York: John B. Pierce Foundation, 1944); "A Communication, Mr. Mumford, Mr. Haskell and the Factory-Built House," *New Republic,* July 2, 1931.

36. Wright, *USA,* 129.

37. Macy, "Architect's Office of the Tennessee Valley Authority."

38. Alfred Clauss Portable Workmens' House (Memo from Louis Grandgent to Caroll A. Towne, August 9, 1937), Reservoir Properties Papers, Box 34, Folder B30d, Misc. Architecture 1940–42, NAA.

39. "Basic Reports of Land Planning & Housing Division, Tennessee Valley Authority, May 1, 1936," Engineering Project Histories Papers, Box 40, NAA.

40. "Truckable Unit House, November 23, 1934, L.P. & H.—T.V.A.," George Richardson Files, Box 14, Folder Prefabrication—Truckable Unit House, NAA.

41. Ibid.

42. Future Work and Policy (Grandgent to Towne, August 25, 1937), 5, George Richardson Files, Box 14, Folder Prefabrication—Truckable Unit House, NAA.

43. Ibid.

44. "Truckable Unit House, November 23, 1934," George Richardson Files, Box 14, Folder Prefabrication—Truckable Unit House, NAA.

45. Ibid.

46. Emphasis in the original. Future Work and Policy (Grandgent to Towne, August 25, 1937), George Richardson Files, Box 14, Folder Prefabrication—Truckable Unit House.

47. Oral History of the TVA, Towne Interviews, circa p. 18, MVA.

48. Postwar Reconversion of TVA Prefabricated Houses (Menhinick to Ager, December 18, 1943), General Manager's Office Papers, Box 586, Folder 622.101, Low Cost Houses in General, NAA.

49. "TVA Demountable Cottages, May 15, 1941," George Richardson Files, Box 17, Folder Vacation Cabins, NAA.

50. Oral History of the TVA, Towne Interviews, 18, MVA.

51. Request for Loan of Service of Louis Grandgent from United States Housing Authority (Memo from George Slover to Arthur S. Jandry, January 15,1941), Board of Directors Papers, Box 107, Folder 050-113.6, US Housing Authority, NAA.

52. Towne, "Portable Housing," 49.

53. Margaret Crawford, "Daily Life on the Home Front: Women, Blacks, and the Struggle for Public Housing," in *World War II and the American Dream,* ed. Donald Albrecht and Margaret Crawford (Washington, DC: National Building Museum, 1995).

54. Job Descriptions 1941–42 (Multiple Memos Arranged in Folder), Reservoir Properties Papers, Box 20, Folder Job Descriptions 1941–42, NAA.

55. "The Problems and the Methods of General Management in a Multi-Purpose Regional Agency," by Gordon R. Clapp, May 22, 1941, Board of Directors Papers, Box 220, Folder 913, Regional Planning, Social Planning Economic & National, NAA.

56. Towne, "Portable Housing."

57. The Library of Congress Prints and Photographs Division has images of these houses. See, for example, accessed July 20, 2022, www.loc.gov/item/2017871887/.

58. Job Descriptions 1943 (Multiple Memos Arranged in Folder), Reservoir Properties Papers, Box 20, Folder Job Descriptions 1943, NAA.

59. Job Descriptions 1941–42 (Multiple Memos Arranged in Folder), ibid.

60. Hyun-Tae Jung, "'Technologically' Modern: The Prefabricated House and the Wartime Experience of Skidmore, Owings and Merrill," in *Sanctioning Modernism: Architecture and the Making of Postwar Identities,* ed. Vladimir Kuli, et al. (Austin: University of Texas Press, 2014).

61. "Description of TVA Prefarbicated Houses Types E-1, E-2, and F-3 (n.d.)," George Richardson Files, Box 10, NAA.

62. "Aménagemet De La Vallée Du Tennessee," *L'Architecture D'aujourd'hui,* no. 12, Techniques Américaines Urbanisme et Habitation (Juillet 1947); "Maison Préfarbriquée De La T.V.A," *L'Architecture D'aujourd'hui,* no. 12, Techniques Américaines Urbanisme et Habitation (Juillet 1947).

63. Mennel, "Miracle House Hoop-La."

64. Future Work and Policy (Grandgent to Towne, August 25, 1937), George Richardson Files, Box 14, Folder Prefabrication—Truckable Unit House, NAA.

65. Oral History of the TVA, Menhinick Interview, 20–22, MVA; "Demountable and Trailer Houses" (February 1, 1943), George Richardson Files, Box 10, NAA.

66. "Demountable and Trailer Houses" (February 1, 1943), George Richardson Files, Box 10, NAA.

67. "Prefabricated Houses Designed by Tennessee Valley Authority by C. A. Towne, August 14, 1943," George Richardson Files, Box 10, File Research Program (General), NAA.

68. Nye, *Electrifying America,* 323.

69. Mary Heaton Vorse, "Yesterday, Today, and Tomorrow," *Pencil Points* 23, no. 12 (December 1942): 28–31.

70. Rural Electrification Program (Memo from George W. Kable to H. A. Morgan, July 27, 1937), Board of Directors Papers, Box 238, Folder 951.9, Rural Electrification thru 1937, NAA.

71. Lilienthal, *TVA: Democracy on the March* (10th anniversary ed.), 90–91.

72. TVA, *Annual Report for the Fiscal Year Ended June 30, 1945,* 8.

73. TVA, *Annual Report for the Fiscal Year Ended June 30, 1946,* 69–70.

74. See, for example, Library of Congress Prints and Photographs Division, accessed June 18, 2022, https://www.loc.gov/item/2017832435/.

75. Rovang, "Modernization and Architecture."

76. Schaffer, "Environment and TVA," 352.

77. Reyner Banham, "The Great Gizmo," *Industrial Design* 12, no. 9 (September 1965): 54.

78. "The Land Planning Program, Fiscal Year 1935–1936," 19–20, Board of Directors Papers, Box 162, Folder 321-75-4 (2), NAA.

79. Letter from L. W. Schad to A. Twitchell, June 3, 1934, in MM.1984.003, Tennessee Valley Authority (TVA) housing projects, 1934–38, McClung Historical Collection.

80. Oral History of the TVA, Draper Interview, 14, MVA.

81. "Annual Report of the Division of Land Planning & Housing, for Fiscal Year July 1, 1935 to June 30, 1936," 28, Engineering Project Histories Papers, NAA.

82. "Annual Report LP&H, 1937," Engineering Project Histories Papers, NAA.

83. "TVA Thermal Research, 1943," George Richardson Files, Box 10, Folder TVA Projects, NAA.

84. "Annual Report of the Department of Regional Planning Studies, for the Fiscal Ended June 30, 1938," Regional Studies Papers, Box 9, Folder 4G1, NAA.

85. Louis Grandgent, "Heating at Norris, TN: A Study of Thermal Efficiency in Housing," 1938, George Richardson Files, Box 12, Folder Research—General: Heating at Norris, TN, NAA.

86. "Annual Report of the Department of Regional Planning Studies Fiscal Year 1939," Regional Studies Papers, Box 9, Folder 4G1, NAA.

87. Oral History of the TVA, Tour Interview, 16, MVA.

88. They would both go on to work with Mario Bianculli after the end of the war.

89. Tennessee Valley Library Council Meeting, October 25, 1944 (Memo, Menhinick to Rothrock, November 6, 1944), Mary Rothrock Papers, Box 31, Folder 726, McClung Historical Collection.

90. Small Structures Research (n.d., c. 1944), George Richardson Files, Box 10, Folder—Research Program General, NAA.

91. Letter from W. H. Purnell to R. L. Davison, June 5, 1941, Reservoir Properties Papers, Box 33, Folder B-30A Misc.—General Jan. June 1941, NAA.

92. Letter from W. H. Purnell to Vernon Demars, January 25, 1944, George Richardson Files, Box 13, Folder Prefabrication Design, NAA.

93. Letter to Schult Corporation from Howard P. Vermilya, May 26, 1944, George Richardson Files, Box 13, Folder Prefabrication Design, NAA.

94. Report of Trip to New York, Hartford, and Pittsburgh (Memo from Carl Koch to Vernon Demars, December 11, 1943), George Richardson Files, Box 13, Folder Non TVA Research General, NAA.

95. Use of Cotton in House Construction (Memo from Tracy B. Augur to C. A. Towne, December 19, 1940), Reservoir Properties Papers, Box 34, Folder B30d, Misc. Architecture 1940–46, NAA.

96. "Prefabricated Houses Designed by by C. A. Towne, August 14, 1943," George Richardson Files, Box 10, File Research Program (General), NAA.

97. Carroll A. Towne, "Portable Housing: TVA Experience Leads to Trailer-Houses," *New Pencil Points* 23, no. 7 (1942): 49–56. See also "The Trailer House: TVA's New Approach to Mobile Shelter," by the staff of the DRS, TVA, *Architectural Record* 93, no. 2 (1943): 49–52.

98. Carroll A. Towne, "Design for Prefabrication—Some Personal Observations," *Pencil Points* (March 1944): 74–76.

99. Authorization of Salary Increase within Grade to Maximum Rates for Employees at TVA Salary Grades 14 and above (Memo from Arthur S. Jandrey to Board of Directors, July 21, 1944), Board of Directors Papers, Box 134, Folder 221.31, NAA.

100. Burnham Kelly, *The Prefabrication of Houses: A Study by the Albert Farwell Bemis Foundation of the Prefabrication Industry in the United States* (Cambridge, MA: Technology Press of MIT and John Wiley and Sons, 1951).

101. "Wartime Housing: An Exhibition in 10 Scenes, Presented at the Museum of Modern Art, Sponsored by the National Committee on the Housing Emergency, and Prepared in Cooperation with the National Housing Agency, April [22]–June [21], 1942," *Bulletin of the Museum of Modern Art* 9, no. 4 (May 1942).

102. "TVA Builds Portable Houses: 3-Section Cottages Are Shop-Fabricated and Trucked to Site," in *Defense Homes Handbook: Portfolio of Low Cost Homes and Rental Housing Units* (Chicago: Simmons-Boardman, 1943); DRS, TVA, "The Trailer House: TVA's New Approach to Mobile Shelter"; "Homes for Tomorrow: Prefabricated and Pre-Engineered Machines for Living Are Visible Signs on the Road to Social Progress," *The Technocrat* 12, no. 12 (December 1944): 6–10.

103. "Well Built Knoxville Homes: Home Builders in the Tennessee Region, Offer Low Cost, Thoroughly Insulated, Electrically and Oil Heated Units," in *Defense Homes Handbook: Portfolio of Low Cost Homes and Rental Housing Units* (Chicago: Simmons-Boardman, 1943).

104. Avigail Sachs and Tricia A. Stuth, "Innovation and Tradition: Eighty Years of Housing Construction in Southern Appalachia," *Construction History* 28, no. 1 (2013).

## 6. Regional Development

1. MacKaye, "Appalachian Trail."

2. Ibid., 325.

3. Geddes, *Cities in Evolution,* 99.

4. Ibid., 94.

5. Garrett Dash Nelson, introduction to reprint of "An Appalachian Trail: A Project in

Regional Planning," *Places Journal* (April 2019), accessed May 14, 2020, https://placesjournal.org/article/an-appalachian-trail-a-project-in-regional-planning/.

6. "Report on the Appalachian Project," *Journal of the American Institute of Architects* 11, no. 7 (July 1923): 292–93.

7. TVA, *Annual Report for the Fiscal Year Ended June 30, 1935.*

8. Ronald Foresta, "Transformation of the Appalachian Trail," *Geographical Review* 77, no. 1 (January 1987): 76–85.

9. Anderson, *Benton MacKaye.*

10. Oral History of the TVA, Draper Interview, 78, MVA.

11. Maher, *Nature's New Deal.*

12. Koppes, "Efficiency/Equity/Esthetics," 132.

13. *Report of the Secretary of Agriculture in Relation to the Forests, Rivers, and Mountains of the Southern Appalachian Region, December 19, 1901* (Washington, DC: Government Printing Office, 1901).

14. Taylor, "Building the Back of Beyond."

15. Maher, *Nature's New Deal.*

16. Schaffer, "Environment and TVA," 340.

17. TVA, *Scenic Resources of the Tennessee Valley,* 3.

18. Larsen, *Enduring Pastoral.*

19. Droze, "TVA and the Ordinary Farmer," 194.

20. Baker and Landess, "Education for Sustained Regional Productivity."

21. TVA, *Annual Report for the Fiscal Year Ended June 30, 1935,* 43.

22. Kenneth J. Seigworth, "Reforestation in the Tennessee Valley," *Public Administration Review* 8, no. 4 (Autumn 1948): 280–85.

23. Maher, *Nature's New Deal.*

24. Seigworth, "Reforestation in the Tennessee Valley."

25. Baker and Landess, "Education for Sustained Regional Productivity."

26. *Annual Report of the Director of the Civilian Conservation Corps, Fiscal Year Ended June 30, 1939* (Washington, DC: Government Printing Office), 76.

27. *Annual Report of the Director of the Civilian Conservation Corps, Fiscal Year Ended June 30, 1941* (Washington, DC: Government Printing Office), 37.

28. *1937 Yearbook: Park and Recreation Progress, United States Department of the Interior, National Park Service* (Washington, DC: Government Printing Office), v.

29. Tennessee Valley Library Council Meeting, October 25, 1944 (Memo, Menhinick to Rothrock, November 6, 1944), 2, Mary Rothrock Papers, McClung Historical Collection.

30. Ibid., 3.

31. Schaffer, "Environment and TVA," 351.

32. "Proposed Statement, 'Recreational Development on TVA Reservoir Lands,'" Board of Directors Papers, Box 271, NAA.

33. "Suggested Content of a Legislation Defining Policy of Recreation Lands," Board of Directors Papers, Box 271, NAA.

34. Ibid.

35. Cutler, *Public Landscape of the New Deal,* 8.

36. Galen Cranz, *The Politics of Park Design: A History of Urban Parks in America* (Cambridge, MA: MIT Press, 1982), 62.

37. Cindy S. Aron, *Working at Play: History of Vacations in the United States* (New York: Oxford University Press, 1999).

38. Draves, "It's Easier to Pick a Tourist."

39. *Investigation of the Tennessee Valley Authority,* 3714.

40. Robert M. Howes, "Controversy and Consequence: A Personal Look at TVA," *Jackson Purchase Historical Society* 2, no. 1, Article 8 (1974): 40.

41. "Annual Report LP&H, 1937," Engineering Project Histories Papers, NAA.

42. DRPS, *Recreational Development of the Southern Highlands Region,* ix.

43. Oral History of the TVA, Towne Interviews, second interview, 12, MVA.

44. "Annual Report LP&H, 1937," Engineering Project Histories Papers, NAA.

45. "Suggested Categories for a Series of Leaflets on the Tennessee Valley" (with Maps by Benton MacKaye and Robert M. Howes), Regional Studies Papers, Box 9, Folder 4G1, NAA.

46. Anderson, *Benton MacKaye.*

47. "Basic Reports of Land Planning & Housing Division, Tennessee Valley Authority, May 1, 1936," Engineering Project Histories Papers, Box 40, NAA.

48. Draper, "Demonstration Parks in the Tennessee Valley."

49. "A Summary of Transportation Studies Conducted by the Department of Regional Planning Studies, Submitted by E. Bruce Wedge," Board of Directors Papers, Box 267, NAA.

50. TVA, *Scenic Resources of the Tennessee Valley,* 2.

51. Schaffer, "Benton MacKaye: The TVA Years."

52. TVA, *Annual Report for the Fiscal Year Ended June 30, 1937,* 48.

53. TVA, *Scenic Resources of the Tennessee Valley,* 35.

54. Ibid., xi.

55. Minutes of Meeting Recreational Policy Committee of the Regional Planning Council, October 12, 1939, Board of Directors Papers, Box 221, Folder 913.4, Recreational Development thru 1939, NAA.

56. "Annual Report of the Department of Regional Planning Studies, for the Fiscal Ended June 30, 1938," Regional Studies Papers, Box 9, Folder 4G1, NAA.

57. "Regional Planning in the Tennessee Valley, Knoxville, Tennessee, August 8, 1938," Board of Directors Papers, Box 288, Folder 221.31, NAA.

58. *Investigation of the Tennessee Valley Authority,* 3708.

59. TVA, *Annual Report for the Fiscal Year Ended June 30, 1937.*

60. "Annual Report of the Division of Land Planning & Housing, for Fiscal Year July 1, 1935 to June 30, 1936," 31, Engineering Project Histories Papers, NAA.

61. Maher, *Nature's New Deal.*

62. Allen R. Coggins, "The Early History of Tennessee's State Parks, 1919–1956," *Tennessee Historical Quarterly* 43, no. 3 (Fall 1984): 295–315.

63. Draper, "Demonstration Parks in the Tennessee Valley," 126.

64. See this image in the Library of Congress Prints and Photographs Division, accessed June 18, 2022, www.loc.gov/item/2017873068/.

65. Cutler, *Public Landscape of the New Deal,* 77.

66. Macy and Bonnemaison, *Architecture and Nature.*

67. Albert H. Good, *Park and Recreation Structures* (Washington, DC: Government Printing Office, 1938).

68. Larsen, *Enduring Pastoral.*

69. Smith, "Almost Fully Modern."

70. Ibid.

71. "Norris Buildings Report," Construction Project Reports, Box 3, NAA.

72. "Annual Report LP&H, 1937," Engineering Project Histories Papers, NAA.

73. Draper, "Demonstration Parks in the Tennessee Valley," 126.

74. "Annual Report of the Division of Land Planning and Housing for Fiscal Year July 1, 1934 to June 30, 1935," Regional Studies Papers, Box 9, Folder 4G1, NAA.

75. "Annual Report LP&H, 1937," Engineering Project Histories Papers, NAA.

76. Draper, "Demonstration Parks in the Tennessee Valley," 126.

77. TVA, *Scenic Resources of the Tennessee Valley,* 118–19.

78. "Small Structures Research" (c. 1944), George Richardson Files, Box 10, Folder Research Program General, NAA.

79. "Norris Buildings Report," Construction Project Reports, Box 3, NAA.

80. TVA, *Annual Report for the Fiscal Year Ended June 30, 1937.*

81. DRPS, *Recreational Development of the Southern Highlands Region.*

82. Oral History of the TVA, Towne Interviews, second interview, 4–5, MVA.

83. *Investigation of the Tennessee Valley Authority,* 3708.

84. "Annual Report LP&H, 1937," Engineering Project Histories Papers, NAA.

85. "Annual Report of the Department of Regional Planning Studies Fiscal Year 1939," Regional Studies Papers, Box 9, Folder 4G1, NAA.

86. "Annual Report LP&H, 1937," Engineering Project Histories Papers, NAA.

87. "Review of Report and Comments on a Negro Park Development on Norris Lake, Summarized by the Department of Regional Planning Studies for Consideration by the TVA Board, January 20, 1938," Board of Directors Papers, Box 286, NAA.

88. Larsen, *Enduring Pastoral.*

89. Oral History of the TVA, Towne Interviews, second interview, 6, MVA.

90. "Annual Report of the Division of Land Planning and Housing for Fiscal Year July 1, 1934 to June 30, 1935," Regional Studies Papers, Box 9, Folder 4G1, NAA.

91. Ibid.

92. *1941 Yearbook: Park and Recreation Progress* (Washington, DC: Government Printing Office), iii.

93. Oral History of the TVA, Menhinick Interview, 40, MVA.

94. Oral History of the TVA, Frincke Interview, part 2, pp. 7–8, MVA.

95. TVA, *Scenic Resources of the Tennessee Valley,* 155.

96. Ibid., 147–48.

97. "Annual Report LP&H, 1937," Engineering Project Histories Papers, NAA; Lawrence Logan Durisch, "Local Government and the T.V.A. Program," *Public Administration Review* 1, no. 4 ( Summer 1941): 326–34.

98. "Annual Report of the Division of Land Planning & Housing, for Fiscal Year July 1, 1935 to June 30, 1936," 13, Regional Studies Papers, Box 9, Folder 4G1, NAA.

99. "Some Recent Work of the Tennessee Valley Authority, Roland A. Wank, Principal Architect—Including a Visitors' Building, a Concession Building and Comfort Station, an Overlook Building, and a Harbor Master's Office, Harrison S. Gurnee and Mario Bianculli, Designers, under Supervision of Carroll A. Towne and George L. Richardson," *Pencil Points* 22, no. 7, July (1941): 175–82.

100. Robert M. Howes, "Recreation," in *TVA: The First Twenty Years, a Staff Report,* ed. Tennessee Valley Authority and Roscoe C. Martin (Tuscaloosa: University of Alabama Press, 1956), 208.

101. Oral History of the TVA, Towne Interviews, second interview, 7, MVA.

102. "Notes on Messers. Menhinick and Towne's Attendance at the National Recreation Congress in Cleveland, September 30—October 4" (Second Draft, C.A.T. October 22, 1940), Reservoir Properties Papers, Box 33, NAA.

103. "Small Structures Research" (c. 1944), George Richardson Files, Box 10, Folder Research Program General, NAA.

104. Letter from C. T. Barker to Lieutenant H. H. Green, March 17, 1943, Reservoir Properties Papers, Box 33, Folder B30, Misc. Jan–March 1943, NAA.

105. Lilienthal, *TVA: Democracy on the March* (10th anniversary ed.), 115.

106. Preparation of Standard Plans for Recreation Facilities (Memo from R. M. Howes to H. K. Menhinick, March 4, 1940), Reservoir Properties Papers, Box 34, NAA.

107. "List of Examples of TVA Plans for Structures and Facilities for Recreational Developments," George Richardson Files, Box 12, Folder Master Copy of List of Recreational Examples, NAA.

108. Collection of Material Re: Vacation Cabins, George Richardson Files, Box 12, Folder Camping, Tourist Cottages, NAA.

109. "Construction Requirements for Summer Cabins Recreational Areas (Glr, 6/7/39)," Reservoir Properties Papers, Box 33, Folder B30, Misc. Jan–March 1943, NAA.

110. Postwar Reconversion of TVA Prefabricated Houses (Memo, Menhinick to Ager, December 18, 1943), General Manager's Office Papers, Box 586, Folder 622.101, Low Cost Houses in General, NAA.

111. Plan for Vacation Cabin (Memo from Harry H. Wilkerson to A. D. Rieger, December 3, 1945), George Richardson Files, Box 16 Folder Research—TV-34897—Charlie G. Cloar, NAA.

112. Collection of Material Re: Vacation Cabins, George Richardson Files, Box 17, Folder Vacation Cabins, NAA.

113. *Larsen, Enduring Pastoral,* 91.

114. "Proposed Resolution Authorizing the Leasing of Certain Cabin Sites in Norris Reservoir Area, July 12, 1939" (Misc. Documents), Board of Directors Papers, Box 198, Folder 680.33, Camp Grounds and Parks, NAA.

115. Oral History of the TVA, Frincke Interview, part 2, p. 15, MVA.

116. Ibid., part 2, pp. 11–12.

117. A Departmental Project Proposal (Memo from George L. Richardson to Carroll a Towne, April 11, 1940), Reservoir Properties Papers, Box 34, Folder B30-d Misc. Architecture 1940–42, NAA.

118. Ibid.

119. Howes, "Recreation," 211–12.

120. TVA, *Annual Report for the Fiscal Year Ended June 30, 1940.*

121. *Recreation Development of the Tennessee River System: Message from the President of the United States Transmitting a Report on the Recreation Development of the Tennessee River System* (Washington, DC: Government Printing Office, 1940).

122. Howes, "Recreation," 211–12.

123. Draves, "It's Easier to Pick a Tourist."

124. National Resources Planning Board, *Regional Planning, Part XI: The Southeast* (Washington, DC: Government Printing Office, 1942).

125. Lepawsky, "Government Planning in the South," 554.

126. Lilienthal, *TVA: Democracy on the March* (10th anniversary ed.), 114.

127. Howes, "Recreation," 212.

128. "Review of Norris Reservoir Properties to Determine Surplus Land, by the Department of Property and Supply, Land Division, August 1945," Board of Directors Papers, Box 281, NAA.

129. Downs, *Transforming the South.*

130. Joseph J. Seneca, Paul Davidson, and F. Gerard Adams, "An Analysis of Recreational Use of the TVA Lakes," *Land Economics* 44, no. 4 (November 1968): 529–34.

131. Draves, "It's Easier to Pick a Tourist," 88.

## Conclusion

1. *Report to the Congress on the Unified Development of the Tennessee River System, Submitted by the Board of Directors of the Tennessee Valley Authority, March 1936* (Knoxville: Tennessee Valley Authority, 1936).

2. Droze, "TVA and the Ordinary Farmer."

3. Lowitt, "The TVA, 1933–1945."

4. Drumright, "A River for War."

5. Ekbladh, "Mr. TVA," and "Meeting the Challenge from Totalitarianism."

6. McCraw, "Triumph and Irony—the TVA."

7. Hargrove, *Prisoners of Myth.*

8. William C. Harvard Jr., "The Images of TVA: The Clash over Values," in *TVA: Fifty Years of Grass-Roots Bureaucracy,* ed. Erwin C. Hargrove and Paul K. Conkin (Urbana: University of Illinois Press, 1983), 309.

9. W. H. Droze, "The TVA, 1945–80: The Power Company," in ibid.

10. Lawrence Logan Durisch, "The TVA Program and the War Effort," *Journal of Politics* 8, no. 4 (November 1946): 536.

11. TVA, *Annual Report for the Fiscal Year Ended June 30, 1950.*

12. Report on Status of Work (Memo from Malcolm J. Rand to Howard K. Menhinick, August 28, 1946), Regional Studies Papers, Box 9, Folder 4G (A-Z), NAA.

13. "Tracy Baldwin Augur, Operated Plans Office," *Washington Post,* June 24, 1974.

14. David F. Krugler, *This Is Only a Test: How Washington, D.C., Prepared for Nuclear War* (New York: Palgrave Macmillan, 2006).

15. Memo from Howard K. Menhinick to Dr. H. A. Morgan, June 23, 1947, Board of Directors Papers, Box 162, Folder 9321-75-4 (2), Regional Studies Division, Duties, Activities, Policy and Procedures, Etc., NAA.

16. Roland B. Greeley, "Regional Conference at Fontana," *Journal of the American Institute of Planning* 12, no. 4 (1946): 42–45.

17. Kyle, *Building of TVA.*

18. "TVA Buildings," *Progressive Architecture* 32, no. 11 (November 1951): 62–71.

19. Moffett, "Looking to the Future: Architecture of Roland Wank."

20. Roland A. Wank, "The Plant as a Place to Work," *Architectural Record* 10, no. 6 ( December 1946): 94.

21. John Shearer, "Modernism Architecture," Chattanoogan.com, July 19, 2011, http://www.chattanoogan.com/2011/7/19/205375/John-Shearer-Modernism-Architecture.aspx.

22. Oral History of the TVA, Bianculli Interview, MVA.

23. Bianculli, "Planning and the Architect," *Tennessee Planner* 11, no. 2 (October 1950): 42–46.

24. "Study of Library for Rural Communtiies Type I" (Plan Drawn by H. Gurnee, Dated April 11, 1944), Mary Rothrock Papers, FL 9–12, Q 3, McClung Historical Collection.

25. Pioneering Women of American Architecture, s.v. "Jane West Clauss," by Avigail Sachs, accessed May 31, 2022, https://pioneeringwomen.bwaf.org/jane-west-clauss/.

26. *Planning the Neighborhood: Standards for Healthful Housing* (Chicago: American Public Health Association, Public Administration Service, 1948).

27. Conover, *Grounds Maintenance Handbook.*

28. Civil Service Commission, *Official Register of the United States: Persons in the Civil, Military, and Naval Service, Exclusive of the Postal Service,* 1948, GovInfo.gov, accessed May 31, 2022, https://www.govinfo.gov/app/details/GOVPUB-CS1-c8a32080209c260c6988fbc61590627a.

29. Oral History of the TVA, Tour Interview, 44, MVA.

30. Civil Service Commission, *Official Register,* 1953, GovInfo.gov, accessed May 31, 2022, https://www.govinfo.gov/app/details/GOVPUB-CS1–77f482ea6566c699067b84cd47438113.

31. Gray and Johnson, *The TVA Regional Planning and Development Program,* 89.

32. "TVA Buildings."

33. Report on Status of Work (Memo, Rand to Menhinick, August 28, 1946), Regional Studies Papers, Box 9, Folder 4G (A-Z), NAA.

34. Ibid.

35. Conkin, "Intellectural and Political Roots," 4.

36. Creese, "TVA as an Allegory," 62.

37. Lowitt, "The TVA, 1933–1945," 51.

38. McDonald and Muldowny, *TVA and the Dispossessed,* 272.

39. Dahir, *Region Building,* 13.

40. Albert Lepawsky, "The Progressives and the Planners," *Public Administration Review,* 31, no. 3, Special Symposium Issue: Changing Styles of Planning in Post-Industrial America (May–June 1971): 302. Emphasis added.

41. Avigail Sachs, "The Postwar Legacy of Architectural Research," *Journal of Architectural Education* 62, no. 3 (2009): 55–68; and "Marketing through Research: William Caudill and Caudill Rowlett Scott (Crs)," *Journal of Architecture* 14, no. 1 (2009): 737–52.

42. Editorial Board Page, *Journal of the American Institute of Planners* 6, no. 4 (1942).

43. Tracy B. Augur, "Does the Planner's Field Have a Boundary? Discussion," *Planners' Journal* 6, no. 3 (1940): 77.

44. Ian L. McHarg, *Design with Nature* (Garden City, NY: Doubleday/Natural History Press, 1969).

45. Sachs, *Environmental Design.*

46. Arthur E. Morgan, "Tennessee Valley Becomes Laboratory for the Nation," *New York Times,* March 25, 1934.

47. Morgan and Landless, "The Common Mooring," 117.

48. Fitch, "Rise of Technology," 75.

# BIBLIOGRAPHY


## Archives

CALVIN M. MCCLUNG HISTORICAL COLLECTION, KNOX COUNTY PUBLIC LIBRARY, KNOXVILLE, TN

APD 0013, Norris, Tennessee, and other Tennessee Valley Authority architectural plans and drawings by Osborne H. Graves

Mary U. Rothrock Papers

PC 0066, Gilbertsville Camp photographs

MISSISSIPPI VALLEY ARCHIVES (MVA)

Oral Histories of the Tennessee Valley Authority, John Willard Brister Library, Memphis State University

NATIONAL ARCHIVES OF ATLANTA (NAA)

Board of Directors Papers. RG 142, TVA, Office of the General Manager's Office Records of the Board of Directors, Curtis-Morgan-Morgan, General Correspondence, 1933–57

Chairman and the Members of the Board Papers. RG 142, TVA, Records of the Chairman and the Members of the Board of Directors, 1930–57, James P. Pope, Raymond R. Paty

Construction Project Reports. RG 142, TVA, Records of the Chief Administrative Office, Construction Project Reports on Structures at Dams and Other Construction Projects

Engineering Project Histories Papers. RG 142, TVA, Office of Engineering, Design and Construction

General Manager's Office Papers. RG 142, TVA, Records of the General Manager's Office Administrative Files, 1933–57

George Richardson Files. RG 142, TVA, Regional Studies Department, Architectural Records, 1940–48

Regional Studies Papers. RG 142, TVA, Office of Economic and Community Development, Regional Studies Dept. General Correspondence, 1940–48

Reservoir Properties Papers. RG 142, TVA, Division of Reservoir Prop. Recreation/Reservation Site Planning and Defense Housing, 1950–58

### Sources

"1,946,970 Door and Operating Means Therefor (Patented Feb. 13, 1934)." Edited by United States Patent Office.

*1937 Yearbook, Park and Recreation Progress.* Washington, DC: Government Printing Office, 1937.

"1940 Institute Roster." *Journal of the American Institute of Planners* 6, no. 1 (1940): 25–28.

*1941 Yearbook, Park and Recreation Progress.* Washington, DC: Government Printing Office, 1941.

"AIP Code of Professional Conduct." *Journal of the American Institute of Planners* 14, no. 2 (Spring 1948): 47–48.

Alderman, Derek H., and Robert N. Brown. "When a New Deal Is Actually an Old Deal: The Role of TVA in Engineering a Jim Crow Racialized Landscape." In *Engineering Earth: The Impacts of Megaengineering Projects,* edited by S. D. Brunn, 1901–16. Dordrecht: Springer Science+Business Media B.V, 2011.

"Aménagemet de la Vallée du Tennessee." *L'Architecture D'aujourd'hui,* no. 12, Techniques Américaines Urbanisme et Habitation (July 1947): 16–17.

American Library Association. *Books for the South.* Chicago: American Library Association, 1933.

Anders, Mary Edna. *The Tennessee Valley Library Council, 1940–1949: A Regional Approach to Library Planning.* Atlanta: Southeastern Library Association, 1960.

Anderson, Larry. *Benton MacKaye: Conservationist, Planner, and Creator of the Appalachian Trail.* Baltimore: Johns Hopkins University Press, 2002.

*Annual Report of the Director of the Civilian Conservation Corps, Fiscal Year Ended June 30, 1939.* Washington, DC: Government Printing Office, 1939.

*Annual Report of the Director of the Civilian Conservation Corps, Fiscal Year Ended June 30, 1941.* Washington, DC: Government Printing Office, 1941.
Aron, Cindy S. *Working at Play: A History of Vacations in the United States.* New York: Oxford University Press, 1999.
Augur, Tracy B. "Does the Planner's Field Have a Boundary? Discussion." *Planners' Journal* 6, no. 3 (1940): 76–77.
———. "Industrial Growth in America and the Garden City." MLA thesis, Harvard University, Cambridge, MA, 1921.
———. "Planning Principles Applied in Wartime: Planning the Postwar Community . . . What It Promises to Be and How It Can Be Made That Way." *Architectural Record* 93, no. 1 (January 1943): 71–77.
———. "The Planning of the Town of Norris." *American Architect* 148 (1936): 19–26.
———. "The Size and Spacing of Urban Communities." *Journal of the American Institute of Planners* 15, no. 3 (1949): 42–43.
Bacon, Mardges. "The Federation of Architects, Engineers, Chemists and Technicians (FAECT): The Politics and Social Practice of Labor." *Journal of the Society of Architectural Historians* 76, no. 4 (December 2017): 454–63.
———. "Le Corbusier and Postwar America: The TVA and *Beton Brut.*" *Journal of the Society of Architectural Historians* 74, no. 1 (2015): 13–40.
Baker, Willis M., and William M. Landess. "Education for Sustained Regional Productivity." *Journal of Educational Sociology* 15, no. 3, The TVA Program—The Regional Approach to General Welfare (November 1941): 160–74.
Ball, Carlton R. *A Study of the Work of the Land-Grant Colleges in the Tennessee Valley Area in Cooperation with the Tennessee Valley Authority.* [Place unknown]: Tennessee Valley Agricultural Correlating Committee, 1939.
Banham, Reyner. "The Great Gizmo." *Industrial Design* 12, no. 9 (September 1965): 48–59.
Barde, Robert E. "Arthur E. Morgan, First Chairman of TVA." *Tennessee Historical Quarterly* 30, no. 3 (1971): 299–314.
"Basic Principles of Healthful Housing: Preliminary Report of the Committee on Hygiene of Housing, American Public Health Association." *American Journal of Public Health and the Nation's Health* 28, no. 3 (March 1938): 351–72.
"Basic Reports of Land Planning and Housing Division, Tennessee Valley Authority, May 1, 1936." Engineering Project Histories Papers, Box 40, NAA.
Bauer, Catherine. *Modern Housing.* Boston: Houghton Mifflin, 1934.
Bianculli, Mario. "Planning and the Architect." *Tennessee Planner* 11, no. 2 (October 1950): 42–46.

Black, Brian. "Organic Planning: Ecology and Design in the Landscape of the Tennessee Valley Authority, 1933–1945." In *Environmentalism in Landscape Architecture,* edited by Michel Conan, 71–95. Washington, DC: Dumbarton Oaks Research Library and Collection, 2000.

Bond, J. Max [Sr.]. "The Educational Program for Negroes in the TVA." *Journal of Negro Education* 6, no. 2 (April 1937): 144–51.

Boyce, Ronald Reed. "Geographers and the Tennessee Valley Authority." *Geographical Review* 94, no. 1 (January 2004): 23–42.

Bruce, Alfred, and Harold Sandbank. *A History of Prefabrication.* New York: John B. Pierce Foundation, 1944.

Cannavò, Peter F. "American Contradictions and Pastoral Visions: An Appraisal of Leo Marx, the Machine in the Garden." *Organization & Environment* 14, no. 1 (March 2001): 74–92.

Cater, Casey P. *Regenerating Dixie: Electric Energy and the Modern South.* Pittsburgh, PA: University of Pittsburgh Press, 2019.

Cebul, Brent. "Creative Competition: Georgia Power, the Tennessee Valley Authority, and the Creation of a Rural Consumer Economy, 1934–1955." *Journal of American History* (June 2018): 45–70.

Chapin, F. Stuart. *Communities for Living, Prepared for the Advisory Panel on Regional Materials of Instruction for the Tennessee Valley.* Athens: University of Georgia Press, 1941.

Chase, Stuart. "TVA: The New Deal's Greatest Asset, II. Broadening the Exchange Base." *The Nation,* June 10, 1936, 738–40.

Civil Service Commission. *Official Register of the United States: Persons in the Civil, Military, and Naval Service, Exclusive of the Postal Service,* 1948. GovInfo.gov. Accessed May 31, 2022. https://www.govinfo.gov/app/details/GOVPUB-CS1-c8a32080209c260c6988fbc615906 27a.

———. *Official Register of the United States: Persons in the Civil, Military, and Naval Service, Exclusive of the Postal Service,* 1953. GovInfo.gov. Accessed May 31, 2022. https://www.govinfo .gov/app/details/GOVPUB-CS1–77f482ea6566c699067b84cd47438113.

Clapp, Gordon R., and Howard K. Menhinick. "The Approach of the TVA to the Solution of Regional Problems." *Journal of Educational Sociology* 15, no. 3, The TVA Program—The Regional Approach to General Welfare (1941): 136–49.

Coggins, Allen R. "The Early History of Tennessee's State Parks, 1919–1956." *Tennessee Historical Quarterly* 43, no. 3 (Fall 1984): 295–315.

"A Communication: Mr. Mumford, Mr. Haskell and the Factory-Built House." *New Republic,* July 2, 1931, 180–81.

"Community Buildings: Architectural Record's Building Types Study Number 113." *Architectural Record* 99, no. 5 (May 1946): 97–111.

Conkin, Paul K. "Intellectual and Political Roots." In *TVA: Fifty Years of Grass-Roots Bureaucracy,* edited by Erwin C. Hargrove and Paul K. Conkin, 3–34. Urbana: University of Illinois Press, 1983.

———. *A Revolution Down on the Farm, Transformation of American Agriculture since 1929.* Lexington: University of Kentucky Press, 2008.

Conover, Herbert S. *Grounds Maintenance Handbook.* New York: F. W. Dodge Corp., 1958.

———. "Improvement and Maintenance Techniques at Certain TVA Dams, Areas 'Built for the People of the Unite States.'" *Landscape Architecture* 39, no. 2 (January 1949): 53–59.

Coyle, David Cushman, ed. *Electric Power on the Farm: The Story of Electricity, Its Usefulness on Farms, and the Movement to Electrify Rural America* Washington, DC: Government Printing Office, 1936.

Cranston, Clayton. "The TVA and the Race Problem." *Opportunity, Journal of Negro Life* 12, no. 4 (April 1934): 111.

Cranz, Galen. *The Politics of Park Design: A History of Urban Parks in America.* Cambridge, MA: MIT Press, 1982.

Crawford, Margaret. "Daily Life on the Home Front: Women, Blacks, and the Struggle for Public Housing." In *World War II and the American Dream,* edited by Donald Albrecht and Margaret Crawford. Washington, DC: National Building Museum, 1995.

———. "Earle S. Draper and the Company Town in the American South." In *The Company Town: Architecture and Society in the Early Industrial Age,* edited by John S. Garner, 139–71. New York: Oxford University Press, 1992.

Creese, Walter L. "TVA as an Allegory." In *Built for the People of the United States: Fifty Years of TVA Architecture,* edited by Marian Moffett and Lawrence Wodehouse, 59–63. Knoxville: Art and Architecture Gallery, University of Tennessee, 1983.

———. *TVA's Public Planning: The Vision, the Reality.* Knoxville: University of Tennessee Press, 1990.

Cromley, Elizabeth. "Domestic Space Transformed, 1850–2000." In *Architectures: Modernism and After,* edited by Andrew Ballantyne, 163–201. Oxford: Blackwell, 2003.

Culvahouse, Tim, ed. *The Tennessee Valley Authority: Design and Persuasion.* New York: Princeton Architectural Press, 2007.

Cutler, Phoebe. *The Public Landscape of the New Deal.* New Haven, CT: Yale University Press, 1985.

Dahir, James. *Region Building—Community Development Lessons from the Tennessee Valley.* New York: Harper & Brothers, 1955.

D'Anieri, Phillip. "A 'Fruitful Hypothesis'? The Regional Planning Association of America's Hopes for Technology." *Journal of Planning History* 1, no. 4 (2002): 279–89.

"Demountable Housing for Defense Workers." *American Builder and Building Age (1930–1948)* 64, no. 3 (March 1942): 76.

Department of Regional Planning Studies, TVA. *Recreational Development of the Southern Highlands Region: A Study of the Use and Control of Scenic and Recreational Resources.* Knoxville: Tennessee Valley Authority, 1938.

Department of Regional Studies, TVA. "The Trailer House: TVA's New Approach to Mobile Shelter." *Architectural Record* 93, no. 2 (1943): 49–52.

"Design Awards for First Term, 1909–1910." *Technology Architectural Record, Published Quarterly by the MIT Architectural Society* 3, no. 2 (March 1910).

Downs, Matthew L. *Transforming the South: Federal Development in the Tennessee Valley, 1915–1960.* Baton Rouge: Louisiana State University Press, 2014.

Draper, Earle S. "Demonstration Parks in the Tennessee Valley." *Architectural Record* (June 1937): 126–27.

———. "The TVA Freeway." *American City* 49, no. 2 (February 1934): 47–48.

———. "The TVA's Forgotten Town: Norris, Tennessee." *Landscape Architecture* 78, no. 2 (March 1988): 96–100.

———. "TVA's Yardstick for Housing." *Architectural Forum* 63, no. 3 (September 1935): 162–70.

———. "Urban Development in the Southeast: What of the Future?" *Social Forces* 19, no. 1 (October 1940): 17–22.

Draves, Ian. "'It's Easier to Pick a Tourist Than It Is a Bale of Cotton': The Rise of Recreation on the Great Lakes of the South." *Southern Cultures* 20, no. 3, Southern Waters (2014): 87–104.

Droze, W. H. "The TVA, 1945–80: The Power Company." In *TVA: Fifty Years of Grass-Roots Bureaucracy,* edited by Erwin C. Hargrove and Paul K. Conkin, 297–315. Urbana: University of Illinois Press, 1983.

———. "TVA and the Ordinary Farmer." *Agricultural History* 53, no. 1, Southern Agriculture since the Civil War: A Symposium (January 1979): 188–202.

Drumright, William Wade. "A River for War, a Watershed to Change: The Tennessee Valley Authority during World War II." PhD diss., University of Tennessee, Knoxville, 2005.

Dümpelmann, Sonja. "Three Men in Search of a Modern Arcadia: Landscape Architecture, Planning, and Conservation between Tradition and Modernism (Review Essay)." *Journal of Planning History* 6, no. 2 (May 2007): 166–86.

Durisch, Lawrence Logan. "Local Government and the T.V.A. Program." *Public Administration Review* 1, no. 4 (Summer 1941): 326–34.

———. "The TVA Program and the War Effort." *Journal of Politics* 8, no. 4 (November 1946): 531–37.

Editorial Board Page. *Journal of the American Institute of Planners* 6, no. 4 (1942).

Ekbladh, David. "Meeting the Challenge from Totalitarianism: The Tennessee Valley Authority as a Global Model for Liberal Development, 1933–1945." *International History Review* 32, no. 1 (2010): 47–67.

———. "'Mr. TVA': Grass-Roots Development, David Lilienthal, and the Rise and Fall of the Tennessee Valley Authority as a Symbol for U.S. Overseas Development, 1933–1973." *Diplomatic History* 26, no. 3 (2002): 335–74.

Conover, H. S. *Public Grounds Maintenance Handbook.* Knoxville: Tennessee Valley Authority, Site Planning Section, Division of Reservoir Properties, 1953.

Coyle, David Cushman, ed. *Electric Power on the Farm: The Story of Electricity, Its Usefulness on Farms, and the Movement to Electrify Rural America* Washington, DC: Government Printing Office, 1936.

Falkner, Max H. *Planning the Rural Home.* Circular 38, November 1937. Agricultural Extension Service, University of Tennessee, Knoxville, 1937.

Field, Gregory B. "'Electricity for All': The Electric Home and Farm Authority and the Politics of Mass Consumption, 1932–1935." *Business History Review* 64, no. 1, Government and Business (Spring 1990): 32–60.

Fitch, James Marston. "The Rise of Technology: 1929–1939." *Journal of the Society of Architectural Historians* 24, no. 1 (1965): 75–77.

Foresta, Ronald. "Transformation of the Appalachian Trail." *Geographical Review* 77, no. 1 (January 1987): 76–85.

Gabler, Carole. "Philadelphians at Home: The Clausses Drew a Blueprint for a Happy, Working Marriage." *Sunday Bulletin* (October 30, 1960): 7–8.

Geddes, Patrick. *Cities in Evolution: An Introduction to the Town Planning Movement and to the Study of Civics.* London: Williams & Norgate, 1915.

———. "The Twofold Aspect of the Industrial Age: Paleotechnic and Neotechnic." *Town Planning Review* 3, no. 3 (October 1912): 176–87.

Good, Albert H. *Park and Recreation Structures.* Washington, DC: Government Printing Office, 1938.

"Graduates of the Class of 1911." *Technology Architectural Record, Published Quarterly by the MIT Architectural Society* 4, no. 3 (June 1911).

Grant, Nancy L. *TVA and Black Americans: Planning for the Status Quo.* Philadelphia: Temple University Press, 1990.

Grantham, Dewey W. "TVA and the Ambiguity of American Reform." In *TVA: Fifty Years of Grass-Roots Bureaucracy,* edited by Erwin C. Hargrove and Paul K. Conkin, ix–xviii. Urbana: University of Illinois Press, 1983.

Graves, Osborne H. "TVA Land Planning: Landscape Architecture in a Resource Development Agency." *Landscape Architecture* 53 (July 1953): 154–61.

Gray, Aelred J., and David A. Johnson. *The TVA Regional Planning and Development Program: The Transformation of an Institution and Its Mission.* Aldershot, UK: Ashgate, 2005.
Gray, Aelred J., and Victor Roterus. *The Tennessee River Valley: A Case Study.* Washington, DC: [Housing Division, International Cooperation Administration], 1960.
Greeley, Roland B. "Regional Conference at Fontana." *Journal of the American Institute of Planning* 12, no. 4 (1946): 42–45.
Gutheim, Frederick Albert. *One Hundred Years of Architecture in America, 1857–1957: Celebrating the Centennial of the American Institute of Architects.* New York: Reinhold Publishing, 1957.
———. "Roland Wank, 1898–1970." *Architectural Forum* 133, no. 2 (September 1970): 58–59.
Hall, Peter. "The Neotechnic Vision." *Built Environment* 8, no. 4, Classics Revisited (1982): 217–18.
Hamlin, Talbot F. "Architecture of the TVA." *Pencil Points* 20, no. 11 (November 1939): 721–31.
Hargrove, Erwin C. *Prisoners of Myth: The Leadership of the Tennessee Valley Authority, 1933–1990.* Princeton, NJ: Princeton University Press, 1994.
Harvard, William C., Jr. "The Images of TVA: The Clash over Values." In *TVA: Fifty Years of Grass-Roots Bureaucracy,* edited by Erwin C. Hargrove and Paul K. Conkin, 297–315. Urbana: University of Illinois Press, 1983.
Haskell, Douglas. "Architecture of the TVA." *The Nation,* May 17, 1941, 592–93.
———. "Bringing Shelter up to Date: II Unchaining the House from Land." *The Nation,* May 23, 1934, 586–87.
———. "The House of the Future." *New Republic,* May 13, 1931, 344–45.
Hastings, Loren C. "Fontana . . . Top Find in Low Cost Vacations." *Better Homes and Gardens,* April 1947, 128–30.
Hays, Samuel P. *Conservation and the Gospel of Efficiency: The Progressive Conservation Movement, 1890–1920.* Pittsburgh, PA: University of Pittsburgh Press, 2015.
Heaton Vorse, Mary. "Yesterday, Today, and Tomorrow." *Pencil Points* 23, no. 12 (December 1942): 28–31.
Henderson, G. E., and Jane A. Roberts. *Wiring and Lighting the Farmstead: A Combined Text and Laboratory Manual.* Knoxville: Tennessee Valley Authority, 1939.
Herbert, Gilbert. *The Dream of the Factory-Made House: Walter Gropius and Konrad Wachsmann.* Cambridge, MA: MIT Press, 1984.
Higgins, Benjamin. "The American Frontier and the TVA." *Society* 32, no. 3 (1995): 34–42.
Hodge, Clarence Lewis. *The Tennessee Valley Authority: A National Experiment in Regionalism.* Washington, DC: American University Press, 1938.
"Homes for Tomorrow: Prefabricated and Pre-Engineered Machines for Living Are Visible Signs on the Road to Social Progress." *The Technocrat* 12, no. 12 (December 1944): 6–10.

Howard, Ebenezer. *Garden Cities of To-Morrow (Being the Second Edition of "To-Morrow: A Peaceful Path to Real Reform").* London: S. Sonnenschein & Co., 1902.
Howard, T. Levron. "The Social Scientist in the Tennessee Valley Authority Program." *Social Forces* 15, no. 1 (October 1936): 29–34.
Howes, Robert M. "Controversy and Consequence: A Personal Look at TVA." *Jackson Purchase Historical Society* 2, no. 1, Article 8 (1974).
———. "Recreation." In *TVA: The First Twenty Years, a Staff Report,* edited by Tennessee Valley Authority and Roscoe C. Martin, 206–18. Tuscaloosa: University of Alabama Press, 1956.
Hubbard, Theodora Kimball, and Henry Vincent Hubbard. *Our Cities Today and Tomorrow: A Survey of Planning and Zoning Progress in the United States.* Cambridge, MA: Harvard University Press, 1929.
Hubka, Thomas C. *How the Working-Class Home Became Modern, 1900–1940.* Minneapolis: University of Minnesota Press, 2020.
Hubka, Thomas C., and Judith T. Kenny. "Examining the American Dream: Housing Standards and the Emergence of a National Housing Culture, 1900–1930." *Perspectives in Vernacular Architecture* 13, no. 1 (2006): 49–69.
Hudson, G. Donald. "Geography and Regional Planning." *Journal of Geography* 34 (October 1935): 267–77.
"Huge Crowds Visit Norris Dam Project." *Knoxville News-Sentinel,* May 18, 1934.
Huxley, Julian. *TVA, Adventure in Planning.* Surry: Architectural Press, 1943.
*Investigation of the Tennessee Valley Authority: Report of the Joint Committee on the Investigation of the Tennessee Valley Authority, Pursuant to Public Res. No. 83 (75th Congress) Creating a Special Joint Congressional Committee to Make an Investigation of the Tennessee Valley Authority.* Washington DC: Government Printing Office, 1939.
"J. Max Bond Sr., 89, an American Who Headed Liberian University." *New York Times,* December 18, 1991.
Jung, Hyun-Tae. "'Technologically' Modern: The Prefabricated House and the Wartime Experience of Skidmore, Owings and Merrill." In *Sanctioning Modernism: Architecture and the Making of Postwar Identities,* edited by Vladimir Kuli, Timothy Parker, Monica Penick, and Dennis P. Doordan. Austin: University of Texas Press, 2014.
Kargon, Robert H., and Arthur P. Molella. *Invented Edens: Techno-Cities of the Twentieth Century.* Cambridge, MA: MIT Press, 2008.
Katz, Barry M. "Ideology and Engineering in the Tennessee Valley." In *The Tennessee Valley Authority: Design and Persuasion,* edited by Tim Culvahouse, 80–95. New York: Princeton Architectural Press, 2007.
Kelly, Burnham. *The Prefabrication of Houses: A Study by the Albert Farwell Bemis Foundation of*

*the Prefabrication Industry in the United States.* Cambridge, MA: Technology Press of MIT and John Wiley and Sons, 1951.

Koppes, Clayton R. "Efficiency/Equity/Esthetics: Towards a Reinterpretation of American Conservation." *Environmental Review: ER* 11, no. 2 (Summer 1987): 127–46.

Krugler, David F. *This Is Only a Test: How Washington, D.C., Prepared for Nuclear War.* New York: Palgrave Macmillan, 2006.

Kyle, John H. *The Building of TVA: An Illustrated History.* Baton Rouge: Louisiana State University Press, 1958.

"Landscape Architectural Exhibition at the Pennsylvania State College." *Pencil Points* 10, no. 12 (December 1929): 872.

Larsen, Torben Huus. *Enduring Pastoral: Recycling the Middle Landscape Idea in the Tennessee Valley.* Amsterdam: Rodopi, 2006.

Lepawsky, Albert. "Government Planning in the South." *Journal of Politics* 10, no. 3 (1948): 536–67.

———. "The Progressives and the Planners." *Public Administration Review,* 31, no. 3, Special Symposium Issue: Changing Styles of Planning in Post-Industrial America (May–June 1971): 297–303.

Lilienthal, David E. "The TVA, An Experiment in the 'Grass Roots' Administration of Federal Functions." Address before the Southern Political Science Association, Knoxville, TN, November 10, 1939.

———. *TVA: Democracy on the March.* New York: Harper, 1944.

———. *TVA: Democracy on the March.* 10th anniversary ed. New York: Harper & Row, 1953.

Longstreth, Richard W. *The Drive-in, the Supermarket, and the Transformation of Commercial Space in Los Angeles, 1914–1941.* Cambridge, MA: MIT Press, 1999.

"Louis Grandgent." *Journal of Housing* 16, no. 10 (1959): 350.

"Low Cost Houses." *Architectural Forum* 84 (April 1946): 117–28.

Lowitt, Richard. "The TVA, 1933–1945." In *TVA: Fifty Years of Grass-Roots Bureaucracy,* edited by Erwin C. Hargrove and Paul K. Conkin, 35–65. Urbana: University of Illinois Press, 1983.

Macfadyen, Dugald. "Sociological Effects of Garden Cities." *Social Forces* 14, no. 2 (December 1935): 250–56.

MacKaye, Benton. "An Appalachian Trail: A Project in Regional Planning." *Journal of the American Institute of Architects* 9, no. 9 (September 1921): 325–30.

———. "Regional Planning and Ecology." *Ecological Monographs* 10, no. 3 (July 1940): 349–53.

———. "Tennessee—Seed of a National Plan." *Graphic Survey* (May 1933): 251–54, 293–94.

Macy, Christine. "The Architect's Office of the Tennessee Valley Authority." In *The Tennessee Valley Authority: Design and Persuasion,* edited by Tim Culvahouse, 26–51. New York: Princeton Architectural Press, 2007.

———. *Dams.* New York: Norton & Co., 2009.

Macy, Christine, and Sarah Bonnemaison. *Architecture and Nature: Creating the American Landscape.* London: Routledge, 2003.

Maher, Neil M. *Nature's New Deal: The Civilian Conservation Corps and the Roots of the American Environmental Movement.* Oxford: Oxford University Press, 2008.

"Maison Préfarbriquée De La T.V.A." *L'Architecture D'aujourd'hui,* no. 12, Techniques Américaines Urbanisme et Habitation (July 1947): 23.

Martin, Reinhold. "Abolish Oil: From Green New Deal to Green Reconstruction." *Places Journal* (June 2020). https://placesjournal.org/article/abolish-oil/.

Marx, Leo. "The American Ideology of Space." In *Denatured Visions: Landscape and Culture in the Twentieth Century,* edited by Stuart Wrede and William Howard Adams, 62–78. New York: Museum of Modern Art, 1994.

———. "The Idea of Nature in America." *Daedalus* 137, no. 2, On Nature (Spring 2008): 8–21.

———. *The Machine in the Garden: Technology and the Pastoral Ideal in America.* Oxford: Oxford University Press, 1964.

McCraw, Thomas K. "Triumph and Irony—the TVA." *Proceedings of the IEEE* 54, no. 9 (September 1976): 1372–80.

———. *TVA and the Power Fight, 1933–1939.* Philadelphia: Lippincott, 1971.

McCullough, Erin. "City Hall Added to National Register of Historic Places." (Tullahoma, TN) *Times,* August 17, 2018.

McDonald, Michael J., and John Muldowny. *TVA and the Dispossessed: The Resettlement of Population in the Norris Dam Area.* Knoxville: University of Tennessee Press, 1982.

McHarg, Ian L. *Design with Nature.* Garden City, NY: Doubleday/Natural History Press, 1969.

Meikle, Jeffrey L. "Leo Marx's the Machine in the Garden." *Technology and Culture* 44, no. 1 (2003): 147–59.

Menhinick, Howard K. "The Tennessee Valley and Its Development." *Journal of the American Institute of Architects* 6, no. 4 (1946): 147–55.

Menhinick, Howard K., and Henry V. Hubbard. "Editorial." *1,* no. 1 (1935): 10.

Menhinick, Howard K., and Lawrence Logan Durisch. "Tennessee Valley Authority: Planning in Operation." *Town Planning Review* 24, no. 2 (1953): 116–45.

Mennel, Timothy. "'Miracle House Hoop-La': Corporate Rhetoric and the Construction of the Postwar American House." *Journal of the Society of Architectural Historians* 63, no. 3 (2008): 340–61.

Miller, Ernest I. *Buildings for Small Public Libraries: Remodeled and Adapted, Including New Designs for Branches.* Chicago: American Library Association, Committee on Library Architecture and Building Planning, 1950.

Minteer, Ben A. *The Landscape of Reform: Civic Pragmatism and Environmental Thought in America.* Cambridge, MA: MIT Press, 2006.

Mock, Michelle. "The Electric Home and Farm Authority: 'Model T Appliances,' and the Modernization of the Home Kitchen in the South." *Journal of Southern History* 80, no. 1 (February 2014): 73–108.

Moffett, Marian. "Looking to the Future: The Architecture of Roland Wank." *ARRIS, Journal of the Southeast Chapter of the Society of Architectural Historians,* no. 1 (1989): 5–17.

———. "Wank, Roland." Oxford Art Online. Published 2003. https://doi.org/10.1093/gao/9781884446054.article.T090648.

Moffett, Marian, and Lawrence Wodehouse. "Noble Structures Set in Handsome Parks: Public Architecture of the TVA." *Modulus* 17 (1984): 75–83.

"Moon, Mist Afford Unusual View of Dam." *Knoxville News-Sentinel,* September 10, 1937.

Morgan, Arthur E. "Social and Economic Implications of TVA." *Civil Engineering* 5, no. 12 (December 1935): 754–57.

———. "Tennessee Valley Becomes Laboratory for the Nation." *New York Times,* March 24, 1934.

———. "Vitality and Formalism in Government." *Social Forces* 13, no. 1 (October 1934): 1–6.

Morgan, Harcourt A., and William M. Landless. "The Common Mooring—a Working Philosophy." *High School Journal* 30, no. 3, Health Educators at Work (May 1947): 115–17.

Moutoux, John T. "Architects and Engineers Unite Talents on TVA Dams." *Knoxville News-Sentinel* magazine, November 28, 1937.

Mumford, Lewis. "The Architecture of Power." *New Yorker,* June 7, 1941, 58–60.

———. *The Culture of Cities.* New York: Harcourt, Brace, 1938.

Munger, George D., Carroll A. Towne, and Philip W. Voltz. "Education in the Adaptation of the Valley People to New Factors in the Environment." *Journal of Educational Sociology* 15, no. 3, The TVA Program—The Regional Approach to General Welfare (November 1941): 174–84.

Nash, Linda. "The Changing Experience of Nature: Historical Encounters with a Northwest River." *Journal of American History* 86, no. 4 (2000): 1600–1629.

National Resources Planning Board. *Regional Planning, Part XI: The Southeast.* Washington, DC: Government Printing Office, 1942.

Nelson, Garrett Dash. Introduction to reprint of Benton MacKaye, "An Appalachian Trail: A Project in Regional Planning." *Places Journal* (April 2019). https://placesjournal.org/article/an-appalachian-trail-a-project-in-regional-planning/.

"News." *Architectural Forum* 80, no. 4 (April 1944): 65–70.

"Norris Dam Draws 230,000 Visitors from out-State." *Knoxville News-Sentinel,* September 3, 1937.

"Norris Leads Boulder Dam." *Knoxville Journal,* September 18, 1934.

Nye, David E. *American Technological Sublime.* Cambridge, MA: MIT Press, 1994.

———. *Electrifying America: Social Meanings of a New Technology, 1880–1940.* Cambridge, MA: MIT Press, 1990.

"One Hundred Years of Significant Building." *Architectural Record* 121, no. 4 (1957): 201–4.

Parsons, Kermit C. "Collaborative Genius: The Regional Planning Association of America." *Journal of the American Planning Association* 60, no. 4 (Autumn 1994): 462–82.

*Planning the Neighborhood; Standards for Healthful Housing.* Chicago: American Public Health Association, Public Administration Service, 1948.

"Power & Beauty." *Knoxville News-Sentinel* magazine, November 28, 1937.

"Power Board and Municipal Building." *Architectural Forum* 84, no. 3 (March 1946): 139.

"REA Headquarters Buildings for a Program of Rural Electrification." *Architectural Forum* (February 1943): 79–88.

*Recreation Development of the Tennessee River System: Message from the President of the United States Transmitting a Report on the Recreation Development of the Tennessee River System.* Washington, DC: Government Printing Office, 1940.

"The Regional Planning Association of America." *Journal of the American Institute of Architects* 11, no. 7 (July 1923): 292.

*Report of the Secretary of Agriculture in Relation to the Forests, Rivers, and Mountains of the Southern Appalachian Region, December 19, 1901.* Washington, DC: Government Printing Office, 1902.

"Report on the Appalachian Project." *Journal of the American Institute of Architects* 11, no. 7 (July 1923): 292–93.

*Report to the Congress on the Unified Development of the Tennessee River System, Submitted by the Board of Directors of the Tennessee Valley Authority, March 1936.* Knoxville: Tennessee Valley Authority, 1936.

"Residence of Dr. R. B. Taft, Belmont, Mass. Grandgent & Elwell, Architects." *Architectural Record* 47, no. 2 (February 1920): 178–80.

Rook, Robert. "Race, Water, and Foreign Policy: The Tennessee Valley Authority's Global Agenda Meets 'Jim Crow.'" *Diplomatic History* 1 (January 2004): 55–81.

Rorty, James. "TVA's H. A. Morgan, Made the TVA Safe for the Tennessee Valley." *The Commonweal* June 18, 1948, 226–30.

Rothrock, Mary U. "Tomorrow's Rural Libraries." *Bulletin of the American Library Association* 31, no. 13 (December 1937): 961–64.

Rothrock, Mary U., and Helen M. Harris. "A Regional Library in the Tennessee Valley." *ALA Bulletin* 35, no. 12 (1941): 658–64.

Rousey, Eric L. "The Worker's Life at Kentucky Dam, 1938–1945." *Filson Club History Quarterly* 71, no. 3 (July 1997): 347–66.

Rovang, Sarah K. "Modernization and Architecture under the Rural Electrification Administration, 1935–1945." PhD diss., Brown University, Providence, Rhode Island, 2016.

"Rural Activities Center, Tenn. Valley." *Architectural Forum* 80, no. 4 (April 1944): 89–93.

Ryan, Paul E., and Raymond F. Leonard. "Industrial Studies in Physical Regional Planning." *Planners' Journal* 2, no. 2 (1936): 29–34.

Sachs, Avigail. *Environmental Design: Architecture, Politics, and Science in Postwar America.* Charlottesville: University of Virginia Press, 2018.

———. "Jane West Clauss." Pioneering Women of American Architecture. Accessed May 31, 2022. https://pioneeringwomen.bwaf.org/jane-west-clauss/.

———. "Marketing through Research: William Caudill and Caudill Rowlett Scott (CRS)." *Journal of Architecture* 14, no. 1 (2009): 737–52.

———. "The Postwar Legacy of Architectural Research." *Journal of Architectural Education* 62, no. 3 (2009): 55–68.

Sachs, Avigail, and Tricia A. Stuth. "Innovation and Tradition: Eighty Years of Housing Construction in Southern Appalachia." *Construction History* 28, no. 1 (2013): 65–82.

Samuels, M. M. "Electricity Puts Its Hand to the Plow." *Pencil Points* 23, no. 12 (December 1942): 60–62.

Schaffer, Daniel. "Benton MacKaye: The TVA Years." *Planning Perspectives* 5, no. 1 (1990): 5–21.

———. "Environment and TVA: Toward a Regional Plan for the Tennessee Valley, 1930s." *Tennessee Historical Quarterly* 43, no. 4 (1984): 333–54.

Seigworth, Kenneth J. "Reforestation in the Tennessee Valley." *Public Administration Review* 8, no. 4 (Autumn 1948): 280–85.

Selznick, Philip. *TVA and the Grass Roots: A Study in the Sociology of Formal Organization.* Berkeley: University of California Press, 1949.

Seneca, Joseph J., Paul Davidson, and F. Gerard Adams. "An Analysis of Recreational Use of the TVA Lakes." *Land Economics* 44, no. 4 (November 1968): 529–34.

Shanken, Andrew M. *194X: Architecture, Planning, and Consumer Culture on the American Home Front.* Minneapolis: University of Minnesota Press, 2009.

———. "The Visual Culture of Planning." *Journal of Planning History* 17, no. 4 (2018): 300–319.

Shapiro, Henry D. *Appalachia on Our Mind: The Southern Mountaineers in the American Consciousness, 1870–1920.* Chapel Hill: University of North Carolina Press, 1978.

Shearer, John. "Modernism Architecture." Chattanoogan.com, July 19, 2011. http://www.chattanoogan.com/2011/7/19/205375/John-Shearer-Modernism-Architecture.aspx.

"Smith Creek Village, Community Center." *Pencil Points* 25, no. 2 (February 1944): 44–46.

Smith, Todd. "Almost Fully Modern: The TVA's Visual Art Campaign." In *The Tennessee Valley Authority: Design and Persuasion,* edited by Tim Culvahouse, 80–95. New York: Princeton Architectural Press, 2007.

"Some Recent Work of the Tennessee Valley Authority, Roland A. Wank, Principal Architect—Including a Visitors' Building, a Concession Building and Comfort Station, an Overlook Building, and a Harbor Master's Office, Harrison S. Gurnee and Mario Bianculli, Designers, under Supervision of Carroll A. Towne and George L. Richardson." *Pencil Points* 22, no. 7 (July 1941): 175–82.

Spann, Edward K. *Designing Modern America: The Regional Planning Association of America and Its Members.* Columbus: Ohio State University Press, 1996.

Taylor, Stephen Wallace. "Building the Back of Beyond: Government Authority, Community Life, and Economic Development in the Upper Little Tennessee Valley, 1880–1992." PhD diss., University of Tennessee, Knoxville, 1996.

"Tennessee System Headquarters Has Many New Features." *Rural Electrification News* 5, no. 10 (June 1940): 24.

"Tennessee Valley Authority." *Architectural Forum* 71, no. 2 (August 1939): 73–113.

Tennessee Valley Authority. *Annual Report of the Tennessee Valley Authority for the Fiscal Year Ended June 30, 1934.* Washington, DC: Government Printing Office, 1934.

———. *Annual Report of the Tennessee Valley Authority for the Fiscal Year Ended June 30, 1935.* Washington, DC: Government Printing Office, 1935.

———. *Annual Report of the Tennessee Valley Authority for the Fiscal Year Ended June 30, 1937.* Washington, DC: Government Printing Office, 1937.

———. *Annual Report of the Tennessee Valley Authority for the Fiscal Year Ended June 30, 1938.* Washington, DC: Government Printing Office, 1938.

———. *Annual Report of the Tennessee Valley Authority for the Fiscal Year Ended June 30, 1940.* Washington, DC: Government Printing Office, 1940.

———. *Annual Report of the Tennessee Valley Authority for the Fiscal Year Ended June 30, 1942.* Washington, DC: Government Printing Office, 1942.

———. *Annual Report of the Tennessee Valley Authority for the Fiscal Year Ended June 30, 1945.* Washington, DC: Government Printing Office, 1945.

———. *Annual Report of the Tennessee Valley Authority for the Fiscal Year Ended June 30, 1946.* Washington, DC: Government Printing Office, 1946.

———. *Annual Report of the Tennessee Valley Authority for the Fiscal Year Ended June 30, 1950.* Washington, DC: Government Printing Office, 1950.

———. *How Cheap Electricity Pays Its Way—TVA.* Washington, DC: Government Printing Office, 1938.

———. *The Kentucky Project: A Comprehensive Report on the Planning, Design, Construction, and Initial Operations of the Kentucky Project, Technical Report No. 13.* Washington, DC: Government Printing Office, 1951.

———. *Navigation and Economic Growth, Tennessee River Experience: A Report Prepared*

*Pursuant to Section 22 of the TVA Act and Executive Order No. 6161 (June 8, 1933).* Knoxville: Tennessee Valley Authority, 1966.

———. *The Norris Project: A Comprehensive Report on the Planning, Design, Construction, and Initial Operations of the Tennessee Valley Authority's First Water Control Project, Technical Report No. 1.* Washington, DC: Government Printing Office, 1940.

———. *The Scenic Resources of the Tennessee Valley: A Descriptive and Pictorial Inventory.* Washington, DC: Government Printing Office, 1938.

———. *The Watts Bar Project: A Comprehensive Report on the Planning, Design, Construction, and Initial Operations of the Watts Bar Project, Technical Report No. 9.* Washington, DC: Government Printing Office, 1949.

"Tennessee Valley Authority Architecture." *Pencil Points* 20, no. 11 (November 1939): 690–744.

Thomas, Bruce. "Nature and the City in 1920s America: Sunnyside Gardens, Queens, New York." In *Rural and Urban: Architecture between Two Cultures,* edited by Andrew Ballantyne, 134–44: London: Taylor & Francis, 2009.

Tour, Harry B. "Engineers and Architects Cooperate on TVA Projects (Letter to the Editor)." *Civil Engineering* 11, no. 5 (1941): 309–10.

Towne, Carroll A. "Design for Prefabrication—Some Personal Observations." *Pencil Points* 25, no. 3 (March 1944): 74–76.

———. "Portable Housing: TVA Experience Leads to Trailer-Houses." *New Pencil Points* 23, no. 1 (1942): 49–56.

Townsend, Gavin. "Mario Bianculli, Chattanooga's First Modernist." *ARRIS, Journal of the Southeast Chapter of the Society of Architectural Historians* 21 (2010): 4–19.

"Tracy Baldwin Augur, Operated Plans Office." *Washington Post,* Jun 24, 1974.

Turner, Frederick Jackson. *The Significance of the Frontier in American History.* Madison: State Historical Society of Wisconsin, 1894.

"T.V.A. Architecture and Design." *Bulletin of the Museum of Modern Art* 8, no. 4 (April–May 1941): 8–9.

"TVA Architect and First Mayor of Pioneer New Town, Norris; Winner of Many Honors (Obituary for Harry B. Tour)." *AIA Journal* 56, no. 5 (November 1971): 62.

"TVA Buildings." *Progressive Architecture* 32, no. 11 (November 1951): 62–71.

"TVA Builds Portable House: 3-Section Cottages Are Shop-Fabricated and Trucked to Site." In *Defense Homes Handbook: Portfolio of Low-Cost Homes and Rental Housing Units,* 100–101. Chicago: Simmons-Boardman Publishing, 1943.

"TVA Camp Presents Model Night Life." *Knoxville News-Sentinel,* July 8, 1934.

"TVA Creates a New Form of Display, Designed by Alfred Clauss." *Architectural Record* 82, no. 2 (July 1937): 86–88.

"TVA Steam Plant." *Progressive Architecture* 35, no. 11 (November 1954): 79–83.
US Department of Agriculture. *Rural Library Service: Farmers' Bulletin No. 1847.* Washington, DC: Government Printing Office, 1949.
Walker, Melissa. "African Americans and TVA Reservoir Property Removal: Race in a New Deal Program." *Agricultural History* 72, no. 2, African Americans in Southern Agriculture: 1877–1945 (1998): 417–28.
Wank, Roland A. "Architecture in Rural Areas: A Report on TVA Experience." *Pencil Points* 23, no. 12 (December 1942): 47–53.
———. "Co-Op Buildings Typify Progressive Democracy: REA Headquarters Buildings Are Community Centers." *Rural Electrification News* 6, no. 10 (1941): 6–9.
———. "Demountable Houses: Smith Creek Village, Appalachia Dam, TVA." *Pencil Points* 25, no. 3 (1944): 77–79.
———. "Planned Communities: A Speculative Survey of Their Future." *Architectural Record* 93, no. 2 (February 1943): 44–48.
———. "The Plant as a Place to Work." *Architectural Record* 10, no. 6 (December 1946): 91–94.
———. "Time to Choose Our Destiny: Planning or Disintergration?" *Pencil Points* 23, no. 6 (June 1942): 44–47.
"Wartime Housing. An Exhibition in 10 Scenes, Presented at the Museum of Modern Art, Sponsored by the National Committee on the Housing Emergency, and Prepared in Cooperation with the National Housing Agency, April [22]–June [21], 1942." *Bulletin of the Museum of Modern Art* 9, no. 4 (May 1942).
Weil, Martin. "Frederick Gutheim Dies." *Washington Post,* October 4, 1993.
"Well-Built Knoxville Homes: Home Builders in the Tennessee Region, Offer Low Cost, Thoroughly Insulated, Electrically and Oil Heated Units." In *Defense Homes Handbook: Portfolio of Low-Cost Homes and Rental Housing Units,* 106–9. Chicago: Simmons-Boardman Publishing, 1943.
Welter, Volker M. *Biopolis: Patrick Geddes and the City of Life.* Cambridge, MA: MIT Press, 2002.
Wildavsky, Aaron. "TVA and Power Politics." *American Political Science Review* 55, no. 3 (1961): 576–90.
Williams, Harry B. "The County Agent Teaches Resource Use." *High School Journal* 29, no. 3 (May 1946): 167–71.
Wright, Gwendolyn. *USA.* Modern Architectures in History Series. London: Reaktion Books, 2008.

# ILLUSTRATION CREDITS

Photographs by the author: fig. 2, fig. 3, fig. 5, figs. 7–9, fig. 19, figs. 23–32, figs. 35–39, fig. 42, fig. 43, fig. 65, fig. 67, fig. 68, fig. 70, fig. 83, fig. 86, fig. 89, fig. 93, fig. 98, fig. 100

Courtesy of the Alabama Department of Archives and History: fig. 18

APD 0013, Norris, Tenn., and other TVA architectural plans and drawings by Osborne H. Graves, T 12, Fountain City, TN, Calvin M. McClung Historical Collection, Knox County Public Library: fig. 4, fig. 92

PC 0066, Gilbertsville Camp photographs, TVA, Calvin M. McClung Historical Collection, Knox County Public Library: fig. 44, fig. 45, fig. 47, fig. 49, fig. 50, fig. 51, fig. 54

Prints and Photographs Division, Farm Security Administration/Office of War Information Black-and-White Negatives, Library of Congress: fig. 34

RG 82, Tennessee Department of Conservation Photograph Collection, 1937–76, Tennessee State Library and Archives: fig. 16, fig. 21, fig. 87, fig. 88, fig. 90

RG 142, TVA, Regional Maps, 1942–56 Land Planning and Housing, National Archives at College Park, MD: fig. 85

RG 142, TVA, Chief Administrative Officer, Construction Project Reports on Structures at Dams and Other Construction Projects, National Archives at Atlanta: figs. 11–13, fig. 22, fig. 69

RG 142, TVA, Division of Reservoir Prop. Recreation/Reservation Site Planning & Defense Housing, 1950–58, National Archives at Atlanta: fig. 96

RG 142, TVA, Engineering Design Division, Original Presentation Drawings, Architectural Support Branch, National Archives at Atlanta: fig. 17, fig. 20, fig. 33, fig. 63, fig. 64, fig. 66, fig. 91, fig. 99

RG 142, TVA, Office of Engineering, Design and Construction, National Archives at Atlanta: fig. 52

RG 142, TVA, Office of Engineering, Design and Construction, Engineering Project Histories and Reports, National Archives at Atlanta: fig. 6

RG 142, TVA, Regional Studies Department Architectural Records 1940–48, George Richardson Files, National Archives at Atlanta: fig. 10, fig. 14, fig. 40, fig. 41, fig. 48, fig. 53, figs. 55–62, figs. 71–82, fig. 94, fig. 95, fig. 97

RG142, TVA Regional Studies Department General Correspondence 1940–48, National Archives at Atlanta: fig. 84

# INDEX

*Page numbers in italics refer to illustrations.*

Midcentury: Architecture, Landscape, Urbanism, and Design

*Rethinking Frank Lloyd Wright: History, Reception, Preservation*
Neil Levine and Richard Longstreth, editors

*The Architecture of Suspense: The Built World in the Films of Alfred Hitchcock*
Christine Madrid French

*Monumental Jesus: Landscapes of Faith and Doubt in Modern America*
Margaret M. Grubiak

*Traces of J. B. Jackson: The Man Who Taught Us to See Everyday America*
Helen Lefkowitz Horowitz

*American Autopia: An Intellectual History of the American Roadside at Midcentury*
Gabrielle Esperdy

*Indoor America: The Interior Landscape of Postwar Suburbia*
Andrea Vesentini

*Environmental Design: Architecture, Politics, and Science in Postwar America*
Avigail Sachs

*Detached America: Building Houses in Postwar Suburbia*
James A. Jacobs